THE EVERYTHING
Green Living Book

Dear Reader,

I've been interested in the environment ever since I was a teen growing up on the west coast of Florida. While other girls my age read fashion monthlies, I kept my nose in nature magazines. Learning about the environment made me feel grounded and connected to a part of everything.

We're all interconnected with each other and the environment. But as we watch troubling environmental news make the headlines, it can be overwhelming. Please don't be dismayed or disheartened with the news. Each of us may only be one living creature, but together we can make a difference. Remember the story of Swimmy? When the little fish swam separately, they were gobbled up by the big fish, but when they all swam together, they were invincible.

We are each stewards in our own right, taking care of the earth. Our roles may be minor, but we're all part of the big show and this planet we call home. Sometimes it's hard to get a basic understanding of all the different issues. I hope this book gives you that, an introduction, some insight, and an idea about where we all fit in the big picture today.

Here's to a greener life,

Diane Gow McDilda

The EVERYTHING® Series

Editorial

Publisher	Gary M. Krebs
Innovation Director	Paula Munier
Editorial Director	Laura M. Daly
Executive Editor, Series Books	Brielle K. Matson
Associate Copy Chief	Sheila Zwiebel
Acquisitions Editor	Kerry Smith
Associate Development Editor	Elizabeth Kassab
Production Editor	Casey Ebert

Production

Director of Manufacturing	Susan Beale
Production Project Manager	Michelle Roy Kelly
Prepress	Erick DaCosta
	Matt LeBlanc
Interior Layout	Heather Barrett
	Brewster Brownville
	Colleen Cunningham
	Jennifer Oliveira
Cover Design	Erin Alexander
	Stephanie Chrusz
	Frank Rivera

Visit the entire Everything® Series at *www.everything.com*

THE
EVERYTHING®
GREEN LIVING BOOK

Easy ways to conserve energy,
protect your family's health,
and help save the environment

Diane Gow McDilda

▲

Adams Media
Avon, Massachusetts

To everyone who wants to leave the world a better place.

An Everything® Series Book.
Everything® and everything.com® are registered trademarks of F+W Publications, Inc.

Published by Adams Media, an F+W Publications Company
57 Littlefield Street, Avon, MA 02322 U.S.A.
www.adamsmedia.com

ISBN-10: 1-59869-425-1
ISBN-13: 978-1-59869-425-3

Printed in the United States of America.
The pages of this book are printed on 100% post-consumer recycled paper.

J I H G F E D C

Library of Congress Cataloging-in-Publication Data
McDilda, Diane Gow.
The everything green living book / Diane Gow McDilda.
p. cm.
Includes index.
ISBN-13: 978-1-59869-425-3 (pbk.)
ISBN-10: 1-59869-425-1 (pbk.)
1. Environmental protection—Citizen participation. 2. Human ecology. I. Title.
TD171.7.M375 2007
640—dc22
2007018982

This publication is designed to provide accurate and authoritative information with regard to the subject matter covered. It is sold with the understanding that the publisher is not engaged in rendering legal, accounting, or other professional advice. If legal advice or other expert assistance is required, the services of a competent professional person should be sought.

—From a *Declaration of Principles* jointly adopted by a Committee of the American Bar Association and a Committee of Publishers and Associations

Many of the designations used by manufacturers and sellers to distinguish their products are claimed as trademarks. Where those designations appear in this book and Adams Media was aware of a trademark claim, the designations have been printed with initial capital letters.

This book is available at quantity discounts for bulk purchases.
For information, please call 1-800-289-0963.

Contents

Acknowledgments

To my husband Alton and my daughters Katelin and Cassidy. They came through in the crunch, making this book a team effort. There were times I felt like I was living with my own personal cheerleaders. And thanks to my mom, Susanne, who decades ago taught me how to write, explaining patiently from another room that the letter "t" looked like a telephone pole.

Thanks to the many environmentally conscious people in this and earlier generations who broke ground on this diverse and important topic. We owe a debt of gratitude to the scientists, engineers, and journalists who brought important issues to light so that we can all work together to solve them.

Foreword

For more than a century, conservationists have spent time striving to save the world. They have written letters, marched, protested, and even celebrated in pursuit of that cause. For twenty years, I've worked for The Nature Conservancy, whose mission is to preserve the world's plants, animals, and natural communities. We save great places to protect nature and preserve life. Yet after all the acres saved, species protected, laws passed, and regulations enacted, something more is needed to save our planet. In short, people need to have a conservation ethic: to care about the environment and know what they can do about it. That is why this book, *The Everything® Green Living Book*, is so important; it helps instill that conservation ethic and shows us how to live accordingly.

The expression "Think globally, act locally" describes an effective approach to conservation, but it could be improved to include individual actions people can take to live more lightly on the earth. To me, acting locally to preserve the environment means neighborhood cleanup projects, recycling activities, and community gardens. In this book, Diane McDilda guides people to the next step of making their personal lives more environmentally friendly. She describes everyday actions that each individual can take to preserve our planet and its amazing natural resources. Thus, a new expression might be to "dream globally, join in locally, act personally" because it conveys the idea that people need to visualize a greener world, participate in community improvement activities, and make their own lives compatible with a healthy environment.

The timing is just right for *The Everything® Green Living Book*. People are starting to realize that caring about the environment is not just a once-per-year activity on Earth Day; nor is it a "mom and apple pie" idealism that is quickly forgotten when they make choices about consumer products, home improvements, transportation, and political candidates. Caring for the environment needs to be an integral part of everyday life.

In recent years I have questioned Earth Day and our schools' environmental education because after almost forty Earth Days and millions of students becoming adults, we should have more to show for it. Sure, the air and water are cleaner, yet the earth is warming, resources are being depleted, species face extinction, and in politics and business, the environment consistently comes after other concerns. But, as people are becoming more aware of global warming and its human causes, they want to do things in their own lives to address the problem. They are beginning to realize that a new and widely held conservation ethic will move us to the next phase of saving our planet.

When my son was in kindergarten, the teacher taught him about choices: a bad choice brings trouble and a good choice earns rewards. *The Everything® Green Living Book* is a book about choices. Make bad choices, and we will all suffer and possibly not survive. Make good choices, and this beautiful world, full of bountiful life and amazing possibilities, will be hospitable for humans and our fellow travelers for thousands of years to come. Let's make good choices.

Christopher J. Maron
Champlain Valley Program Director
The Nature Conservancy—Adirondack, New York Chapter

Top 10 "Green" Things You Will Know after Reading This Book

1. Putting up solar panels or even a windmill can provide enough power to supply your home, and you can sell the extra electricity to the power utilities.

2. The quality of the air inside your house may be worse than the air outside.

3. If you are getting around on gasoline, there are ways to increase your gas mileage and lower your emissions.

4. You can buy centuries-old reclaimed lumber to use for projects in your home.

5. Death can be green; use an earth-friendly casket.

6. Supermarkets can be adopted and encouraged to carry organic products.

7. Antibiotics are used to keep feedlot cattle healthy because their diets and confinement make them sick.

8. Babies can sleep safely on beds made of natural latex; it's hypoallergenic and resistant to dust mites.

9. Joining a car-sharing group means you can have a car when you need one without the regular expense.

10. If you take an ecovacation, you'll be helping the environment while supporting a local economy and having a great time.

Introduction

▶ THE ENVIRONMENTAL MOVEMENT has been gaining momentum for decades, but with so much at stake now with global climate change, genetically modified foods, pesticides, and the like, many people are looking at it for the first time. It can be overwhelming. Green living and the environment touch every aspect of your life, and that is a lot of information to process—not to mention the decisions you will have to make. It sounds deep, but learning comes in parts—and chapters.

This book is an introduction to green living. It includes background on different environmental topics so you can understand why things are the way they are and how situations came to be. For instance, why do power plants pollute? What are some of the challenges with petroleum production and the country's dependency on it? Part of the process of getting a little greener is learning enough to make informed decisions. You will be able to decide what measures you want to take and get some ideas on how you can tread a little lighter and leave a smaller footprint on the planet.

As big as the environmental movement has become, it still has a way to go. Common marketing campaigns urge everyone to buy this and consume that, but more thought needs to be given to what goes into popular products—the process, the means, and the ends. Anyone, any consumer, can read labels to learn about products and make informed purchase decisions. Anyone who is concerned or curious about a product or process can research the company and its policies and practices.

Sometimes all it takes is an e-mail or a phone call to find out just how green a product is.

Many people would just like to learn more about what is going on with the environment and what they can do to help the planet—and that's who this book is written for. If you have decided today is the day you will start living a greener life, that's great. But understand that doesn't mean throwing away all your furniture, altering your entire diet, and buying all new clothes. Anyone can switch to a greener lifestyle gradually—changing a habit here, selecting a different product there, reading a magazine, or checking out a different Web site. Think of it as gradual greening. You can make changes slowly over time and focus on the ones that are most important to you. Pick a topic and see how it fits with your lifestyle.

Many people may be surprised at what topic piques their interest. Maybe they'll decide that organic farming or developing a recycling program is something they'd like to tackle. Maybe they'll even take a stab at politics or join a community organization. That's one thing about the green movement—by becoming part of it, you're never alone. It's a group that spans generations and crosses economic and racial divides, and what this movement shares is a desire, a dream, a goal to leave the world a better place.

For now, sit back and enjoy the book and give yourself a big pat on the back for taking the first step in leading a greener life.

Chapter 1

The Earth and the Environment

The state of the environment has been a controversial topic for many years. There are disappearing flora and fauna, depleted stores of natural resources, rising temperatures worldwide—and many fingers pointing at who or what is to blame. Collective care and nurturing of the planet has waxed and waned over the decades, but today more people seem to want to get involved. Where do you start if you're looking to live a greener life? The truth is, there are plenty of places. For example, become familiar with the background of the environment and get a feel for what's going on with the world and what can be done to help.

The Momentum of Earth Day

Although it wasn't the first such rally, the first Earth Day on April 22, 1970, succeeded like never before in raising awareness about the earth, natural resources, and pollution. Politicians, citizens, and school kids became involved, organizing antilitter campaigns and working to save endangered species. That same day, a televised public service announcement aired, showing Chief Iron Eyes walking over a shoreline covered in trash and watching as drivers threw garbage from their car windows. A single tear ran down his cheek as the announcer said, "People start pollution. People can stop it."

Although Earth Day may have helped galvanize political movements, these issues and concerns were not new. Rachel Carson's *Silent Spring* was published in 1962. Carson's work is cited as one of the mainstream books that introduced the nation to the problems with pesticides. A woman ahead of her time, Carson pointed out the importance of the food chain and the impact insect-controlling pesticides had on birds and fish. While critics saw her as a menace to organized agriculture, segments of the population understood—and respected—her need to protect the environment.

FACT

The original "tree-huggers" are thought to be the Bishnois in India, who live by a set of principles that instruct them not to kill trees or animals. In the 1700s, the Bishnois wrapped themselves around trees to protect them from being cut down. Although more than 300 of the Bishnois were killed, that protective act later became a successful way to spare trees, and it continues today.

To many, Earth Day and environmental protection were associated with war protestors, teens and young adults, and hippies looking for a cause. But today, increasing numbers of common folk are looking to the planet as a resource that needs to be sustained—a difficult task that cannot be undertaken only one day a year. Taking on one act at a time, choosing sustainable options over more damaging ones, thinking about purchases and their impact on the environment, seeking to raise generations with respect for the planet—any of these actions will help make every day Earth Day.

The World Today

Earth has three main components: the air we breathe, the land we live on, and the water that nourishes us. All of them have been affected by pollution, but there are ways to minimize future damage.

It's in the Air

Although the complex mechanics of air quality were not understood until recently, air quality has been an issue dating back to medieval times, when coal-burning furnaces choked peoples' lungs. In recent decades, the quality of the outside air arose as a concern, but now indoor air pollution is becoming more of a problem as well.

The world's largest stationary air polluters are power plants, followed by factories, dry cleaners, and degreasing operations used to clean metal equipment and machine parts. Add to that mobile sources of air pollution such as cars, buses, planes, and trains. Some air pollutants impact local conditions, and others travel upward and then float on air currents until they settle elsewhere. Individually, people can alter their driving habits and become involved politically to maintain or improve the air quality in their town, city, or state.

The U.S. Congress passed the Clean Air Act in 1970, followed by amendments and complementary legislation in the following years and decades. The goal was to lower air pollution by reducing emissions of many common pollutants. Industries and corporations had to meet set standards for their own operations and products. Individual states have their own regulations aimed at curtailing pollution within their borders.

The Foundation for Clean Air Progress estimates that it would take twenty modern cars to produce the same amount of pollution as one car from the 1960s. This improvement, along with reduced air emissions from factories and power plants, is reflected by the decrease in the number of poor-air-quality days in many metropolitan areas.

Indoor air pollution is a concern in many households. From formaldehyde in furniture to dangerous chemicals in fragrances and even hazardous radon in building materials, indoor air quality can't be taken for granted anymore. Some commercial cleaners and pesticides have harmful chemicals that contribute to indoor air pollution as well. Armed with information, people can choose to make changes in the way they live, the way they furnish their houses, and in other activities that potentially impact the air quality they breathe in every day. To help lower indoor air pollution levels, consider the products you use before you buy them and make sure your home is well ventilated.

The Land

It's easy to take soil for granted, but dirt is definitely more than a reason to run the vacuum. It sustains life both on the surface and belowground. Soil controls the flow of water over land, filters chemicals, and stores nutrients. It supports the structures that people live and work in. When the soil is neglected, the life that depends on it is damaged as well.

Soil is the outermost layer of the planet. In a way, it functions as the planet's skin, a protective layer. It's made from rocks, plants, and animals that have decayed over hundreds of years—just one inch of topsoil takes up to 500 years to form. Beneath the surface, a complex ecosystem comprised of minerals, water, air, fungi, bacteria, and plant material works together.

Earthworms are essential to soil health. Living at different depths underground, these animals digest organic matter like plant litter, leaving behind casts that become a vital part of the soil. For more information on earthworms, check out ✐*www.backyardnature.net.*

Contamination from human activities weighs heavily on the soil. Industrial impacts include unremediated chemical spills, pesticide contamination from agricultural practices, and runoff from livestock farms with cattle operations. Also devastating are mining activities that alter the surface and subsurface. Not only are the ecosystems living in the soil destroyed, but drainage patterns on the surface are distorted and waste products from mines often degrade the quality of the soil and even nearby water bodies. Even old unlined landfills can leach liquids into the ground, contaminating groundwater as well as soil. Erosion also impacts the soil. When the uppermost layer of soil detaches, it takes with it nutrients and composition needed to sustain plants and structures.

Strides are being made in protecting the soil. As people become more aware of their individual impacts on the planet and more industries are held accountable, improvements in protection are becoming the norm rather than the exception. Industries that work with hazardous chemicals and other materials can take advantage of plant designs and barrier systems that are intended to prevent accidental spills from contaminating nearby soil and water. Agricultural techniques, such as leaving plant materials from previous harvests on the field, help reduce erosion and improve soil quality.

Deep in the Ocean

The world's oceans are home to some of the largest, smallest, and most diverse animal populations on the planet. They are majestic environments that hold unknown mysteries humans are only beginning to discover.

FACT

In 1943, French oceanographer Jacques Cousteau partnered with Emile Gagnan to develop the first self-contained underwater breathing apparatus, or SCUBA. This invention allowed divers all over the world to observe underwater beauty and gain an understanding of its complexities. His television show, *The Underworld Sea of Jacques Cousteau*, ran from 1968 through 1976 and introduced this fragile world to the masses.

Humans impact the oceans through destructive fishing practices, ocean dumping, and industrial discharge to the air and the water. Because so many countries share ocean coastlines, it's not always easy coming to a consensus on the best way to protect them, or even on defining what exactly needs protecting. One country may see harvesting sea life as a necessity while others watch on in disgust. Marine mammals may beach themselves in one area as a result of activity in another. The sea is a complex environment, but there are stewards and backers who work endlessly to protect it. Environmental groups lobby governments and international organizations such as the United Nations for policy changes to protect the oceans.

It's in the Water

Protecting resources like drinking water is paramount for society, but it often comes only after shortages are permanent. In areas all over the United States, especially in the Southwest and now the Southeast, water wars are frequent as rising populations strain limited supplies.

Water sources like rivers, streams, and aquifers have been tapped for irrigation. The demand has forced water management districts and environmental protection agencies to deny new well construction permits. In certain cases, however, the impact has not been all bad. As the price for water has increased, the use of treated wastewater effluent has become more acceptable. Where perfectly good drinking water was pumped miles away to fields of crops, pipelines are now placed so effluent, or graywater, can be used for irrigation. Not only does this alleviate an added strain on the water table, it provides an outlet for effluent rather than discharging it into estuaries and bays.

Water flushed from household toilets and drained from residential washing machines can be converted to graywater with minimal treatment and reused for irrigation. Individual graywater systems are being approved for residents, with states like Arizona leading the way. Not only does graywater offset the demand for treating water to the highest potable standard, it may actually be beneficial to plants as it's likely to contain nitrogen and phosphorus.

The quality of some water supplies has been negatively impacted as a result of poorly run industries, old landfills, septic tanks, pesticides and fertilizers used on crops, and other common causes. Regulators and watchdog groups alike try to monitor water quality, ensuring that no one is in harm's way.

Global Climate Change

It's practically impossible to listen to the radio, watch television, or read a newspaper without hearing about global climate change. The majority of scientists agree that action needs to be taken to stop, and eventually reverse, the trend of global warming. Economists debate the cost of solutions versus the financial benefits of adaptation to new climate conditions.

The Greenhouse Effect

Agents causing global warming work collectively to increase the earth's temperature. Greenhouse gases—such as carbon dioxide, methane, nitrous oxide, and ground-level ozone—trap heat within the atmosphere, causing a warming effect similar to that in a greenhouse. Changes in land use have also impacted global climate change but not to the degree that greenhouse gases have. Clearing forest land for development increases the warming. Since trees absorb carbon dioxide and convert it to oxygen, cutting them down without replacing them means more carbon dioxide stays in the atmosphere.

The result is global warming and an increased potential for far-reaching consequences. Storms may become more severe, biodiversity may be adversely affected as ecosystems change, and polar icecaps may melt, causing ocean water levels to rise. Large-scale environmental impacts can increase potential dangers to public health.

QUESTION?

Will global warming lead to increased numbers of hurricanes or stronger hurricanes?

Not necessarily, according to a 2007 report from the Intergovernmental Panel on Climate Change. The IPCC found inconclusive evidence that global warming contributed to the number of hurricanes. However, the IPCC reported better than two-to-one odds that human activities contributed to the intensity of hurricanes.

The World Community

The world today seems much smaller than it was mere decades ago. Little can happen in one part of the globe that doesn't eventually affect another place half a world away. No one person, no one country, no one continent is truly independent.

World agencies recognize this fact and work together toward consensus on topics such as protecting sensitive coral reefs and diverse ocean populations, managing forests to allow logging while maintaining sustainable growth, ensuring air quality not just for individual communities but the world over, reducing the damaging effects of fossil fuel, and understanding the impacts of chemicals on people and the environment. However, individual efforts are essential to help improve all aspects of the environment. No one person is independent of other living things, and no one ecosystem is independent of the others.

In 1997, under the auspices of the United Nations, representatives met in Kyoto, Japan, to discuss global air quality. The result was the Kyoto treaty, an international framework for managing greenhouse gases and improving air quality. The agreement binds nations to restrict their greenhouse gas emissions over time. Developed nations must submit to more stringent restrictions than developing nations. The goal is for each developed nation to release fewer greenhouse gases by 2012 than it did in 1990. The target emissions rates were negotiated on a country-by-country basis. Developing nations are exempt from reducing emissions until 2012. To date, more than 160 nations have ratified the treaty, including 35 developed nations. The United States and Australia have refrained from ratifying the treaty, claiming it would cost jobs and hurt their domestic economies.

Countries in the European Union, in compliance with the Kyoto treaty, limit the amount of carbon dioxide individual power plants and other large sources of emissions are allowed to produce within a certain time frame. Facilities whose emissions fall below the emissions cap can sell credits to facilities that overshoot their target emissions. The amount of carbon dioxide facilities are allowed to produce will be gradually reduced over time, resulting in fewer emissions. Since carbon dioxide is one of the principle culprits in global warming, carbon trading has been lauded as a way to offset emissions. In 2008, the European Union is expected to phase in regulations incorporating more industries and more greenhouse gases.

California is one of the largest producers of greenhouse gas emissions in the world. The state has committed to reducing emissions to 80 percent below 1990 levels by the year 2050. The reduction will be implemented by enforcing emission caps and implementing sector-specific regulatory programs. Rather than hurting the economy, these changes could potentially increase job growth as new industries and technologies develop to support this goal.

In the United States, some states are looking to renewable energy sources—wind, water, and solar energy—for electricity. To date, twenty-three states and the District of Columbia have set standards for how much of their electricity must be generated by renewable sources. Individuals can offset their own carbon production using a variety of measures. They can determine their impact on global warming by calculating the amount of carbon dioxide they produce. Calculations are based on size of household, miles driven and types of cars, air miles flown, and the amount of garbage generated. Web sites such as *www.conservationfund.org* not only assist people with the calculations, they also accept donations to plant the number of trees needed to offset a household's carbon production. In theory, the trees produce enough oxygen to make up for the amount of carbon dioxide individuals generate.

The Chemicals of Concern

It seems the world is inundated with human-made chemicals. They are in the food, the air, and the water. Are all synthetic chemicals bad? Many manufactured chemicals, such as pesticides and food preservatives, were developed solely to protect people and were lauded for their success. Although pesticides have been invaluable in eradicating diseases like malaria, they've become burdensome as a group. Many don't easily break down in the environment and have been linked to cancer and birth defects in humans.

Preservatives were used initially to make sure food would remain safe and could be stored over longer periods. They now include colorants and flavorings that go beyond maintaining safety, allowing the foods to keep their looks and taste. Levels of preservatives, with chemical names such as butylated hydroxyanisole (BHA) and butylated hydroxytoluene (BHT), are regulated by the U.S. Food and Drug Administration (FDA) and are permitted to be used at concentrations generally recognized as safe (GRAS). Recently, the public has been clamoring for fresher and less chemically preserved food, not just to avoid preservatives but also to gain health benefits such as nutrients and fiber from whole food. Another motivation for the organic food movement is to protect the environment. People concerned with the production and application of pesticides on crops and antibiotics in animals are looking to organic foods to encourage a more earth friendly way to raise food. Statistics kept on file by the U.S. Department of Agriculture Economic Research Service show that the amount of land used for organic farming or grazing has increased considerably over the years. In 1992, there were about 532,050 acres of organic pasture. That area increased to 2.2 million by 2005. In the same time span, organic cropland increased from 403,400 acres to 1.7 million acres.

FACT

Diseases caused by mosquitoes, including West Nile virus and encephalitis, continue to be a health problem in the United States. Because of these diseases, local governments see the controlled use of pesticides as an important part of managing the mosquito population and resultant diseases.

Some chemicals are introduced not for their potential health benefits but for product improvement and better performance. Phthalates such as dibutyl phthalate (DBP) and dihexyl phthalate (DEHP) are added to plastics to make them flexible and to extend the life of the material. Now these chemicals have been identified as suspected endocrine disruptors that mimic hormones in the bodies of animals. There has been some evidence that young male animals exposed to high phthalate concentrations have reduced sperm counts. Serious situations like these rally scientists and the general public alike to evaluate the best way to simultaneously meet the goals of convenience and health.

Degradation of Natural Resources

The disappearance of natural resources damages an area and limits its ability to sustain a population. The population could be trees, sea grass, animals, or even people. Often, this damage is the result of beneficial activities performed irresponsibly. Wastewater discharged into an estuary can alter the salinity, affecting the lifecycle of sea grass and fish nurseries. If fishing is a source of income for a community, not only will improper treatment and disposal of wastewater damage natural resources, but it will harm the local economy as well.

On a larger scale, natural resources can be impacted to a point that they can no longer be repaired. Species cannot be brought back and populations can no longer survive on the land. Damage from deforestation impacts biodiversity, causes soil erosion, and limits the farming of an area.

Degradation of natural resources often has a chain effect. For example, consider the impact that clearing acres of rain forest for farming has on the environment—both local and global. The soil cannot support crops that are harvested on a yearly basis and its productivity quickly diminishes. As income decreases along with the crop yield, farmers abandon the land in search of more fertile fields, increasing pressure on local resources. The deforested land does not absorb rainwater as before, so rainfall causes more water to flow into nearby rivers all at once, flooding downstream villages and cities. However, drought is also an outcome of deforestation. Part of the reason rain forests are so wet is that trees play a vital role in supplying water to the atmosphere through transpiration; without trees, the water to produce rain simply isn't there. Haphazard deforestation results in patches of remaining forest separated by cleared land. Plants and animals are effectively marooned, isolated from their species. Fewer options can result in inbreeding, weakening the gene pool. Larger species, usually predators, are especially vulnerable to population loss simply because there are so few of them. A bad breeding year, a natural disaster, or a disease can wipe them out. On a global scale, deforestation contributes to a buildup of greenhouse gases; fewer trees mean more carbon dioxide is left in the atmosphere.

However, people are gaining a better understanding that one system cannot operate at the expense of another. Conservation of natural resources has become a priority for businesses and governments, which tout sustainability as a way to strike a balance between helping the environment and preventing economic or personal hardship.

Sustainability: The Word of the Day

Sustainability is the balance between people and the environment. Air, water, and land are all impacted by the behavior and actions of human beings, but these impacts can be controlled so they do not cause as much damage while allowing all involved to maintain a comfortable existence. The art of sustainable living is the ability to support communities today without jeopardizing the environment for tomorrow.

Sustainability touches every aspect of life, from food to housing to how corporations conduct business. The Global Reporting Initiative (GRI) is an organization that sets a framework for global companies to report on their sustainable practices, as measured by economic, environmental, and social factors. Currently, close to 1,000 companies from more than sixty different countries participate in this voluntary program. Members include professionals worldwide who work with government, corporations, and social organizations. As a result, companies have been acknowledged not just for participating in the reporting but for including sustainability in their mainstream operating practices. The Dow Jones Sustainability Index manages the criteria and takes charge of monitoring which companies are listed on its index or on other socially responsible investment funds. The Dow Jones Sustainability World Index tracks the top 250 sustainable corporations from the 2,500 largest companies in the Dow Jones Global Index. Some of the companies included on the Sustainability Index include General Electric, BP, and Toyota.

ALERT!

A 2006 study by Brian Halweil of Worldwatch Institute recommends that consumers lead the drive in saving the world's oceans by choosing fish that support a sustainable marine environment. Suggestions include purchasing fish from smaller operations that are less likely to use damaging practices, avoiding threatened species, and eating lower on the food chain (i.e., oysters, clams, and smaller species).

Maintaining sustainability isn't just up to corporations and governments, however; individuals bringing it into their everyday lives make an impact. Sustainability is making decisions with a new set of values—not a value set that hangs over your head like a cloud, but an understanding that there's a great deal you can do to preserve the environment for future generations while providing for yourself today. By making personal choices in what you buy, how you drive, and what kind of energy you use, you can support a more sustainable lifestyle.

Chapter 2

Greening the Grid

The electrical power grid puts energy at your fingertips. Most electricity is generated from burning coal—a limited resource—and even with recent improvements in technology, it can be a detriment to the environment. For this and other reasons, environmentally friendly and renewable ways of generating power are gaining popularity. This chapter gives some insight into the current practices of producing energy and some of the newest innovations and trends in ways of greening the grid.

Traditional Energy and Its Impact

By and large, electricity is generated using coal-fired power plants. Unfortunately, the same process that provides electricity to so many homes is also a major contributor to global climate change.

ALERT!

The EPA reported the ten warmest days recorded took place within the last fifteen years. This warming has resulted in measurable melting of polar icecaps and a decrease in ice in the Arctic Ocean. The past 100 years have also seen an increase in sea levels of four to eight inches. Like the majority of forecasts, the change in ocean level is calculated with mathematical models that use estimated variables in different scenarios. The variables used—such as the estimated level of carbon dioxide in the atmosphere and ocean temperatures—are based on existing data that have been extrapolated for future estimates. This results in a range, rather than an absolute, change in ocean levels.

Fossil fuels are the carbon-based power behind today's society. The name *fossil fuels* isn't an arbitrary choice. Formed about 300 million years ago, fossil fuels are made from plants and trees that died, fell into swamps and oceans, and were covered by more and more dead plants and trees. Eventually, sand and clay piled up and turned to rock, squeezing any remaining water out of the decayed plants and trees. After exposure to heat and pressure in the earth's crust over hundreds of millions of years, fossils turn into common fuels: coal, oil, and natural gas. The U.S. Energy Information Administration reports that the national average of electricity generated can be broken down by source as follows:

- **Coal**—49.7 percent
- **Nuclear**—19.3 percent
- **Natural gas**—18.7 percent
- **Hydroelectric**—6.5 percent
- **Petroleum**—3.0 percent

- **Renewables**—2.3 percent
- **Other gases**—0.4 percent
- **Other**—0.1 percent

Coal

Coal is a hard, black sedimentary rock that is actively mined in the United States and in other countries all over the world. One reason coal is used widely as a power source in the United States is that it is such a plentiful domestic resource. It's the primary feedstock in power plants today; 50 percent of all electricity is produced by coal. When it's burned to produce electricity, coal generates wastes like sludge and ash. Additionally, a significant amount of water is needed to complete the process.

The Union of Concerned Scientists estimates there about 600 coal-fueled power plants operating in the United States today, and the push is on to bring more online, possibly to construct plants before stronger air compliance legislation is enacted that could inhibit permitting of these plants. Coal gasification plants, while also relying on fossil fuel, burn much cleaner than standard coal power plants, but the initial cost to build these plants is about 20 percent higher. As a result, coal gasification plants have not become as popular as proponents had hoped.

However, more cities and institutions are turning to renewable resources for their energy, a trend that is likely to continue as public awareness increases. In addition, reducing energy use and improving efficiency can control electricity production demands.

Oil and Petroleum

Beyond producing electricity, fossil fuels are also the prime power behind cars. Oil, or petroleum, was initially used to light lamps, to treat frostbite, and to waterproof canoes. In the United States, more than 50 percent of the oil used comes from other countries. Crude oil is imported and then refined by heating and separating out the different petroleum compounds. The American Petroleum Institute (API) estimates that one 42-gallon barrel of crude oil can actually produce 44.2 gallons of petroleum products. This net gain isn't magic, however; it's a result of other chemicals added to the crude oil to synthesize certain compounds. At least twelve different compounds are produced from refining crude oil. From one barrel, about 19.5 gallons of crude are converted to gasoline, 9.2 gallons to diesel, and 4.1 gallons to jet fuel. The remaining compounds are used to make everything from plastics to pesticides to clothing.

Unfortunately, before crude oil ever makes it to the processing facility, it's already impacted the environment. Crude oil, a fossil fuel, is formed by the decomposition of tiny plants and plankton. They lived and died in ancient seas, accumulating in limestone and sandstone. Locating the oil's position, sandwiched between layers of impermeable rock miles below the surface, is complicated. Different methods are employed to ferret out the reservoirs, including magnetometers that measure changes in the earth's magnetic field, sniffers that smell out hydrocarbons, and seismology that reads shock waves originating on the surface to determine if oil is hidden in the depths.

Once found, wells are drilled either on land or in the ocean, and the crude is pumped to the surface using an industrialized process. On land, miles of roads and pipeline and hundreds of drilling pads are needed at the site of the wells. Pump stations are constructed along with pipe line routes. In the ocean, rigs are constructed on sensitive ocean floors, and tankers are used to convey the crude. The construction of oil wells produces drilling mud that must be treated. Spills of crude oil can occur during pumping or transporting, and these spills have the potential to contaminate the oceans, soil, groundwater, and surface water. Sludge and wastewater produced during refinement have to be treated and carefully disposed.

In areas with high mineral reserves and little environmental regulation, drilling for oil can have devastating effects on the local culture. Rain forests and indigenous cultures in remote locations such as the Ecuadorian rain forest have been destroyed by drilling.

In the United States, the Arctic National Wildlife Refuge (ANWR) has been considered a viable source for sustaining domestic oil supply. Supporters believe drilling domestically will increase U.S. independence from foreign oil. Opponents argue the environmental impact is too great to justify the potential volume of oil in the ANWR. They estimate that a volume equivalent to as few as six months' worth of oil could be gleaned from the area. The drilling also carries the potential to impact animal populations of caribou, polar bears, musk oxen, snow geese, and other birds and mammals.

Problems with Traditional Power Sources

Burning fossil fuels produces the energy necessary to run homes, offices, and automobiles. In the process, they release pollutants and contribute to global warming. Two of those pollutants—sulfur dioxide and nitrogen oxide—react with water or moisture in the air to form nitric and sulfuric acids. These chemicals fall to the earth in the form of acid rain, damaging trees, soil, and waterways.

Mercury that escapes coal-burning power plants through smoke stacks may wind up settling on rivers, lakes, estuaries, and bays. Fish absorb the mercury and then pass it along to humans who eat the fish. The EPA and local health departments publish warnings on mercury content in different types of fish. Mercury is especially harmful to the nervous systems of unborn fetuses, babies, and young children.

Urban ozone, or smog, is also a by-product of coal-burning power plants. Smog can be detrimental to people, particularly children and the elderly, in whom it can cause wheezing, shortness of breath, and coughing.

For these and other reasons, people have started to look at alternatives when it comes to providing electricity. Geographic information systems (GIS), for example, help municipalities and utilities determine the best sustainable energy method for them. While GIS are best known for providing maps, the system has been expanded to include real data points that can be used to perform calculations specific to certain geographical points. This allows organizations like the National Renewable Energy Laboratory (NREL) to coordinate sustainable energy sources such as wind, solar, and geothermal generators with population information to determine potential energy sources for a specific area.

Solar Power

Solar power converts energy from the sun into electricity. There are two basic methods of using solar power to generate electricity: concentrated solar power (CSP) plants and photovoltaic cells (PV). The CSP plants are more mechanical in nature. Sunlight is used to heat a fluid, which then operates a generator and produces electricity. It operates much like a conventional power plant, but the energy source is sunlight rather than fossil fuels such as coal or natural gas. The PV uses sunlight to move electrons in a solar cell, which produces electricity. There are few mechanical or moving parts with this type of operation.

CSP plants are the larger of the two. They can accommodate the needs of a small community or can generate enough electricity to flow into the grid and supplement power generated by other means. Parabolic troughs are curved collectors that concentrate light onto a receiver that heats up transfer fluid located within the trough. The heated fluid then runs a generator, which produces electricity. Troughs can operate in parallel to make a collector field. The troughs are rounded so they can collect sunlight from all angles, eliminating the need to move as the day progresses. The trough systems in operation are hybrid facilities that use both solar power and fossil fuel to run generators. Towers use mirrors to track the sun and collect light. Dish systems use a solar dish to collect sunlight, which produces electricity through a generator.

Nanosolar, a private company that is committed to providing affordable solar panels, is at the forefront of solar technology. The company was started with money from Google founders Larry Page and Sergey Brin and other investors in 2002. Headquartered in Palo Alto, California, Nanosolar came one step closer to its goal of being the global leader in its field in December 2006 when it announced its plans to carry out research and manufacturing at two new facilities in California and Germany.

PV operations are generally limited to smaller electricity production. They are becoming more common on houses and are used in a wide variety of systems where a power source is needed, but connection to a grid is not feasible. Such is the case with some flashing traffic signals, cell phones, and direct television. Homeowners who are able to generate more solar power than they need have the ability in some locations to sell the power back to their local utilities.

Solar power is still slightly more expensive than traditional fossil fuel options, but the cost for solar power is expected to decrease as more private and public utility plants appear and solar cell technology advances.

Many municipalities have installed solar power systems at locations with high energy demands, such as schools and municipal administration buildings. For example, Santa Clara, California, encourages residents and businesses to use solar energy for heating water. As part of the program, the city will install and maintain solar water-heating systems for swimming pools and domestic hot water. Businesses can also utilize the service for heating process water.

Oakland, California, uses one of the state's largest municipal solar projects to provide electricity to over 1,000 homes. What's called the 1.1 Megawatt City project uses more than 6,000 solar electric tiles and is estimated to eliminate 385 tons of carbon dioxide emissions a year.

Federal, state, and local organizations and governments fund incentives and rebate programs for homeowners who install residential solar units. These programs help offset the cost of installing home solar units. A variable sometimes left out of the economic calculation is that once a solar unit is paid for, the electricity is free.

Wind Power

Throughout history, windmills have been used primarily as grinding mills, sawmills, or even water-pumping mills. Today they are used to harness the wind's kinetic energy. Wind moves the mill's blades, which rotate a shaft that in turn moves gears connected to a generator. The generator creates electricity.

Not only is wind renewable, it's clean, and it doesn't produce any deleterious by-products that other forms of energy do. Wind energy doesn't depend on process water as do coal and nuclear power. Wind power is generated domestically; there is no dependence on other countries to produce energy for local use. Also, harnessing wind power doesn't require mining operations as coal does, but there are some drawbacks to wind energy, including the negative impact of windmills on wild bird populations. Individual birds may be killed or injured by flying into rotating windmill blades.

Wind is the fastest-growing energy source, and per kilowatt, it is coming close to the cost to generate electricity using fossil fuels. The cost of installing windmills is recouped more quickly than other emerging technologies.

Wind turbines require an extensive amount of land, which can make them more difficult to site in urban areas. Beside land availability, wind turbine sites must be located within high wind energy areas either on land or over the water. Wind power also brings clean, high-tech jobs to the farmlands of the American West, rural Appalachia, and possibly coastal communities as well.

Research continues to improve this technology, making it more affordable. It's expected that wind power could eventually produce 20 percent of the electricity used in the United States. According to the U.S. Department of Energy, wind-produced energy totaled 11,603 megawatts of electricity in 2006. That's enough to provide for 2.9 million homes. Wind farms are more prevalent in the western United States than in any other part of the country. California has the most windmills, followed by Texas.

Puget Sound Energy owns and operates two wind farms in Washington State. The Hopkins Ridge farm has 83 turbines and supplies electricity to 50,000 homes. The Wild Horse wind farm is near completion. It will have 127 wind turbine generators capable of supporting 73,000 homes with electricity.

ALERT!

Some opponents of wind farms cite the danger to bats, migratory birds, and raptors like red-tailed hawks and eagles. Companies are working more with local bird authorities to ensure that migratory populations are considered and that safer design elements are included to help birds steer clear of the turbines.

Xcel Energy is the largest supplier of wind energy in the country with customers in Colorado, New Mexico, and Minnesota. In 2006 the company produced 1,100 megawatts, and in 2007 the company expects to increase production to 2,300 megawatts. By 2012, it expects to add another 1,700 megawatts to the grid.

While not yet constructed, there are proposed plans for building offshore wind farms. On the Atlantic side, the Nantucket Sound wind farm, called Cape Wind, would include 130 wind turbines, and a wind farm in Buzzards Bay would have 90 to 120. The state of Texas currently has plans for a wind farm off Galveston Island and could possibly be the country's first offshore wind farm. Some of the challenges to these offshore wind farms include the visual impact on the landscape. Those living by the coast do not always favor offshore wind farms.

Offshore wind farms proposed for the United States are relatively close to shore, which helps restrain costs. While wind speeds are much higher farther off the coast, the wind turbine foundations must be constructed to withstand deeper water and higher waves, making construction more expensive. Another factor is the distance power must be relayed when farming offshore.

Organizations like the American Wind Energy Association (*www.awea.org*) are looking at safe wind farm designs that take marine life into account. They are comparing the potential dangers associated with constructing and operating offshore wind farms to other marine activities and other methods of generating electricity.

If you live in an apartment or other location where installing solar panels or windmills isn't an option, contacting the local electric utility is a good place to start. Some utilities offer green electricity that's generated from renewable sources, which often costs slightly more than standard electricity. Because green electricity goes to the grid along with electricity produced from nonrenewable sources, customers choosing the green alternative are not necessarily receiving only green electricity. They are, however, supporting the utility's effort to produce electricity from renewable or more environmentally friendly methods. Another option would be to consider approaching the building's owner or the homeowners' association about the possibility of adding solar panels or windmills to the apartment or condominium. Any local, state, or federal rebates or tax incentives would then go to the owner or association.

Biomass and Methane

Biomass is a collective term that means producing energy from plants or animals. One common method is burning plant material to heat water and generate electricity. Feedstock for biomass power facilities generally includes agricultural waste left over from harvesting, energy crops grown specifically for use as biomass, forestry remains after timber harvesting, and wood left over from mill operations. To provide the most sustainable alternatives, it's best to use plant material waste that is close to the biomass plant to avoid transportation impacts. Trees commonly farmed for use in biomass in the northern United States include hybrid poplars and willow; in the southeast, sycamore and sweet gum work well. These trees are amenable as feedstock because they grow quickly and will grow back after being harvested close to the ground. Grasses are also used as feedstock—mostly frequently, switchgrass, sugar cane, and elephant grass. Corn remains from harvesting for the food market are also used as a feedstock for biomass energy production. Corn specifically for use as fuel is not as sustainable as other plants because it requires pesticides, fertilizers, and energy to grow and frequently has to be transported to energy facilities, often negating the benefits of using it as a renewable resource.

Facilities can operate with either a pure biomass feedstock or with combined biomass and coal. Although biomass material does contain sulfur and nitrogen compounds, these are present at lower concentrations than coal and emit lower levels of sulfur dioxide and nitrogen oxides when burning.

The other common method of creating biomass includes digesting organic material like sludge or manure to produce methane, which is then burned, or flared, to produce electricity. Wastewater treatment plants are beginning to digest sludge at their facilities and then use the methane generated to help operate the treatment plant. In New York City, the North River facility uses electricity generated from digested methane to run some of the plant's operations.

FACT

The EPA runs two programs that assist with converting methane into electricity. The AgSTAR program works with swine and dairy farmers who are interested in purchasing and operating methane digesters. The Landfill Methane Outreach Program (LMOP) works to forge relationships between landfill owners and electric utility business. More information is available at the EPA's Web site at *www.epa.gov.*

In Marin County, California, the Straus Family Creamery uses the electricity generated from methane digesters not only to run their organic dairy but to charge up Albert Straus's electric car. And the dairy didn't stop with organic farming and digesting methane. The backup generator and the feed truck have both been converted to biodiesel. The family is in the process of converting all their farm vehicles to biodiesel.

Methane can also be obtained from landfills. The decomposition of waste produces methane, which can be collected and piped to generators where it is then converted to electricity and put out on the grid. The Omaha Public Power District uses methane that's generated by the decomposition of landfill waste as fuel. By utilizing the methane, the utility is able to generate 3 million watts of electricity—enough to run about 2,000 homes.

The Tennessee Valley Authority utilizes three sources of renewable energy, generating electricity from wind-powered turbines, solar generation sites, and methane gas from a wastewater treatment plant.

Geothermal Power

For every 100 meters you go belowground, the temperature of the rock increases about 3 degrees Celsius. Deep under the surface, water sometimes makes its way close to the hot rock and turns into boiling hot water or steam. Wells, some shallow and some miles deep, are drilled into the reservoirs and bring hot water or steam to the surface. Geothermal energy is most abundant and more easily accessible in places like Hawaii and Alaska where the geothermal reservoirs are closer to the surface. The shifting and moving tectonic plates in these areas enable the water heated from the magma below to escape more easily to the surface. Geothermal electricity is available virtually anywhere but is located much deeper, making retrieval less cost-effective. Geothermal energy is most heavily utilized in California and Nevada.

With geothermal energy, there are no air emissions. The only discards are salts and minerals that are discharged back into the reservoir with the excess water. To protect water supplies, reinjection takes place below the aquifers. Solids are generated at some geothermal plants, which extract minerals like silica and zinc and sell them. Proponents of using geothermal energy believe that reinjecting water into the reservoirs will provide steam as long as the earth's core continues to heat the water. However, experts with the U.S. National Renewable Energy Laboratory (NREL) have stated that individual reservoir heat diminishes over time and that reservoirs shouldn't be expected to last longer than thirty years.

California currently has the greatest number of power plants operating on geothermal energy, the most prolific plant being The Geysers. Located north of San Francisco, The Geysers came on line in 1960, spans 30 miles and now includes twenty-one power plants supplying approximately 750 megawatts of electricity, or enough to supply 750,000 homes. The Geysers is the sole source of power for Sonoma, Lake, and Mendocino counties, and it also supplies a portion of the power for Marin and Napa counties.

When not used to generate electricity, the hot water can be used directly to warm greenhouses and fish farms, clean industrial laundry, and dehydrate food like onions and garlic. People in Klamath Falls, Oregon, walk on sidewalks cleared of snow using geothermal heat piped underground.

Hydropower

Hydropower plants harness the kinetic energy of flowing water to power machinery or make electricity. There are typically three different types of hydropower facilities: impoundment, diversion, and pumped storage. The most common is impoundment in a dam that stores the water in a reservoir. Water flowing through the dam spins a turbine, which uses a generator to make electricity and sends it out to the grid. A diversion facility does not use a dam but instead diverts a portion of the river. Pumped storage requires the pumping of water from a lower reservoir to a higher reservoir so the water can be released when electrical demands are high.

Because water is not destroyed in the process of creating energy, it is considered a renewable resource. It doesn't produce pollutants like fossil fuels, and the dams are often used for flood control. Unfortunately, because hydropower relies on the natural water cycle, energy production can be impacted during dry seasons or times of drought. Hydroelectric plants also interfere with the natural flow of rivers and everything that moves along with them, including spawning fish and river and tributary flows. Another consideration with dams is "thermal pollution," because the water released on the other side of the turbine is often warmer than the water entering. This can have a negative effect on aquatic life that is suited to narrow temperature ranges.

Some companies and power utilities are incorporating the use of renewable resources into their conventional systems. ConEdison *Solutions* now includes a combination of wind and hydropower, offering customers an alternative to traditional power. By signing up for green power, customers receive a rebate and don't have to pay sales tax on the delivery of their power.

The National Geographic Society uses Africa's Zambezi River and the floodplain created by the Cahora Bassa Dam in a hydropower educational program. Students in grades nine through twelve are asked to consider the benefits, including the electricity produced for villages and irrigation water for farms, along with detrimental effects to the elephant population and teak trees. More information can be found at *www.nationalgeographic.com/geographyaction/ga45.html.*

On the downside, dams can also infuse the water with nitrogen and dissolved oxygen, causing problems with fish that are comparable to what divers call "the bends." At deeper depths, the gases are absorbed by the blood; when the fish surface, however, the bubbles come out of the blood and form on the eyes, skin, and gills with deadly results. Fish ladders and elevators can be installed on the upriver side of the dam, allowing safe passage for the fish upstream. This is particularly important when fish are migrating upstream to spawn. In some situations, fish are trapped and hauled upriver by truck. This is usually seen as a temporary measure and not relied on to protect fish populations long-term. Other concerns include the creation of floodplains in otherwise dry areas and the displacement of wildlife.

Nuclear Power

Although a bane to many environmentalists, nuclear power is still considered a viable option when it comes to considering alternatives to coal-powered facilities. Nuclear power is usually created by splitting either a uranium or plutonium atom, but other radioactive elements can be used. The splitting releases an incredible amount of energy, which is used to heat water and drive a steam turbine. The power plants are usually very clean and safe when operated correctly. However, problems associated with nuclear power include the partial meltdown of a reactor at Three Mile Island near Middletown, Pennsylvania, in 1979, and the explosion and widespread radioactive contamination experienced at the Chernobyl nuclear power plant in the former Soviet Union in 1986.

More than 100 nuclear power plants are currently operating in the United States. Waste produced from nuclear power plants includes high-level and low-level radioactive waste. High-level waste is the spent fuel. Although it's depleted, it continues to be radioactive for tens of thousands of years or longer and must be handled using remote-control equipment. The spent fuel is stored temporarily in water-cooled pools and dry casks at nuclear power plants across the country. Permanent storage requires burial of the material deep underground, and there are currently no permanent storage facilities in the United States. The U.S. Department of Energy identified Yucca Mountain in Nevada as a suitable location for permanent storage. The governor of that state opposed the selection but was overruled. Licensing and permitting of the facility has been delayed. So for now, only temporary storage of nuclear waste is available. Environmental concerns regarding the storage of nuclear waste generally stem from the transportation to the facility and the potential for a nuclear accident, spill, or terrorist attack. Nuclear waste is generally transported by rail to a place for storage, which because of its inherent dangers can impact the real-estate value along the transportation route as well as in the vicinity of the storage unit.

Low-level radioactive waste consists of items contaminated by radioactivity like rags, discarded clothing, and equipment. Low-level waste can be stored in shallow burials for upward of fifty years until radioactive levels are low enough for disposal of the material as a solid waste. The federal government allows states and tribal programs to operate storage facilities as long as they abide by standards at least as strict as the federal requirements. There are currently only four active locations approved for disposal of low-level radioactive waste.

ALERT!

According to the Union of Concerned Scientists (UCS), the Nuclear Regulatory Commission (NRC) does not require nuclear facilities to be adequately prepared in the event of a terrorist attack. The UCS wants to see potential attacks from airplanes, trucks, and boats considered when designing safety features. They also encourage the distribution of potassium iodide, an agent used in radiation emergencies, to all nearby residents.

Mining for radioactive minerals can also be a dirty business. Mill tailings generated as part of the mining process contain low levels of radioactivity but have long half-lives, up to tens of thousands of years. The tailings are sandy, silty material that will emit radon as it decays—the second leading cause of lung cancer.

The NRC and other federal agencies including the EPA, Occupational Safety and Health Agency, the Food and Drug Administration, and the Department of Transportation regulate laws governing different aspects of the nuclear industry. Title 10, Part 20 of the *Code of Federal Regulations* (CFR) includes standards for protection against radiation and dose limits for radiation workers and the public, monitoring and labeling of radioactive materials, posting of radiation areas, and reporting when radioactive material has been stolen or lost.

Chapter 3

Building or Buying Your Green House

If you are looking to relocate, build a house, or even remodel your house, you can take into account different locations and attributes that might make the change more environmentally friendly. With a public upsurge in environmental concerns, many cities and states have taken the initiative to make improvements and make themselves a haven for environmentally friendly citizens. If you know where you are going to live, you can choose to use more environmentally friendly home designs and construction materials. This chapter outlines the ways and means to find a green city or build a green house.

Green Cities and States

Many mayors are taking it upon themselves to be good stewards of the environment. They are taking actions to improve air quality, reduce electrical use and production, encourage green building construction, allocate more green space, support nontraditional transportation, and set aside or improve areas for recreational activities.

The U.S. Conference of Mayors is just one coalition working to improve cities in a variety of ways. In an effort to improve air quality, 238 cities have pledged accordance with the Climate Protection Agreement, a pact that encourages each city to reduce greenhouse gas emissions by 7 percent from 1990 levels by the year 2012. The organization shares ideas and outcomes from programs they have implemented, providing a network of environmental actions and results for others to learn from. This is just one example of how communities are working together to improve conditions in their own cities and towns.

When it comes to good stewardship, Austin, Texas; San Francisco, California; Portland, Oregon; Boulder, Colorado; Seattle, Washington; and many others have been identified by organizations like the Green Guide as showing success. Chicago, Minneapolis, and Honolulu are very conscientious when it comes to encouraging clean air and water, promoting green building, and ensuring parks and open spaces are protected. Eugene, Oregon, got the top spot in the Green Guide's list for 2006 because of its numerous bike trails, open space, and commitment to renewable resources. Eighty-five percent of the city's power is provided by hydroelectricity and wind power.

If you are looking for an official list, review The Top 10 Green Cities List put out annually by National Geographic's *The Green Guide*, a resource that provides information for consumers so they can make informed environmental choices in their daily lives. Check out the Web site and the list at *www.thegreenguide.com*.

States may not be involved on the same level as cities, but they still take measures to make themselves more environmentally friendly to homeowners. States on both coasts have come together to reduce greenhouse gas emissions. The West Coast Governors' Global Warming Initiative, including California, Oregon, and Washington, puts limits on greenhouse gas emissions and commits the states to using increasing amounts of renewable energy. Nine states on the other side of the country—Connecticut, Delaware, Maine, Massachusetts, New Hampshire, New Jersey, New York, Rhode Island, and Vermont—formed the Regional Greenhouse Gas Initiative with similar aims to reduce greenhouse gas emissions.

ALERT!

If California, Oregon, and Washington were a country, they would rank seventh in the world in terms of greenhouse gas emissions. California alone would rank twelfth.

Federal and state tax incentives or local utility rebates may be available for energy-efficient products purchased and installed in your home. Energy Star–rated appliances like solar water heaters, photovoltaic cells, and windows can be deducted from federal income tax. The North Carolina Solar Center publishes a list of state incentives and programs. The state-by-state list is available on *www.dsireusa.org*.

There are fifteen states in all where over 20 percent of the homes have qualified for the Energy Star label. Energy Star criteria were created by the EPA and the Department of Energy to give homeowners and contractors guidelines and direction when looking for more sustainable approaches to construction. Energy Star rates homes, businesses, and household products for energy efficiency. The Energy Star Web site, *www.energystar.gov*, has more information.

Finding Your Own Green City

If you are looking for a clean start in a new city, there are a few telltale signs to consider when it comes to making a choice. If environmental stewardship, recreational opportunities, or mass transit systems figured into your decision, tell the community by writing to the mayor's office and local newspapers. If more cities see these factors as magnets drawing people to them, it will reinforce the connection between environmental quality and economic viability.

Air quality is an important consideration when it comes to calling a place home. How does a city rank for fuel exhaust pollution? The EPA maintains an Air Quality Index (*www.airnow.gov*) that scores ozone and particulate matter for different cities across the United States.

Another link to air quality is a city's ability to encourage environmentally friendly transportation. Mass transit systems cut down on the number of personal vehicles on the road, reduce parking and congestion problems, and limit or decrease greenhouse gas emissions and smog. Conscientious cities also provide carpool lanes, designated bicycle lanes, walking trails, and sidewalks and are designed to run efficiently without the need for individually owned vehicles.

Where a city gets its energy correlates not just to the degradation of air quality but to the generation of greenhouse gases as well. If you want to live in a city that's going beyond the norm when it come to energy generation, look for cities that either already use or are making headway with alternative fuels such as biomass, geothermal, hydroelectric, solar, and wind.

There are Web sites you can search for information on cities that use alternative fuels such as *www.sustainlane.us* and *www.eere.energy .gov/greenpower*.

City designers that take into account not just buildings but green space understand an important aspect of improving environmental quality. Green spaces provided by a municipality include athletic fields and parks as well as walking and biking trails along with recreational water and clean water resources. The U.S. Green Building Council (USGBC) runs the Leadership in Energy and Environmental Design (LEED) program, setting criteria for what is considered a green building. LEED takes into account human and environmental health, sustainable site development, water savings, energy efficiency, material selection, and indoor environmental quality. Some builders specifically design houses or developments with sustainability in mind. When looking for a house, find out if the community includes any of these developments. Also, if you're looking for a builder familiar with green construction, visit *www.energystar.gov* where builders familiar with environmentally friendly home construction are listed by city and state.

Municipal recycling programs are also one indication of a city's dedication to the environment. Recycling not only conserves natural resources, it reduces the energy needed to make recycled products. If you're moving, you can consider choosing a city that encourages recycling with curbside programs and recycling centers that go beyond the standard glass, paper, and aluminum. When performed well, recycling programs not only offset the cost of waste disposal but can generate income for an area. Recycling can be a sophisticated business; running a successful operation means keeping up with current trends, technology, and other professionals. There are challenges to recycling, in some cases, when the energy required to transport the reclaimed materials offsets any potential gains.

Portland, Oregon, puts an emphasis on being green. It was the first U.S. city to implement a plan to reduce carbon dioxide emissions. When it comes to power, Oregon relies on hydroelectric means for 44 percent of its energy production. Portland recycles not only the standard glass, metal, and plastic but also accepts residential yard waste and food from businesses for compost.

Feeling safe about the water delivered from the tap is something to consider, too. The EPA requires that municipalities' water quality be documented and reported as part of the Safe Drinking Water Act. The EPA does not maintain the data in a searchable format, but it can direct anyone interested to information on a particular water system. Towns, cities, and utilities should have this information on hand and may even post it on their Web site. Safe drinking water should not contain compounds that are required to be monitored at levels exceeding the Drinking Water Standards. Data that is available for review should note any levels in excess of allowable concentrations.

Finding a Green Location in Any Town

If you already know what town or city you are going to live in, either due to family, work, or environmental reasons, there are still choices about what part of town to live in. If you know where you'll be working, that's a start. Then you can consider all of your commutes—to work, school, the grocery store, and other regular activities. Take into account the frequency of those trips and when they'll be made. What appears to be a great location at two in the afternoon may turn ugly during rush hour. If you are relocating, start looking at places that will give you the shortest trip miles through the week. This strategy will save money that you would spend on fuel and reduce wear and tear on the car, and it may also offer the possibility of biking or walking to some destinations.

If living close to work or school just isn't an option, look at mass transit routes and other transportation opportunities. Is carpooling an option? Or is a subway or train station located nearby? An activity that a family member participates in regularly may also be a controlling consideration. Weigh all the factors.

ALERT!

Although debated by many, urban sprawl is blamed for much of society's woes. Urban sprawl does fragment and destroy wildlife habitat and corridors. The persistent construction of low-density housing developments requires additional roads and cars to navigate them. Unless houses or developments are constructed to be independent from municipal services, other infrastructure systems such as water, wastewater, and electricity have to be expanded to accommodate spreading cities.

A number of larger cities have encouraged the construction of green homes within the city limits to avoid or at least control urban sprawl. Although sprawl may be the bane of society, suburbs can be designed in ways that reduce their potential impact on the environment and conserve natural resources and wildlife habitat. Cities are choosing to develop more efficiently in the suburbs with mixed-use neighborhoods that are bicycle and pedestrian friendly. The aim is that although people may have to drive to work, they should be able to walk or bike about easily once they get home.

Two terms used when it comes to addressing urban sprawl are *new urbanism* and *smart growth*. New urbanism includes compact livable communities—Celebration, Florida, for example—that are traditional neighborhood developments that include various types of housing units as well as professional and entertainment entities. Smart growth is more loosely defined and generally applies to balancing development with natural resources while building single-family homes. It's accomplished through policies and ordinances governing zoning, development buffers, and minimum density requirements.

Home Design

If the location is set and all that's left is to build the house, there are a variety of design considerations to make a dream home a little greener. First off, let Mother Nature help with heating and cooling. In locations with warm climates, the broad side of the house should face north or south to avoid a direct hit—and resulting heat gain—from the sun. Deep overhangs will also help block the sun and reduce excessive heat gains by putting the house in the shade. Tint can be applied to windows, particularly sliding glass doors or large picture windows that can heat up a room quickly and force an air conditioner to work overtime. Without impacting the view, tinting can provide a savings of 5 to 10 percent of the energy needed to cool a house when applied to western-facing windows. Windows facing east also let heat into a house; however, because houses are usually not as hot in the morning when the sun is rising, savings may not be as great as those protecting western windows. In colder climates, take advantage of the sun's heating abilities. Heat provided from the sun can be stored in the concrete or stone walls of a house, helping to keep it warm even after the sun goes down.

If protection from the sun is only needed part of the time, homebuilders can consider retractable awnings and solar screens. There are numerous types and designs available for windows, verandas, and patios. Solar screens reduce heat and glare from the sun but allow the light to enter the house without impeding the outside view.

Of course, there's always the completely organic solution for shading your house—planting a tree. Trees provide nature-made solar protection. Some trees are particularly useful in blocking the sun because of their height and shape. Some grow faster than others, so if time is of the essence when it comes to creating shade, plant a quicker-growing tree. It's important to choose a tree that is native to the location for optimal health and lower maintenance. If it's an option, retain as many of the existing trees as possible when building on a new lot. They'll provide shade and have already proven themselves viable on the property.

When it comes to building a green house, make sure to do your homework. There are sources available online (e.g., ✎www.energystar.gov) and at your local bookstore with information on green building alternatives and designs. Look for contractors and designers with experience in sustainability and find out what other houses they have built. Ask for referrals and then give their clients a call.

Soil can also be an essential source for maintaining the temperature of a home. By building a home partially below grade, you can maintain a more moderate temperature year-round. The earth is usually cooler than above ground, so heating may be necessary to maintain a comfortable temperature in cold weather. However, because the soil provides insulation, the heat will remain in the house rather than escape outside.

When considering the design of a green home, you can work with contractors and architects who are energy conscious and will work with you to achieve your goals. The LEED program tries to educate architects, contractors, and engineers on designing and constructing more energy-efficient and environmentally friendly buildings but does not have a certification course specifically geared toward private homes. Some extension programs work with local builders and designers, providing classes and information in this area.

Rather than starting from scratch, you may be interested in simply renovating an existing home to make it greener. Many of the same new construction considerations apply to renovation. You should be able to discuss alternatives with your contractor to ensure that sustainable elements are brought into the design. Also, if you are demolishing older portions of a home, the material being removed should be reclaimed and reused or handled properly to avoid excessive waste.

If your contractor is not familiar with recycling programs in the area, it may be worthwhile for you to make some phone calls. Habitat for Humanity, a nonprofit organization that builds homes, runs a program called ReStores that accepts donations of used or excess building materials in good condition. Local solid-waste authorities may also have information on specific recyclers in the area. Try calling salvage companies to see what kind of material they are interested in.

Construction Materials

Choosing building materials to preserve natural resources means using elements from renewable resources that help conserve energy and improve the health and well-being of those inside. Qualities to look for in these materials include conserving resources, improving indoor air quality, being energy efficient, and conserving water. Most important, make sure the materials are affordable not just to use for construction but to operate on a month-by-month basis.

Recycled Materials

From the outside in, there are a variety of recycled materials available for building homes. Products made from recycled material require less energy to produce and use ingredients that would otherwise need to be disposed of in a landfill or incinerator.

Starting from the bottom up, the foundation of most homes can be made using concrete that incorporates fly ash (the remnants from coal power plants) and even recycled concrete. Depending on the construction, it could be possible to incorporate the foundation into the finished floor design, which would require fewer building materials than usual.

Recycled paper is being employed in a variety of different home projects. For example, a mixture of cement and paper, called papercrete, is being used to make bricks for home construction. The blocks are strong and provide excellent insulation from weather and sound. A variety of mixes can be used with lesser or greater amounts of cement, depending on your personal preference and the goal.

QUESTION?

How do I buy recycled building products?
If you are shopping for construction materials, look for products with the recycled symbol, three arrows chasing each other in the shape of a triangle. If you are working with a contractor, discuss up-front the need to use recycled materials. Many recycled construction materials are available, including roof material, gypsum board, steel studs, siding, and fascia. Because of customer demand, larger home-improvement stores are beginning to stock more recycled building products.

Concrete isn't without its environmental flaws. It requires the mining of materials such as limestone, which alters the land and surface-water flow and affects inhabitants. Its production is energy intensive, not just in mining and transport but in processing as well; this energy is usually produced by coal-fired power plants. Carbon dioxide is produced by the power plants used to supply electricity to the processing facility and as part of the chemical process of converting limestone into lime. The process also produces sulfur dioxide and nitrous oxides. Particulate matter, or dust, is also created during the mining, storage, and transportation of the materials. Although the mining and processing associated with making concrete has improved over the decades, there are still issues that make reducing the amount produced practical.

Using papercrete reduces the need to purchase and produce cement. The bricks made from papercrete can be used to build straight walls, providing a finished product that looks similar to most standard homes. Papercrete can also be used to construct arches and domes. When constructing domes, the need for roofing materials is eliminated, another advantage to using this building material.

Cellulose, or recycled paper, can also be used in making fiberboard and gypsum-board sheeting material. Cellulose is used for the interior walls of homes. Recycled paper can also be incorporated into insulation. The liquid pulp can be blown into walls or attics, offering an alternative to fiberglass insulation.

High-density polyethylene (HDPE), which comes from used milk jugs, juice bottles, and detergent containers, can be recycled into lumber substitutes. This material is generally not used for indoor construction, but it is becoming more and more popular for outdoor decking and fencing. It's a common component of outdoor amenities such as benches, picnic tables, and trash cans. Not only does HDPE use recycled materials, it avoids the need to use lumber that needs to be treated to withstand weather and insects.

Renewable Materials

Materials that are grown to be harvested are preferable to those whose supply is limited for use in homebuilding and repairs. Examples include wood from forests that are harvested using sustainable methods. These resources are managed so that there is as little impact on the environment as possible. Sustainable products also provide resources and incomes to local populations where they are harvested.

The Forest Stewardship Council (FSC) provides third-party certification for wood products. As part of the certification process, the FSC considers all players involved in the harvesting of wood from forest owners to environmental organizations. The organization ensures that the wood is harvested with minimal environmental impact and fair compensation to local businesses and workers.

Companies offering renewable resources ensure limited use of chemicals and provide conservation zones and protection for rare or threatened species. By growing resources, farmers can properly use the land while providing for their families and villages without damaging the environment and hindering its future use.

Dumpster Diving: The Art of Salvaging

Interior fixtures can be reused just like external building materials. Salvaging or reusing materials has many advantages. Some people who could not afford antiques inherit vintage material such as beautifully grained wood flooring or heavy steel door handles. By looking to demolition sites, builders can obtain material that would otherwise have been disposed of and allow it to live on in someone else's home. When reusing older building materials, for example plumbing and lighting fixtures, they should be checked to ensure they meet current building codes before they're installed.

When designing a new home or remodeling an existing one, homeowners can contact local salvage companies to see what is available. Many carry an evolving and changing stock of cast-iron bathtubs, oak mantels, and stained-glass windows. Contractors working as salvage companies used to be rare entities, but they are becoming more common. The process works best if customers can be patient and wait for just the right piece.

Dumpster diving is more than recycling; it's a social network. In communities all over the country, Dumpster divers meet up online and in person to share stories and tips. But before you go diving in, check your local laws to avoid being cited for trespassing. Divers should never leave a mess; it is not environmentally friendly and will give other divers, or recyclers, a bad name.

Other Construction Considerations

When selecting new materials for building a home, be sure to consider how and where items were made. Does the manufacturer have environmentally sound principles? Do they use recycled materials? Do they recycle their postindustrial materials?

Using locally produced materials eliminates the waste created by transporting the items long distances. This not only reduces the need to use fossil fuels, it reduces the impacts of manufacturing and using petroleum products.

Whatever the purchase, try to buy items that will last and won't need to be replaced within a few years. Purchasing materials with a long life reduces the need to make additional products, thus saving energy and resources—and longer-lasting items can be recycled, salvaged, or passed from generation to generation.

Energy Sources

There are a variety of ways to reduce the amount of power you use in your home. Harnessing power from nature and reducing energy usage may make it possible to get off the power grid. From solar to wind and other alternatives, there are a variety of renewable energy options available for keeping lights bright, food cold, and the temperature just right whether your home is on or off the power grid.

Working Within the Grid

One of the aspects of supplying your own power is how the system will be connected to the grid or electrical network. The national power grid is a network of transmission and distribution systems owned by public companies or investor-owned utilities and cooperatives. Utilities and cooperatives buy and sell power to each other depending on the demand and availability. The network tries to provide redundancy; that means, if there is a problem somewhere in the grid, operations can be rerouted and service can be more easily restored.

If you are generating your own electricity through alternate means, working with your local power company gives you the option of selling any excess energy you may produce. You will need to track your electricity usage; your local power provider can tell you what kind of meter you need to install. Net metering and double metering are the two most common methods of measuring electricity output. You can sell your excess energy to the power company through the same network that delivers electricity. How your power company compensates you depends on the type of metering system.

Net metering uses the typical meters that are installed on most houses. The meter runs forward when electricity is consumed and backward when electricity is generated. With net metering, excess power is banked for the user to access later. This is particularly beneficial for intermittent energy sources like solar and wind power. This system allows customers to receive compensation relatively quickly, and utilities purchase excess power at retail prices. Net metering is relatively easy to administer for the utilities and the customers.

The alternative is double metering. One meter measures the electricity used, and the other measures the electricity generated. This method requires the installation of a second meter and can be cumbersome to administer. Customers are generally paid a lower rate than the retail price for their excess energy.

Another alternative is to bank excess power. Rather than giving excess power back to the utility, the homeowner uses it to charge batteries. When the home system is unable to generate electricity, the power stored in the batteries can be accessed.

Any option allows homeowners to operate independently from the grid when generating their own power. When the grid is down, a home system may continue to operate.

Getting Off the Grid

Of course, there's always the potential to get off the grid completely. Most homes that have been able to disconnect from the grid use either solar or wind power. Wind power tends to work well in the winter and worse in the summer, when solar power is at its best, making hybrid systems worth considering.

Solar Power

Solar energy is produced when the sun shines on photovoltaic (PV) panels. These panels hold semiconductors that use the sunlight to generate electricity in the form of direct current (DC) electricity. Panels are rated in watts, based on the amount of electricity they can produce under ideal sun and temperature conditions. Customers can choose certain panels based on their personal electric demands.

Panels are usually mounted on the roof, on steel poles, or on the ground. Local regulations or neighborhood covenants may dictate the location of solar panels. Mounting the panels on the roof requires using the proper supports. It may be necessary to reinforce the roof support to maintain safety and to be in compliance with local building codes.

The Web site *www.findsolar.com* is a helpful resource if you are considering installing a home solar system. Entering your state, your county, the utility provider, and your energy usage provides you with a breakdown on the estimated size solar system you will need, the estimated installation cost, any rebates that might be available from federal or state agencies or the utility, and the average savings and time to recoup the cost. Beyond monetary savings, the Web site calculates the amount of greenhouse gas, in carbon dioxide equivalents, that will be saved by going solar.

The National Renewable Energy Laboratory also has information for homeowners on renewable alternatives. Readers can check out *A Consumer's Guide: Get Your Power from the Sun* at *www.nrel.gov*.

Wind Power

Depending on where you live, wind can provide the means of powering your house. Maps indicating wind energy potential for the country are available to determine if homes are located within an area where wind power would be an effective method of providing power. The Web site *www.eere.energy.gov/windandhydro/windpoweringamerica/wind_maps .asp* lists wind conditions by state, allowing homeowners to determine if wind power is a suitable alternative for generating their own energy.

When choosing an optimal location for a wind turbine, take topography and terrain into account—and don't forget to consider your local wildlife. Be sure to learn about the local ecology and species habitat and the potential impact your tower might have on your surroundings. The results of your research can minimize negative impacts while providing renewable energy to your home.

Even within areas designated to have appropriate wind speed and resources, homeowners need to consider other factors, such as whether houses are located on top of a hill or in a valley. Wind towers can be configured on either horizontal or vertical axes. The horizontal tower is by far the most common, with blades that rotate about an axis that is parallel to the wind. As a result, they must be oriented with the greatest wind direction in mind. Vertical towers are rare and tend to look like egg beaters. Although their orientation is independent of wind direction, conversion of energy to electricity is less efficient. In either orientation, the blades turn a propeller that captures kinetic energy. A rotor then converts the rotary motion to drive a generator. Unlike a PV used in solar energy, power is captured from moving parts and transferring kinetic energy into electric power.

Heating and Cooling

Two of the biggest energy sinks are the heating and cooling systems. The EPA rates heating and cooling systems using the Energy Star logo to symbolize systems that are more efficient and use less energy. Usually these systems are quieter and have longer lives. Equipment eligible to receive the Energy Star symbol include boilers, furnaces, heat pumps, programmable thermostats, and air conditioners.

FACT

The U.S. Department of Energy reports approximately 45 percent of the average utility bill goes to heating and cooling a home. Heating and cooling dwellings in the United States is responsible for producing 150 million tons of carbon dioxide.

Selecting the correct size system for your living space and choosing an efficient model are two crucial ways to save energy. Maintain your current model by cleaning filters, checking ducts for leaks, and installing programmable thermostats to adjust the times the house is heated and cooled throughout the day. Installing a whole-house fan that pulls cool air in and releases warm air through the attic is another effective measure.

Windows and Doors

Everyone loves a picture window, but it can greatly affect the efficiency of a house. The bigger the window is, the less efficient it is, and the more windows there are in a house, the more energy will be lost. If you are set on having a window overlooking a scenic vista, you can invest in energy-efficient window models to reduce the negative impact of lost efficiency.

Window placement also affects the amount of heat absorbed. Windows on the western side of a house heat up homes like an oven in summertime, but the same window may make that room warm and comfortable during the winter months.

Crank windows that operate using cranks or levers are the most efficient designs, as they allow the window to seal tightly against the frame. Double-hung windows that slide up and down or sideways are less efficient because they must be loose enough to allow sliding, which also means they are loose enough to let air in and out.

Double-pane windows made using two sheets of glass with an air cavity in between are much more efficient than traditional single-pane windows. In cold climates, when the space between the panes is filled with argon and the glass is covered with a low-emissivity coating, heat reflects back into the living area. In warm climates, windows with a similar coating reflect the heat back outside, preventing it from settling in the house. One factor to keep in mind is that the chemicals used to make the coating may be harmful to the environment, causing some of the same problems as pesticides. Windows with low-emissivity coatings may be more difficult to recycle because the treated glass does not easily fuse with other glasses.

The standard skylight design has changed as well, making it more energy efficient. Canister or tube models let light in while eliminating the potential for leaks and heat seepage.

Regardless of what type of windows you get, they need to be installed properly to ensure a tight seal.

Check doors to make sure they shut snugly. This keeps the temperature even inside the house. Doors should fit properly in the frame and can include magnetic weather stripping to decrease drafts. More important, to reduce the time the compressor or furnace is running, shut the door.

Chapter 4

Green House Furnishings

Once a home is built, you still need to make it comfortable. With the increase in environmental awareness, there are options galore when it comes to filling a home with Earth friendly flooring, furniture, appliances, and lighting. Taking the environment into account won't just help the planet; it can save you money through lower electric bills and tax incentives. This chapter gives some insight into how to conserve energy and choose home furnishings with the environment in mind. Making a home green on the inside may just save some green, too.

Conserving Power and Water

You can conserve natural resources by cutting back on utilities such as power and water. Wasting electricity, for example, wastes money as well as the natural resources that produce the power. The majority of homes use energy produced from coal plants that generate pollutants such as particulate matter, which contributes to health conditions like asthma, and carbon dioxide, a greenhouse gas. So when it comes to furnishing and running a home, if you want to reduce your personal impact, or footprint, on the environment, you can cut back on the energy you burn with the added benefit of saving money.

Public water supplies usually use groundwater or surface water, like lakes or rivers, as a source. Water is treated and distributed throughout the city. Just like other services provided by a municipality, if more water is demanded, facilities like water treatment plants will either have to be expanded or new facilities will need to be constructed. Water treatment plants are expensive to build and operate. In addition, they take water from natural rivers, streams, springs, and groundwater. According to the U.S. Geological Survey (USGS), approximately 40 percent of water in the United States goes to supporting agriculture, whereas industry and thermoelectric power combined use 44 percent. Although residential use is only about 13 percent, conserving natural resources is always a good idea. There has been a push for agriculture to use graywater, or treated wastewater, on crops, eliminating a drain on treated water and providing disposal for treated wastewater.

ALERT!

Although the cause is not fully understood, treated wastewater effluent is considered a culprit in the declining health of coral reef systems off the coast of Florida. Tissue samples collected from reefs indicated high levels of proteins associated with reef damage. In addition, the coral lesions where samples were collected were much slower to heal in areas near wastewater discharge. The presence of nitrogen isotopes also supported a strong correlation between sewage and damage to the reefs included in the study.

Used water must also be disposed of. The majority of water from residential and commercial toilets, sinks, washing machines, and dishwashers goes to the sanitary sewer and then on to the wastewater treatment plant. There the water is treated before being discharged, usually to a bay or stream or other body of water. Although the water is treated, there is concern that it impacts the quality of water into which it is discharged.

Not only does conserving power and water save natural resources, it reduces the need to construct costly facilities. As the population expands, additional power plants, water treatment plants, and wastewater treatment facilities are needed. By conserving resources, the need for additional infrastructure can be postponed or in some cases even eliminated.

As water use increases, the demand for wastewater treatment increases as well. In many areas of the country, water is becoming scarce. One approach to alleviating strain on the water system is to pipe treated water, called effluent or graywater, to homes and businesses for use in watering lawns and agricultural fields.

The Energy Star Symbol

The Energy Star label indicates that an appliance or electronic equipment meets certain criteria for being energy efficient. The symbol was introduced by the EPA in 1992 to provide consumers with information to help them choose appliances and electronics that are more efficient and produce fewer greenhouse gases than their traditional counterparts. What started with just a few pieces of equipment grew, and by 1995 the labeling was expanded to include other office equipment and residential heating and cooling equipment. In 1996, the DOE jumped onboard and began working with the EPA. The label now appears on more than thirty-five different kinds of products.

The EPA estimates that approximately 17 percent of the nation's greenhouse gases are produced by the estimated 100 million households in the United States. The Energy Star label means that the appliances were rated objectively, and the label itself includes information on the cost savings for different appliances. Many higher-efficiency home appliances may be more expensive than less efficient ones, so consider what the savings will be over the life of the appliance when you look at the up-front cost.

FACT

Electronics can still drain energy when they are turned off. On average, 40 percent of residential electricity goes to electronic products that are switched off, according to Energy Star. One easy way to eliminate this waste is to unplug electronics when you aren't using them.

Energy Star Homes

When energy savings are achieved throughout the house, the entire building can qualify for the Energy Star label. The EPA has published guidelines for a variety of different types of homes, including single-family and multifamily (duplexes and apartments) units; even modular or log homes can qualify. The EPA lists the criteria needed to achieve Energy Star status, such as effective insulation, high-performance windows, tight construction and ducts, efficient heating and cooling equipment, and the use of Energy Star lighting and appliances. In order to complete the certification process, a licensed third party must verify that these standards have been met. The construction of Energy Star homes or the remodeling of older homes to meet Energy Star guidelines has increased as more contractors become familiar with the objectives. Almost 150,000 new single-family Energy Star homes were built in 2005; that accounts for nearly 10 percent of all new homes built. Owners of Energy Star homes know they are helping conserve natural resources by using less electricity and producing less carbon dioxide.

Energy Audits

Audits can be performed by private companies, electric utilities, or online with homeowners entering household information. A good audit will provide a homeowner with a detailed plan for possible improvements, cost estimates for those improvements, and savings estimates for the improvements over time. Some local utilities offer rebates and incentives for making energy-efficient improvements. It may be necessary to include an official audit with the rebate paperwork.

Let There Be Light

As much as 15 percent of a home's electric bill is spent on lighting. Lighting doesn't come alone, however; it brings a lot of heat with it. In the winter the added heat may be acceptable, even desirable, but during the dog days of summer, the extra heat is just one more indoor temperature demon to fight.

As grateful as you might be to Thomas Edison for lighting the world, his incandescent light bulb wastes upward of 95 percent of the energy as heat, making the lights only about 5 percent efficient. That's right—the main reason to flip the switch is light, but really what is being generated is heat. Halogen lights do not fare much better at only 9 percent efficiency.

At 20 percent efficiency, compact fluorescent lights (CFLs) are four times more efficient than incandescent lights. If your home is already equipped with incandescent lighting, rather than unscrewing the bulbs and tossing them, simply replace the five lights used most frequently. These lights are most likely in the kitchen, dining room, living room, over the bathroom vanity, and on the front porch.

By replacing just five incandescent lights with compact fluorescent lights, a standard household could save up to $60 per year. That may not sound like much, but when it's multiplied by all the households in the United States, the grand total is $6.5 billion a year. The pollution equivalent is that this change would offset the same amount of greenhouse gases as 8 million cars.

CFLs are a little more expensive than incandescent bulbs, but they make up for it in longevity and reduced energy use. Over the span of 10,000 hours, a CFL can cost less than half of an incandescent. In the past CFLs often flickered, but improvements have been made to stop the blinking. New models offer more variety, such as accommodating a dimmer switch.

Even though most people are in the habit of turning off lights every time they leave a room, that's not always necessary with CFLs as they operate within a certain temperature range. You'll see more cost savings if they're used in areas where the lights are frequently left on. If you don't plan to install them in all the light fixtures, consider how much you use a room before you install CFLs.

You need to choose the right CFL for the job. Because CFLs are more efficient, they can operate at a lower wattage. An incandescent light of 40 watts is comparable to a CFL of 14 watts. In addition, when buying CFLs, consider choosing bulbs with a color-rendering index of 80; this will make colors in your home look more natural than bulbs with lower indexes. You can check the label on the package to make sure you're making the best selection.

Here are a few other energy-saving lighting tips:

- Avoid opaque light shades. They trap light and require a stronger bulb.
- Dark paints and flooring don't reflect light as well as lighter colors.
- Clean dust from light fixtures so their light will shine through.
- When reading or performing another task requiring focused lighting, turn off background lights and rely on a small focused lamp instead.

Light-emitting diodes (LEDs) have been around for some time and are frequently seen in roadside lighting. Unlike candescent lighting, LEDs produce specific colors. They are comprised of a semiconductor device that converts electron energy to light. Based on the semiconductor materials, the light will be a certain color. Making an LED produce white light is more difficult, but it can be done in a number of ways. One method manipulates yellow light to appear white. LEDs require much less energy to produce the same amount of luminance, making them appropriate for use with batteries and in places where changing light bulbs is difficult or costly. They are more commonly seen in traffic- and railroad-lighting systems and have been incorporated into flashlight, bike, and motorcycle lights. Because of their relatively high cost, LED lights have not become common in residential lighting systems yet.

Appliances

Advances in technology haven't just provided the masses with MP3 players and high-definition television. There's also been a big push to improve energy and water conservation in more mundane household appliances. Most appliances use water and electricity or natural gas, so buying energy-efficient models conserves all three.

When considering kitchen appliances, look for the Energy Star symbol. While the initial cost of the appliance may be higher than ones without the star symbol, energy savings throughout the life of the appliance will more than cover the additional purchase expense. If you take into account the initial purchase price, maintenance costs, and operational costs for a large appliance, you can expect to save about $200 a year; extending that amount over an expected operating life of five to ten years results in considerable savings.

One other way to reduce energy consumption is to stop using unnecessary appliances, such as the extra stand-alone freezer that runs year-round. Homeowners can consider purchasing fewer frozen food items or only using the extra freezer when needed.

Flooring

Flooring options range from tile to wood, from cork to concrete, from linoleum to laminates—and then, of course, there's carpet. For allergy sufferers, non-carpet options allow good cleaning and easy removal of dust and other allergens. Older flooring options had little to do with environmental impact and more with aesthetics, but that approach has changed. When picking flooring options, people often consider both their health and the environment.

Wood

Wood flooring first came on the scene during the baroque period, around the late 1600s. But by the late 1800s and early 1900s, mass production and Victorian standards made wood the norm for flooring. Over the years, its popularity has waxed and waned. Today, wood is again a popular flooring alternative.

Gibson Guitar Corp. began using sustainable wood from South America back in the 1980s. The company works with the Rainforest Alliance and contracts farmers to supply wood, rather than use a broker who will get them the lowest price. Contractors farming the wood follow a management plan, harvesting the wood using sustainable methods.

Wood flooring generally comes from domestic, exotic, or nondomestic forests. Wood flooring can also be remilled from other wood products and older flooring. Domestic flooring does not require the extensive shipping of exotics. Although hardwood flooring is a renewable resource, you need to be aware of the source of the wood you are considering. Exotic wood is sometimes harvested from forests where conditions of the local ecology and population are not taken into account. This is especially true when low prices and competition encourage irresponsible harvesting. Look for the Forest Stewardship Council (FSC) stamp of approval on wood and let it be a determining factor in your selection. The FSC is an international organization that works to promote responsible stewardship of Earth's forests by bringing together timber users, local foresters, and human rights and environmental organizations. Members include companies such as IKEA and groups such as Greenpeace. Another option in wood is salvaged wood building material; there are companies that sell this wood and will cut it to specifications. Some salvagers have historical information on where the wood was recovered. Imagine walking on the same floor as soldiers from the Civil War.

The laying and sealing of wood flooring requires the application of glues and other materials that contain volatile organic compounds or formaldehyde. These compounds can be released, causing headaches, allergic reactions, or other health problems. Look for adhesives and sealants that contain non-formaldehyde or non-urea-formaldehyde.

Laminate

Laminate, which mimics the traditional wood floor, has become a popular option. It provides the same benefits as wood floor, with a reduction in sealants and the potential for better harvesting practices. Many more styles are available than when compared to its introduction in 1994.

Laminate floors are easier to install than wood floors, and many projects can be done by homeowners over a long weekend. Floating-type flooring offers planks with tongue-and-groove construction, making the planks easier to lock in place over the existing subfloor. There are some designs, however, that do require the use of glue. Laminate floors are also durable and easy to maintain.

Most laminates contain wood that may or may not have been responsibly harvested. The FSC has certified some types of laminates. Other environmental concerns include off-gassing of volatile organics and formaldehyde. These chemicals are used in the manufacturing of laminates and can be released after installation is completed. Because laminate does not contain preservatives or solvents, it is unlikely to spur allergic or asthmatic reactions.

Tile and Stone

Like the other noncarpet alternatives, tile and stone offer the same low-allergen amenities. Their smooth surface is not conducive to a thriving dust mite population and can be cleaned easily. Another consideration is durability. Stone and tile can last decades, meaning that manufacturing resources are conserved.

Depending on the sources of the tile and stone, there can be environmental impacts, however. The EPA requires mines to implement best management practices to avoid affecting stormwater and surface water in the area. Mine reclamation, or repairing the damage to mined lands, is more common now. In addition, depending on how far they are shipped, tile and stone can weigh heavily in terms of the impacts from transportation.

Tile is often made from clay mined throughout the United States. The industry is heavily tied to construction and renovation since the clay is used mainly to make clay floor tiles. The demand for decorative floor tiles has grown, resulting in more sophisticated automation processes within the industry.

Stone flooring comes in a variety of shapes and sizes. From pebbles to large slabs, stone flooring offers consumers a choice of numerous patterns and colors. Stone used in flooring is usually made of porcelain, limestone, marble, or granite. It is installed using relatively benign mortar and grout.

Cleaning ceramic tile floors doesn't have to rely on harmful chemicals. A mixture of a quarter cup of vinegar with one gallon of water can be used with a terry towel to clean up a tile floor. Spills should be wiped up immediately to avoid staining the grout. If the grout does become stained, a mixture of half hydrogen peroxide and half water can be sprayed on the grout and left to sit for ten minutes.

Many tile manufacturers use recycled tiles, glass, and even carpet or plastic fibers in their feedstock. Clear, brown, and green glass can be recycled and used to produce solid-color and decoratively designed tiles. As with wood, laminates are now made that mimic stone and tile flooring. Also like wood laminate, these floorings are produced with tongue-and-groove edges and can be installed to float above the existing floor.

Carpet

In the 1960s, carpet-manufacturing technology improved, and mills moved to the South where cheap labor could mass-produce the flooring. That move started the heyday of wall-to-wall carpet. Before long, shag was the rage, and then smaller loop and cut piles moved in. Carpet was made to be plush and soft.

While carpet does provide more padding and is softer to walk and sit on, it also harbors dirt, dust mites, and other allergens like mold. To avoid allergic reactions to dust mites, carpets must be vacuumed regularly. There is also concern that carpets emit volatile organics and collect pesticides that are used along with other indoor contaminants. To protect your lungs, leave the house while carpet is being installed. Following this with proper ventilation will make carpet installation less of an impact on the lungs.

As other products have included recycled material in their feedstock, so has carpet. Some manufacturers rely solely on recycled plastics to produce flooring. Several different brands are made from recycled soda bottles. Because this production relies on postconsumer material, it avoids disposal of waste products in landfills and incinerators. When choosing flooring options, you may be surprised by the recycled products are available.

Other Green Flooring Alternatives

Relatively new to the flooring world are sustainable cork and bamboo. Cork flooring can be installed in much the same way as laminate and can be manufactured in a variety of colors and appearances, along with a natural cork appearance. It can even be made to look like stone or tile. With different colors available, flooring can be laid in complex or simple designs. An important feature to some is the cork's honeycomb design, which allows it to give slightly and makes it easier on the feet. This is particularly important to those who stand or cook quite a bit. The same honeycomb texture that provides comfort also absorbs noise.

FACT

Cork is harvested from the bark of cork oak trees. Trees must be twenty-five to thirty years old before they can be harvested. They are not harmed in the harvesting process. The cork will grow back and be ready for harvesting in about ten years. Half of the cork harvested for flooring comes from Portugal.

Because cork is giving and flexible, it can be installed on floors that aren't completely level, making it particularly useful in older homes where portions of the floor may have already settled. When choosing cork flooring, check to see that it's formaldehyde-free and that any varnish is water-based.

Bamboo is actually a grass and grows like a weed. It's hearty and can grow in poor-quality soil that is unsuitable for other crops in excess of one foot per day. Bamboo can be harvested in as short a time as three years. The majority of bamboo is grown in China and India; but the environmental impacts from shipping can offset the benefits of using this type of flooring. When manufactured for durable flooring, bamboo maintains the appearance of hardwood but can be tinted different colors. Because it is wood, bamboo requires sealants and protective waxes. Shoppers and installers can check to see that sealants and waxes with little or no volatile organic compounds are used. Companies such as EcoTimber (*www.ecotimber.com*) manufacture bamboo that is made using European adhesive, which is lower in volatile organics.

Bedding

One of the biggest environmental issues when it comes to bedding has to do with the chemicals included with the mattresses. Because so many people died of smoke inhalation and fire as a result of falling asleep while smoking in bed, the government began requiring mattresses to meet the cigarette-ignition testing requirements in 1973.

Flame-retardant chemicals approved by the Consumer Product Safety Commission (CPSC) are of concern to many. Compounds include polybrominated diphenyl ethers (PBDEs). The National Institute of Environmental Health voiced concern about PBDEs as their prevalence in flame-retardant materials and their persistence in the environment rose. Studies performed in Sweden indicated that PBDEs were even present in the breastmilk of nursing mothers. They have also accumulated in fish and other animals. PBDEs bioaccumulate, and tests indicate that concentrations are rising in humans, most predominantly in North America. These chemicals are suspected of causing liver and neurodevelopment toxicity.

The CPSC recently sponsored tests on other flame-retardant chemicals (not PBDEs) and found them to be safe either because a risk analysis showed no discernable effects or because concentrations of the chemicals were not detected in mattresses. The CPSC and other organizations, such as the Sleep Products Safety Council and the International Sleep Products Association, have stated that mattresses treated with flame retardants provide more safety from fire than risk from chemical exposure.

If you want to avoid flame retardant chemicals altogether, consider a wool mattress. Wool is a natural flame retardant and can be marketed without the addition of flame retardants. Organic cotton mattresses are also sold without added chemicals, but they lack natural flame-resistant ability and can only be purchased with the written consent of a doctor.

Bathrooms

Believe it or not, there are several ways to conserve natural resources and money in the bathroom. From the sink to the shower to the toilet, you can make environmental decisions every day.

The Low-Down on Toilets

Along with improvements to other appliances, great strides have been made when it comes to manufacturing more water-conserving toilets. It is estimated that about one-quarter of the water used in an average home goes to flushing the toilet if efficient toilets aren't installed. Homes built before 1992 that haven't had any improvements made are likely to have an old-fashioned 3.5 gallons per flush (gpf)–model toilet. Newer models use only 1.6 gallons for the same flush, and the future may hold even more efficient flushers. Not only does this reduce the amount of water being pumped from aquifers and streams, treated, and piped to the house, it saves on treating and discharging the used water, too.

The ability of a toilet to remove waste can be measured. Just ask the folks at the California Urban Water Conservation Council. The organization uses soybean paste to simulate waste and rates toilets for Maximum Performance, or MaP. The seventh-edition report is available at *www.cuwcc.org.*

Another version of an efficient commode is the composting toilet. These toilets are used mainly in remote locations like weekend getaways and vacation cabins where there is no access to a sanitary sewer and septic systems aren't feasible. Compost toilets are comprised of three components: a throne or seat, a composting chamber, and a drying tray. Some models combine all three components into one enclosure, while other designs have a separate seat. The toilets use bacteria and fungi to decompose waste, turning it into dry, fluffy humus. Regulations vary across the country; in some places, the humus can be used as fertilizer around trees and nonedible plants, but in others it must be buried or disposed of as sewage. These toilets are not supposed to smell, so if one does, chances are there's something wrong. Composting toilets do not need water, so owners reduce their household water usage and production of wastewater.

Showers and Sinks

Beyond taking shorter and colder showers, there are other steps you can take when it comes to conserving water and natural resources while cleaning up. Standard showerheads put out up to 5 gallons per minute (gpm). Low-flow showerheads can cut that in half. If a low-flow shower isn't satisfactory, try using an aerator showerhead. Air is added to the water as it flows from the head, making it feel like a higher-flowing showerhead. Aerators can be added to spigots, reducing a flow of over 2 gpm to about 1 gpm. Aerators are relatively inexpensive and easy to install.

Furniture

The decision to incorporate environmental furniture into a house may be driven by a desire to reduce toxins and improve indoor air quality, to promote recycling, or even to save an old-growth forest and encourage more sustainable wood harvesting.

Run-of-the-mill stuffed furniture, much like mattresses, contains fire-retardant chemicals and formaldehyde. Although regulators have said that the protection afforded by the retardants ranks higher than the potential risk of chemical health problems, you may opt to purchase less chemically protected furniture.

If you are looking to add a bit of flare to your house, check out recycled art—bicycle sprockets made into clocks and used street signs formed into wall hangings. Even discarded tiles are used to make colorful mosaics. If your budget can't afford an artisan's work, consider making your own recycled art project.

Organically grown ramie and cotton are available for upholstering furniture. These materials are beautiful to look at and comfortable to sit on, and those with chemical sensitivities may find it a salvation to home furnishing.

Wood furniture should have the FSC seal to ensure it was forested with the environment and indigenous cultures in mind. Other companies now collect old wood, salvaging it from demolition sites and reworking it to make new wood furniture of both contemporary and more nostalgic styles. One example is Cabin Furniture and Décor (*www.1cabinfurniture.com*), where customers can select hutches, benches, and dining-room tables and chairs made from reclaimed lumber.

As with flooring, bamboo is making headway in furniture construction, too. With its strength and short harvesting time, it's a realistic alternative to traditional wood furniture. Imagine lounging in a bamboo-frame chaise atop organic cotton cushions—green nirvana.

Recycling plastic is the feedstock for some furniture designers and manufacturers. It's made mostly into patio and decking furnishings, but some of the designs are worthy of inside rooms. Seat belts become strapping for loveseats, and corrugated cardboard holds shelves of books. Take your time when choosing any new furnishings. By checking out purchases ahead of time, you can protect the environment while investing wisely in your house.

Chapter 5

Keeping a Green Home and Yard

Maintaining a home that is Earth friendly is usually a combination of conserving energy and being conscientious about the kinds of chemicals you use. You can find many alternatives to help reduce or eliminate the use of chemicals in cleaning supplies and pest control. There are also products available that help conserve energy and water and reduce waste. All of these options conspire to save natural resources. An additional benefit to conservation is that it usually saves you money, too. This chapter gives you a rundown on how to take care of your house while saving the planet and a buck at the same time!

Cleaning House and Product Alternatives

Whoever said dirt was just misplaced matter must not have cleaned it up on a daily basis. Cleaning house requires you to arm yourself with bottles of cleaning solution and various gadgets to help you remove every last speck of dirt. But don't think you have to sacrifice a clean house to be more environmentally friendly. Clean and green aren't mutually exclusive. When you're shopping for environmentally friendly cleaning products, look for a green label and choose natural products that list all their ingredients. Green cleaning products should not contain ingredients such as chlorine, petroleum-based solvents, nonylphenol surfactants, glycol ethers, or dyes. They should be biodegradable and nontoxic. Truly green cleaners are not tested on animals either.

It just takes a little time and effort to find the best cleaning solutions that work for everyone and the environment.

Cleaning Products

When evaluating cleaners, choose one that is safe for everyone in the family, is safe for the environment, conserves natural resources, and—more important—ultimately gets the job done.

When picking out cleansers for the home, try to avoid unnecessary dyes and fragrances and stay away from extra packaging. Be careful with concentrates. Using a cleanser that comes in concentrated form does save on packaging by allowing consumers to mix it up and dilute it at home, but take care to avoid exposing people and the environment to the highly concentrated ingredients.

Simple Can Be Better

People cleaned their houses long before all the fancy products hit the market and the commercials hit the airways. They used common ingredients, and—with a little know-how and mixing—managed to get rid of dirt and dust.

FACT

Baking soda is a wonderful thing. It's sodium bicarbonate, a naturally occurring compound. It's nontoxic. It deodorizes. It's a gentle abrasive—perfect for chrome or enamel. You can mix a quarter cup of baking soda with one quart of warm water to make a cleaning solution. Or you can just shake it directly on what you're cleaning.

A lot of times these cleaning ingredients are less expensive than the new and improved products, often because their prices don't include advertising costs or fancy, colorful bottles.

Here's a list of other more natural and less toxic cleaning ingredients and their uses:

- Mix half a cup of vinegar with a gallon of water to clean floors. (Be careful your floor won't be affected by the pH shift. Some materials like marble and nonwax floors are vulnerable to color change and etchings. Your manufacturer will be able to tell you if vinegar is safe for your floor.)
- Two parts borax mixed with one part lemon juice can be used to clean the toilet. This is especially effective for removing stains. Spray with vinegar to make sure your cleaning solution will remove microbes.
- A mixture of equal amounts of lemon juice and olive oil is great for polishing unvarnished furniture. For varnished furniture, use half a cup of warm water and a few drops of lemon juice.
- Use a quarter cup of rubbing alcohol mixed with half a cup of vinegar and two cups of water to clean windows. Use newspaper to wipe windows instead of paper towels.
- Sprinkle baking soda on your stainless steel, iron, or copper pots and scrub to clean. Don't use baking powder on aluminum pots.

Pest Control

No one wants to see roaches scurrying or ants marching across their kitchen counters. But before using pesticides, consider natural alternatives to control pests. One of the first steps to reducing pests and insects in the house is to remove whatever attracts them. Keep counters and floors clean of food scraps. Avoid dripping faucets and soaking dishes; they serve as a water source enticing insects into the kitchen. Foods that pests find attractive like flour, macaroni, and cornmeal can be kept in the refrigerator or in airtight containers.

There are also some natural remedies to control pests in the house. Here is a list of natural ways to rid your home of some of the more common pests without using pesticides:

- Follow a trail of ants to find where they are coming in. Sprinkle chili pepper, dried peppermint, or borax to steer them away.
- For cockroaches, mix borax, sugar, and flour, and sprinkle it in the infested area, or add water and form the mixture into little balls and leave them for the roaches to eat. Also try sprinkling borax behind light switches, under sinks, and in the back of cabinets to kill roaches.
- Feeding a dog or cat brewer's yeast mixed in with their food deters fleas.
- Look to cedar chips to drive off moths.
- Buy humane traps that allow you to catch and release varmints.
- Pantries can be kept free of moths and other insects with insect traps that use nontoxic adhesives and attractants.
- Diligent vacuuming can eliminate dust mites. If dust mites are in bedding, wash it regularly and cover pillows and mattresses in mite-free mattress cases and pillowcases.

Another benefit of eliminating pesticides is that you will be able to avoid keeping poisons in your home and reduce the possibility of accidental exposure.

Doing the Dishes

There are ways to conserve energy and help the environment while doing the dishes—and you don't have to sacrifice your dishwasher to do it. Researchers at the University of Bonn in Germany determined that using a dishwasher not only cleaned the dishes better, it saved energy and time. Now you can sit back after dinner and relax, guilt-free.

If you are a diehard for washing dishes by hand or if you do not have a dishwasher, the folks in Bonn have recommendations for getting the most out of hand-washing your dishes:

- Remove large pieces of food left on the dishes.
- Don't rinse any of the dishes before washing. This is also true if you are using an automatic dishwasher.
- Use two sinks—one with hot soapy water to wash and one filled with cooler water to rinse.
- Do not go overboard with the soap or detergent. Use only what's needed; it will conserve cleanser and won't over-suds the rinse water.

Phosphorus, an ingredient in many dish detergents, works its way through a wastewater treatment plant, ending up in surface waters and other effluent disposal locations. In the Chesapeake Bay, lawmakers are working to reduce the concentration of phosphorus from the currently allowed 7 percent to 3 percent. It is hoped that the reduction of phosphorus in the detergent will correspond with a similar reduction in the bay's phosphorus levels, improving water quality and avoiding algae outbreaks.

If you are in the market for a new dishwasher, check for Energy Star labels to ensure the model you purchase uses energy efficiently.

Washing and Drying Clothes

There are a few ways to reduce the impact on the environment when doing the laundry. Washing clothes in cold water saves energy and reduces fading. Using the smallest amount of soap or detergent will save money and natural resources.

Soap or Detergent

First things first, it's important to know how soap and detergent work. How do they get the gardening stain off the knees of your britches, or the soy milkshake from your shirt? Surfactants are the key. They are organic molecules that help get in between the grime and fabric, separating the two.

On a small scale, surfactant molecules have two parts: the hydrophilic part loves water, and the hydrophobic part hates it. The two parts work together because the hydrophilic part attaches itself to the water while the hydrophobic part attaches itself to the fabric, helping to reduce surface tension in the water and loosening stain particles.

So what's the difference between soap and detergent? Both soap and detergent use surfactants, which is why they both get stains out. The difference is the source of the surfactants. Soaps tend to be organically based, derived from plant or nut oils and are generally referred to as oleochemicals. Detergents are synthetic and are usually made from petrochemicals.

One reason detergents were developed in the first place was that the surfactants in soaps tended to react with hard water, causing a film or residue. Hard water contains more minerals such as calcium and magnesium that can potentially build up on surfaces and laundry.

Until recently, fossil fuel was relatively inexpensive and easily available, making the synthetics popular ingredients in detergents. However, with fluctuations in the market and concerns about the environmental aspects of obtaining and processing fossil fuels, manufacturers are looking to other surfactant ingredients.

QUESTION?

How do I get out really tough stains?

Stains can be categorized by their base component. Organic or protein stains include blood, sweat, and coffee and can be removed using hydrogen peroxide. Fat or oil stains like salad dressing may come out by dousing and rubbing them with cornstarch. Fruit stains like juice or wine are apt to disappear when drenched in boiling water. Make sure to treat the stain as soon as possible.

Unfortunately, not all vegetable-based or oleochemical surfactants are created equal. Some are obtained from palm and palm kernel oil from Malaysia and others from coconut oil primarily from the Philippines. Care must be taken to conserve the natural resources used to produce these oils. The Soap and Detergent Association has information on sustainable laundry products, including oleochemicals; visit their Web site at *www.cleaning 101.com*.

In the end, using the minimal amount of soap or detergent to get the job done and looking for more environmentally sensitive ingredients is the best approach. Detergents that contain the word *ultra* are concentrated, so you can use less of them to get the same results.

Sun or Electricity

There's no denying that using the sun to dry clothes saves energy, but clotheslines are rare these days. So if you aren't ready to quit using your dryer cold turkey, you may just want to cut back a little. When you do use your dryer, you can take steps to make it more efficient. Don't overdry clothes. Take the clothes out when they are dry. Don't overload the dryer, and do dry similar items together.

Dryer sheets release chemicals as they bounce around in the dryer, making clothes soft and reducing static electricity. They routinely contain chemicals such as chloroform and benzyl acetate that can be harmful to the environment and irritate people's skin.

There are also chemical-free products available that treat static electricity and soften clothes and can be used over and over again. National Allergy (*www.nationalallergy.com*) carries a variety of products for people with sensitivities and allergies, including Static Eliminator Re-usable Dryer Sheets.

Mowing the Lawn or Not

Lawns are getting greener, and it's not just the fertilizer. Taking the environment into account when choosing ground cover and mowing options has become an important issue when it comes to maintaining a healthy yard.

Choosing a Ground Cover

You can decide how much time, effort, and expense you want to put into your yardwork. As with so many other conservation measures, choosing a low-maintenance lawn can also reduce the impact your lawn has on the environment and the amount of natural resources used. It can also reduce the amount of money you spend trying to maintain the perfect bed of grass. Lawns can be planted with a mixture of native tall grasses or plants that require little maintenance. Prairie grasses and flowers will grow taller than standard lawn grass and will beautify the yard with colorful flowers during different times of the year. Other plants and flowers can be added to offer decorative alternatives to grass and give lawns a less manicured and wilder look.

Short-growing plants and ground cover can provide an alternative to standard grass while allowing people to walk and play in the yard. The right grass substitute or no-mow lawn can reduce and possibly even eliminate the need to mow and fertilize altogether.

Multiple companies offer seed mixes of wildflowers and short grasses that can be thrown into the yard. Mixtures can be made according to geographic location, watering and lighting requirements, mowing needs, and soil conditions. These mixtures include ingredients like ryegrass, clover, daisies, lavender, and thyme. Some of the companies that provide no-mow lawn and grass alternatives are listed here:

- **Hobbs & Hopkins Ltd.** is located in Oregon and carries seed mixes like Fleur de Lawn and Fragrant Herbal that are especially for the Pacific Northwest. They work closely with Oregon State University to determine different ecology mixes for lawns and gardens. You can visit their Web site at *www.protimelawnseed.com*.
- **No Mow Grass** can be ordered from the Web site *www.nomow grass.com*. They carry specific seed mixes amenable to the variety of weather conditions in the United States. The Web site also offers preparation and planting instructions. No Mow Grass carries wildflower seed mixes for all types of weather conditions.
- **Prairie Nursery** provides seed mixes for the northern United States and parts of Canada. Their seed mixes include prairie plants and grasses. They also carry lawn mixes that include slow-growing, fine

fescue grass, which grows up to nine inches tall. Due to their slender build, the blades fall over, giving them a height of about four inches. Fescue grasses are good for areas that are too warm for cool-weather grass and too cool for warm-weather grass. Check out the mixtures at *www.prairienursery.com*

- **Wildflower Farm** carries a variety of tall prairie grasses and shorter lawn grasses. Their stock is more appropriate for the central-northern United States. They carry Eco-lawn, a substitute for standard yards that includes a mixture of seven fescue grasses. Visit their Web site at *www.wildflowerfarm.com*.

- **Stepables** are carried in a variety of lawn and garden shops across the United States. Stepables were created by the Under A Foot Plant Company. They offer a wealth of plants that can be selected by zone (location within the United States) at their Web site, *www.stepables .com*. Information on each plant includes a photo, sunlight and watering requirements, information on whether mowing is necessary, and other maintenance requirements.

Maintaining a healthy lawn is even easier if you use native plants when landscaping. Native plants are adapted to local climates and conditions so they don't need a lot of care to thrive—they have been flourishing for years without any help from humans. They are accustomed to local pests, so native plants do not depend on pesticides. Native plants are also acclimated to local weather conditions and rainfall, meaning they don't need excessive watering or protection. Local birds and butterflies are often attracted to native species, making a yard a haven to animals. Native plants will also live longer than exotics, saving time and money, and conserving natural resources. Ultimately, using native plants will cut down on the effort and energy needed to maintain a beautiful lawn.

In the southern and southwestern United States, xeriscape landscaping has become a popular alternative to high-maintenance yards. Xeriscaping uses plants specifically selected for their drought-resistant qualities. In areas where water restrictions are common, these types of plants offer a pleasant alternative to standard lawns. One example is the use of clover instead of grass. Not only is clover drought-resistant, it's tolerant of weeds and insects, requires minimal mowing, and offers a soft cushion for walking.

Choosing a Mower

Either by personal choice or neighborhood covenants many people have lawns of green grass that need to be maintained. That's where choosing the right mower comes in.

FACT

The California Air Resources Board estimates that 2006 model lawn mowers emit 93 times more emissions than 2006 model cars. California is working toward legislation that would require emission standards to be more stringent than those in the other forty-nine states. Lawn mower manufacturers may soon have two lines of mowers, one compliant with California requirements and the other meeting broader requirements for the rest of the country.

If you want to skip a trip to the gym, mow your yard using a reel lawn mower. Reel mowers are the oldest residential lawn mowers. The blades are attached to the wheels, so pushing the mower manually causes the wheels to roll and the blades to rotate, cutting the grass. While some people may choose this type of mower for nostalgic reasons, others may like its simplicity—no engines or ignitions to keep in working order and no fuel mixture to store in the garage. Because they are not dependent on fuel, reel lawn mowers don't produce any emissions.

Electric lawn mowers work well for small yards and gardens. Although they do not produce any emissions, these mowers do get their power from local plants that may burn fossil fuels. Not only are electric mowers friendly for air quality, they're quiet. Some can be equipped with a grass catcher and even have mulch capabilities. Electric mowers are lightweight, and the handles can be folded for easy storage. Cordless mowers can be charged overnight to provide up to forty minutes of mowing time the next day.

Newer power-driven lawn mowers are more efficient than older models, but they can still produce smog-forming chemicals and carbon monoxide. Lawn mowers do not have catalytic converters, which are required on automobiles to treat the exhaust before it escapes and remove nitrogen oxides, volatile organic compounds, and hydrocarbons before they can combine with sunlight to form smog. The EPA is currently working on legislation that would require the installation of catalytic converters in lawn mowers.

Leaves and grass clippings need not be taken to the curb. They can be used in compost and made into mulch or used in planting beds and gardens. The EPA estimates that up to 31 million tons of yard waste is collected, transported, and processed by municipalities every year. Keeping yard trimmings at home for use in the garden reduces waste processing and the need for transportation. If raking isn't your ideal pastime, manual leaf sweepers are available. Composters.com (*www.composters.com*) offers an assortment of lawn sweepers that can be used to collect leaves from yards, sidewalks, and driveways, ready to put in the compost pile.

Lawn Care and Pesticides

When it comes to taking care of the lawn, there are plenty of options and alternatives for eliminating pests and maintaining a healthy strand of grass or ground cover.

Lawn Care

Unhealthy grass and plants are more susceptible to pests. Before turning to pesticides to control bugs, work on getting your plants in shape. One way to pump up plants and get rid of garbage at the same time is to compost.

Compost is made of recycled food scraps, yard trimmings, clean paper, and even ashes from your fireplace. Don't include meat, pet droppings, or oil and grease because they can attract rodents that can carry disease and can kill the beneficial organisms. Commercial compost units can be purchased from lawn and garden centers, online carriers, or even through local extension or utility offices. Compost units can also be made at home using materials like chicken wire, bricks, or buckets. The organic material in the compost bin needs to be turned and watered regularly to mix the contents from the inner portions of the pile to the outer portions. The material in the center of the pile decays as it is kept warm and moist, a perfect atmosphere for degradation. When the mixture turns into a dark brown crumbly material that smells like earth, it's ready to go.

Using compost is a great way to improve soil texture and keep weeds from growing. It increases air and water absorption in the soil and can be used as mulch in the lawn or garden. Compost makes great potting soil.

By joining a group of local growers, green gardeners can exchange information and find out what is working and what is not. Organic gardening has grown in popularity, so joining a group either in person or online is even easier. Extension offices or local garden clubs may have information on groups or meetings in your area.

Beneficial insects and other animals can be very, well, beneficial when it comes to getting rid of pests in your garden. Ladybugs, lacewings, and ground beetles feed on aphids, chinch bugs, and weevils. Lizards, birds, and frogs will likely make a meal out of pesky caterpillars and grubs. But beneficials will not be attracted by the pests alone and sometimes need to be enticed with their favorite plants. Adding bordering flowers will attract beneficial insects by providing shelter and nectar. Not only will there be fewer pests, the beneficial bugs will help pollinate flowers, fruits, and vegetables.

When it comes to countering an invasion in the garden, concerned gardeners may need a more hands-on approach to get rid of weeds and pests. Caterpillars, worms, and beetles can be picked off plants and destroyed. Mixing a few tablespoons of a strong-smelling ingredient like cayenne, garlic, or horseradish with a quart of water and spraying it on plants can drive away some pests. There are also recipes for mildew and fungi treatments that include common kitchen ingredients like baking soda and vinegar.

Here are three simple recipes:

1. Mix three tablespoons of natural apple cider vinegar with one gallon of water. Spray on plants during the cool part of the day.
2. Mix one teaspoon of baking soda, one drop of detergent, and one tablespoon of canola oil in one gallon of water; spray the mixture on plants to treat fungus and mildew.

3. Soak chopped garlic overnight in one pint of mineral oil. Strain the mixture to remove the garlic; then add one pint of water and no more than half a teaspoon of soap remains. Spray the mixture directly on pest infestations.

To make sure that plants won't be adversely affected, use home remedies on just a portion of the plants first.

Pesticides

Rachel Carson's *Silent Spring* educated the world on the dangers of pesticides. The book focuses on the use of pesticides and their impact on the web of life. Pesticides often harm more animals than they mean to. Targeted animals absorb the pesticide, and then a second, unintended animal eats the first and ingests the poison, bringing both populations down. Carson's work highlighted the importance of understanding the impacts of chemicals on the environment. New pesticides developed through Green Chemistry are designed to target specific organisms and will not harm any other living systems.

ALERT!

The EPA has banned the manufacture and use of a number of pesticides previously considered safe. This list includes chlorinated hydrocarbon insecticides such as aldrin and dieldrin. It also includes common pesticides like chlordane, lindane, and toxaphene, which were used as flea control on animals.

Carson's critics claim that without pesticides, civilization would return to the Dark Ages when insects ran rampant and disease was uncontrolled. However, the impacts of many synthetic pesticides are still unknown because many of the effects are long-term. The overuse of pesticides has been acknowledged, and proper application has been taken more seriously by individuals, corporations, and municipalities. People have begun to appreciate chemicals' destructive power and are using more safety precautions and following directions more closely.

The EPA registers pesticides for use on the basis that they do not pose unreasonable risks to people or the environment. Unfortunately, the long-term and synergistic effects are not always known when the chemicals are registered.

The pesticide market is highly competitive; companies are developing new and proprietary compounds every day. It's true that pesticides have allowed an abundance of crops to be grown and incidences of certain diseases to be reduced. When pesticides are used as directed, they can prove beneficial in preventing illness and even death. Pesticides are known to kill bugs that carry diseases like malaria and West Nile virus. They are also praised by the farming community for improving crop health and production by eliminating damaging pests.

FACT

According to the Centers for Disease Control, about 600 pesticide ingredients are currently approved for use and are found in almost 20,000 different products. These products make up the approximately 2 billion pounds of pesticides legally applied in the United States every year. This accounts for one-fifth of global pesticide use.

Exposure to pesticides—or any chemicals—can be acute or chronic. Exposure can occur in a high dosage in a very short time or at lower levels over an extended period. Each type of exposure causes different reactions and effects. The CDC reports that short-term exposure to pesticides has been shown to cause respiratory, gastrointestinal, allergic, and neurological reactions. Long-term exposure may cause cancer and/or damage neurological systems.

There are efforts under way to develop and market safer pesticides. Many that are currently being researched rely on biotechnology to protect plants. These pesticides use chemicals that are less harmful, or more benign, for humans and the environment than more routinely used chemicals.

Checking on the Air Inside

Everyone wants to breathe easily, especially at home. There are a variety of contaminants that can decrease air quality, many of which can be reduced by eliminating the source. From smoking to buying new furniture, contaminants find their way into your airspace.

The following common types of indoor air pollution can be found in most homes:

- **Asbestos** is made up of small carcinogenic particles that can lodge in the lungs. The particles enter the air through deteriorating ceiling and floor tiles, or acoustic materials and fire proofing.
- **Biological pollutants** include mold, mildew, and pet dander. They can cause allergic reactions and asthma.
- **Carbon monoxide** is an odorless gas that is produced during incomplete combustion of carbon and can be lethal. Sources include car emissions, fireplaces, and gas stoves.
- **Pressed-wood products** can emit formaldehyde that can cause headaches and even asthma.
- **Cleaning, maintenance, and hobby products** can contain volatile organic compounds that can cause headaches and also pose a long-term cancer risk.
- **Lead exposure** is generally caused by lead-based paint or contaminated soil. If you are involved in an activity that produces lead dust, be sure to keep children out of the area.
- **Nitrogen dioxide** is produced by unvented kerosene heaters and tobacco smoke.
- **Pesticides** generally include semivolatile organic compounds. Being around pesticides for a long time can irritate the respiratory system and cause damage to the liver and central nervous system.
- **Radon** comes from naturally decaying uranium in soil and water and is the second-leading cause of lung cancer. The U.S. surgeon general has encouraged everyone to have their homes tested for radon.
- **Fireplaces and wood-burning stoves** can produce particles. When burning, try to ventilate the area to avoid irritation to eyes and respiratory systems.

If the sources of indoor air pollution can't be removed, ventilating the area may help decrease the concentrations. Bathroom and kitchen fans can be used to exhaust air directly to the outside and improve the ventilation rate. However, if left open, ventilation fans exchange a considerable amount of air, which requires extra heating or cooling.

ALERT!

If you're getting rid of household products that are labeled poison, danger, warning, or caution, don't throw them in the trash or pour them out. Find out about your local household hazardous waste collection center or pickup service.

A variety of cleaning systems are available to improve the quality of air in homes or workplaces. They vary in size from tabletop models that work in limited areas to models that treat the entire house. Make sure the air purifier you're considering treats the specific contaminant that needs to be eliminated. Air purifiers cannot be used to remove radon from your house; homes have to be mitigated in this instance. Ozone generators are often recommended, but in actuality ozone is not healthy to breathe. Plants have also been found to clean indoor air, so keep your plants healthy and they'll do the same for you.

Chapter 6

Eating Green

The organic food market has grown by leaps and bounds over the past decade. Where organic food was once limited to specialty stores and markets, it's now available almost everywhere. Even Wal-Mart is getting in on the trend, looking to double the number of organic products they sell. Organic food has also become an important part of restaurants, and food services are being revamped in school cafeterias and corporate lunch counters across the country. This chapter delves into what *organic* really means, the benefits of going organic, and the many options for bringing organic food to the table.

The Organic Option

The definition of *organic* varies depending on who is involved in the conversation. Generally, organic refers to the growing, raising, or processing of food without drugs, synthetic chemicals, or hormones, using methods that conserve natural resources and limit the effects on the environment. But how do you know if something is really organic? As organic food increased in popularity, consumers began calling for the standardization of the organic labeling process to ensure that important criteria were met before a label could be obtained.

The call for certification started in the 1970s. Before then, organic farms were small and served local shoppers. As the movement caught on and organic farming expanded with mass production and distribution, however, it became evident that farmers needed to prove that they used organic practices and consumers needed to be reassured of the integrity of organic labels.

QUESTION?

Just because something is labeled organic, how do I know it is safe for the environment?
The USDA regulations for organic production mandate "a production system that is managed in accordance with the Act and regulations in this part to respond to site-specific conditions by integrating cultural, biological, and mechanical practices that foster cycling of resources, promote ecological balance, and conserve biodiversity."

In the 1980s, private and state programs began providing organic certifications, but standards varied from group to group and state to state, and incidences of fraud began to arise. To level the playing field, the federal government stepped in to regulate the industry.

The Organic Foods Production Act of 1990 helped create the National Organic Program (NOP), which is run through the U.S. Department of Agriculture (USDA). The NOP prepared standards, the National Organic Program Regulations, and all organic certifiers were required to be in compliance with these regulations by the end of 2002.

Foods meeting the USDA requirements for being organic have a USDA seal. To obtain the seal, foods must be 95 percent organic. Foods using only organic products and methods may also state "100% organic" on the packaging. A lower level of organic certification is available for foods that are 70 to 95 percent organic. These foods can be labeled as "made with organic ingredients."

To obtain the organic certification, farmers must find a certification agent through either a state or private agency. They must complete an application, documenting information such as pest management practices, seed and seedling sources, storage and handling measures, and monitoring practices. The agent certifies the paperwork and assigns an organic inspector to review operations at the farm. If everything is in place, the certification agent will approve organic certification and the farm can use the organic label.

Organic foods should not be confused with natural or whole foods, although they are all similar in that they steer clear of pesticides and growth hormones. The requirements for a food being deemed organic are well defined while requirements for whole or natural foods are not. Natural foods generally do not include synthetic ingredients, and whole foods tend to maintain their nutrients and fiber because they are processed as little as possible.

Homegrown

If you want to literally put your own fruits and veggies on the table, starting an organic garden or farm might be an option.

Rather than resorting to pesticides, use ladybugs to control aphids, chinch bugs, and alfalfa weevils. These nursery-rhyme warriors of the garden can be purchased through mail-order companies and come in a variety of colors and patterns. Some ladybugs are bedecked with stripes instead of the standard polka dots.

When it comes to organic farming or gardening, local groups can be exceptionally helpful because they are aware of local conditions, what grows well, and what problems you might encounter. Check out cooperatives and extension services associated with nearby universities or county agencies for more information.

Regardless of where you live, you can take simple measures to make your garden truly organic:

- Use natural fertilizers like grass cuttings and leaves to enrich the natural soil.
- Add mulch and compost to help the soil retain water. The less you have to water your garden, the more water you'll conserve.
- Buy organic seeds from local or online retailers. USDA-certified organic seeds will not have any genetic modifications.
- Include plants you can eat like cilantro, dill, and fennel to encourage visits from ladybugs and other predatory insects that will help control pests.
- As your garden grows, use organic methods to keep insect pests, mildew, weeds, and fungus at bay.

Where to Shop

According to the Organic Trade Association, the sale of organic foods increased 16 percent in 2005 alone, bringing in $13.8 million in sales. More and more fresh, whole-food, and organic grocers are popping up across the United States, and traditional grocers and food producers are taking notice.

The Giants

Whole Foods Market started in Austin, Texas, and now operates more than 200 stores in the United States, Canada, and the United Kingdom. Not only are they the world's leading retailer of natural and organic food, *Fortune* magazine consistently lists Whole Foods as one of its top 100 companies to work for. Whole Foods came in at number five in the 2007 list.

The Fresh Market is another chain grocery store that focuses primarily on organic and natural foods. Growing from one location in Greenville, South Carolina, the company now has stores across the Southeast and Midwest.

Feeling pressure from growing specialty organic stores, more mainstream grocery stores are including a variety of organic food in their inventories as well. Brands such as Nature's Best and Newman's Own are common in many conventional grocery stores. Many stores have even started their own lines of organic foods. The Kroger Company, the country's largest supermarket, started the Naturally Preferred line in 2002, which now includes more than 275 items. Even large food producers are getting in on the organic options. Kraft Foods now makes USDA-certified organic macaroni and cheese, and their DiGiorno spinach and garlic thin-crust pizza is made using organic ingredients.

Smaller Grocers

Smaller independent markets consistently buy locally grown fruits and vegetables that are fresh and seasonal. That means the produce people eat spends more time ripening on the vine than traveling across the country— or around the world. Most people are used to having a variety of fruits and vegetables available year-round. But for this to happen, fruits and vegetables have to be trucked and transported, which uses fuel and produces carbon dioxide. A growing movement encourages food labels to include information about how many miles the product traveled from the farm to the store. This information would allow shoppers to purchase more locally grown produce and avoid food that's made a longer haul.

Studies performed by the Leopold Center for Sustainable Agriculture in Iowa compared locally grown produce to fruit and vegetables shipped from different places to the same location. An Iowa-grown apple only traveled about 61 miles from orchard to store, while other apples traveled on average 1,726 miles. Local spinach went about 36 miles while out-of-town spinach tacked on 1,800 miles before landing in the produce case.

Farmers' Markets and Health Food Stores

There are also more specialized farmers' markets and health-food stores where people can purchase lines of organic and natural foods that might not be available elsewhere. The term *farmers' market* can mean anything from an open-air market where farmers and their families sell directly to consumers to full-scale stores utilizing distribution networks to bring a combination of locally and internationally grown produce to their bins. Many cities support locally grown fruits, vegetables, and plants by providing space for weekend markets. These markets often include local entertainment and exhibits, creating a true community event. Farmers or their families are often on hand to answer questions and offer explanations. Larger farmers' markets carry a variety of organic products; however, they do not necessarily carry local produce and tend to bring in many exotic fruits and vegetables.

Health-food stores carry fresh produce similar to what you would find at a farmers' market, but they also offer organic, natural, and whole foods. Items sold at health-food stores range from baby food to breakfast cereal to soups. Stores may also carry special dietary foods such as gluten-free products. Much like conventional grocery stores, health-food stores carry personal items, like shampoo and soap, along with nutritional supplements and homeopathic treatments. Some health-food stores have a café offering a selection of healthful sandwiches and snacks.

Online Alternatives

If you would like your food to come to you, try Community Supported Agriculture (CSA). This program allows you to buy "shares" in a local farm. You will receive a basket of produce every week or month, depending on the farm. You can pick up your basket at a prearranged location or it may be delivered to your home or office. The Web site, *www.localharvest.org/csa*, allows you to find participating farms in your area.

Going Vegetarian or Vegan

Vegetarianism—a lifestyle based on a choice not to consume meat, fish, or poultry—has been practiced for thousands of years. The choice can be based on health, religion, or personal preference, but the well-being of the environment has become another reason to embrace vegetarianism in recent years.

Being a vegetarian does not automatically exclude dairy products or eggs from the diet; that's an individual choice. Vegans are a stricter form of vegetarians. They eat no animal flesh or products and abstain from wearing or using animal products such as leather, silk, wool, lanolin, or gelatin. Then there are dietary vegans who adhere to a strict diet but are amenable to using animal products.

FACT

When he was not calculating the hypotenuse of the right triangle or solving algebraic equations, Pythagoras was a practicing vegetarian. Pythagoras was a member of an organization called the *mathematikoi*. They believed that reality in its purest form was mathematical in nature, and many were vegetarians.

There are a variety of reasons beyond concern for the environment to adopt a vegetarian lifestyle. The quality of life for livestock can be an influential factor. Rather than allowing cows and other animals to graze and forage naturally, they are confined and fed grain and corn grown using pesticides and transported to farms by truck and over rail. Overall, the meat consumes massive amounts of energy, burdening the soil, groundwater, surface water, and air. Health is another reason to give up meat and meat products. Forgoing, or even reducing, meat consumption can be a key factor in lowering cholesterol and limiting the intake of unnecessary chemicals like hormones and antibiotics.

The Dish on Meat

Whether fish, chicken, pork, or beef, meat is still a staple of many meals. More and more information is available to consumers about how animals are raised, allowing them to choose the meat they buy more conscientiously.

Fish

Fish can be a good source of protein without the saturated fats in other meats. Fish also contain essential vitamins and minerals including omega-3 fatty acids, which have been shown to prevent heart disease and may even help brain development. Many fish are caught in the wild; others such as salmon are frequently farm raised.

Wild Fish

Managing the catching of wild fish can be a complicated process because many fish are caught in international waters. More and more organizations are working toward safer practices of catching fish to ensure that marine populations are maintained and are able to flourish over the coming decades.

The Marine Stewardship Council is a nonprofit organization that works internationally to certify fisheries based on the type of fish caught and the methods used to catch the fish. A variety of large chains, looking to support sustainable fishing, have pledged to improve buying practices in this area. In February 2006, Wal-Mart promised that within three to five years, it would only buy and sell fish caught in the wild that met the standards of the Marine Stewardship Council. In Alaska, state officials are monitoring the salmon and at any sign of decline will put a halt to fishing. Studies show that unless fishing is curbed or controlled, many populations are not expected to last until the middle of this century. If precautions are not taken, populations of fish such as orange roughy, Chilean sea bass, Pacific rockfish, sharks, and blue fin tuna may never recover.

Many in the seafood industry understand that their livelihood depends on sustaining the fish population decades into the future, but some populations are in danger of overfishing. Overfishing decreases a population to the point where it cannot replenish itself through natural breeding. This has serious repercussions for the entire ecosystem as species are depleted and are unable to fulfill their traditional roles as predator or prey.

The Monterey Bay Aquarium in California takes an active role in working with the public, educating people on current fishing techniques and better selection of sustainable seafood.

The aquarium also promotes consumer activism in selecting and supporting sustainable fishing practices. Along with other valuable information, pocket guides are available on its Web site (*www.mbayaq.org*) that list the preferable picks of fish as well as those that consumers should avoid. This information allows consumers to flex their spending muscles. One guide spans the United States, and others are divided by region. In addition, the organization offers the following recommendations for consumers and those catching fish themselves:

- Whether in a store or restaurant, ask where the fish came from and how it was caught. Was the salmon raised on a farm or caught wild in Alaska? Farm-raised salmon requires an inordinate amount of protein to feed on, and farms routinely discharge concentrated waste untreated into the ocean. Alaskan fisheries have been rated environmentally responsible by the Monterey Bay Aquarium.
- Opt for oysters, scallops, squid, and clams over grouper, tuna, and shark. Marine life that's lower on the food chain can reproduce more quickly and replenish populations more easily while larger life forms take longer. However, because these animals are bottom feeders, they can ingest toxins from sediments more easily, making selection of farm- versus wild-raised fish more important.
- Don't discard fishing gear in the water. Tangled lines and hooks can hurt or kill unsuspecting marine life such as turtles and sea birds.
- Avoid protected areas, which allow exhausted fish populations to recover. By staying away from them, you can support replenishment of the species.
- Put down that seashell. It's important that people avoid taking certain seashells from the beach or purchasing them from tourist shops and craft stores. Enclosed or "conch" shells are often homes to sea life that depend on them for protection.

Farm Raised

Because of the increased demand for seafood, many commercial anglers are choosing to raise their stock in contained areas rather than fish the open waters. As a result, farming now provides one-third of all seafood sold. Farming, or aquaculture, works best with herbivorous or plant-eating fish such as catfish and carp. However, salmon are carnivorous; they require five times their own weight in fish protein, which usually comes from other fish caught in the wild. Farm-raising fish, if not handled responsibly, can impact the environment. Raising fish like salmon in a net pen is akin to cattle feedlots. Fish are kept in a densely populated area, and because disease transfers easily, antibiotics are needed to control illness. There is also concern that penned fish can escape their environment, harming native fish populations by introducing parasites and diseases and disrupting breeding cycles. One of the best alternatives for farm-raising fish is to locate the fisheries inland away from wild populations and where wastewater can be handled and treated more easily.

Mercury and Fish

Fish offer many nutritional benefits; however, they also carry chemicals and contamination absorbed from feeding and living in the water. Mercury is one particularly adverse element.

The EPA has issued warnings for certain types of sea life and offers guidelines for the amount of fish and shellfish consumers should eat. Certain people, particularly pregnant women and small children, are advised to stay away from fish with high levels of mercury. Mercury hinders neural development, and fetuses, infants, and small children are especially susceptible. Shark, swordfish, king mackerel, and tilefish often contain dangerous amounts of mercury. Shrimp, canned light tuna, salmon, pollock, and catfish have lower levels of mercury and are safe to eat in moderation. More information on the advisory can be found at *www.epa.gov/waterscience/fishadvice*.

Mercury is a naturally occurring element. It is also released into the air by industrial pollution such as waste incinerators. When mercury falls in streams and oceans, bacteria chemically changes some of it to methylmercury, which is absorbed by fish as they feed. The methylmercury is then stored in the tissues; the amount accumulates over time, so older and larger fish are more likely to have higher levels of mercury. Fish that are higher up on the food chain also tend to accumulate more mercury than bottom-dwellers.

Down on the Farm

Animals have long been bred for human consumption. The move to organic meat is bringing to light the treatment of farm animals. Many shoppers are choosing to purchase meat from animals that have been raised more humanely and allowed to graze without the use of hormones and antibiotics.

Researchers at Johns Hopkins University studied the use of antibiotics in poultry farming at one of the largest U.S. producers to determine if the practice was economically beneficial. Based on the results, the drugs did help the chickens grow larger; however, the money made from the larger chickens did not offset the cost of the drugs.

FACT

Dr. Temple Grandin has studied animal behavior, focusing on the handling of animals and animal behavior, and developed a scoring system to measure animal stress. Based on her research, she has designed more humane livestock-handling facilities all over the world. For more information on Dr. Grandin and her work, visit her Web site at *www.grandin.com.*

Organically raised meat is becoming more commonplace, with companies like Coleman Natural Products, the largest natural meat company in the United States, selling its products at over 1,650 stores nationwide. Maverick Ranch Natural Meats, for example, offers a line of meats including beef, chicken, turkey, pork, lamb, and buffalo. Owned by the Moore family, they allow their cattle to forage and graze in pastures free of pesticides. They also refrain from the use of steroids and antibiotics. The animals are all "Certified Humane Raised and Handled" by Humane Farm Animal Care, a nonprofit organization that works to ensure farm animal welfare. While Maverick Ranch and other ranchers like them strive to provide sustainable farming while providing good living conditions for the animals, there are still concerns with many of the animals raised as food.

Cows, poultry, and pigs raised using conventional methods are subject to the same concerns from an environmental standpoint. They are all fed unnatural diets that include hormones and antibiotics. These additives help the animals reach slaughter weight more quickly and decrease disease in animals kept in close quarters. There is concern that animals' bodies do not completely break down the hormones, allowing the hormones to enter the environment through manure and wastewater.

If you are having a hard time finding pasture-raised meat at local grocers, check out *www.eatwild.com*. This searchable Web site allows shoppers to find local pasture-raised meat. Locations are sorted by state along with a summary of the farm and contact information.

Special care must be taken when raising animals in close quarters. Waste and odor management are two important aspects. For example, the Leopold Center for Sustainable Agriculture at Iowa State University has reported on the pros and cons of indoor versus outdoor pig farming. Larger operations tend to use indoor facilities where weather is not a factor and sows tend to produce more babies. However, there are also manure management, health, and odor control issues that must be addressed with indoor farming. When optimally performed, outdoor farming can cost less, as manure and odor management require less attention and herd health is generally better. Also, outdoor raising of pigs provides more flexibility with herd size in that a large structure does not have to be supported by a set number of animals and production. The center assists farmers with design and operational recommendations to ensure profit while protecting the environment and providing good living conditions for the pigs.

Genetically Modified Foods and Hidden Ingredients

Products lining supermarket shelves may not be as innocent as they look. With advances in technology, scientists have been able to manipulate the genes of common foods to bring out positive traits. Similarly, some processed foods have additives that might not be obvious.

Scientists in the Kitchen

Genetic modification got its start from selective breeding, where plants or animals are selected based on certain qualities to breed and reproduce. Selective breeding over hundreds of years gives dog owners the choice of bringing home a Chihuahua or a Great Dane and apple-eaters the option of eating a Golden Delicious or a Bramley.

Genetic modification speeds up the process by inserting specific genes into a plant or animal without going through the trial-and-error process of breeding; that is, breeding good qualities with other good qualities to get the best of both and avoid the undesirable traits. An additional use of genetic modification has been to combine traits from different plants to obtain a very different outcome. This method has been used to grow human insulin in corn for use by diabetics.

The FDA approves genetically modified foods individually based on reports submitted by agricultural companies. If the genetically modified food is shown to be as safe as its unmodified counterpart, approval is granted. The Union of Concerned Scientists has asked the FDA to require labeling of genetically altered food; however, unless reports indicate a difference between the altered and unaltered food, no label is required.

ALERT!

Allergies are caused by certain proteins present in different foods. Scientists are working to eliminate or reduce allergies in foods like peanut, soy, and wheat by removing the proteins. However, there is concern that different allergens might accidentally be created or proteins possibly intensified in the process.

To date, approximately fifty different engineered products have been approved. Chances are if you use canola oil or eat corn, papaya, potatoes, or tomatoes, you have tasted genetically modified food. Numerous crops such as corn, cotton, canola, and soybeans have been genetically altered to be resistant to certain insects.

Objections to the use of genetically modified foods include both environmental and health concerns. It is unsure if plants that are genetically modified for pest resistance could harm unintended and desirable insects. There is also concern that target insects could actually become immune to the pesticides. Environmental concerns include the potential for engineered crops to cross-breed with weeds. Altering crops to resist herbicides could result in mighty weeds undeterred by herbicides. Health concerns include the potential for allergens to be introduced as part of the genetic modification, causing dangerous reactions in some people. Overall, many people are concerned with the unknown effects genetically modified food could have on their health.

Do You Know What's in Your Dinner?

Processed food is likely to contain food additives. Additives help extend the life of some foods, add nutrition, or change a food's consistency. Some additives are relatively straightforward, and by reading the label, you will know what has been added. Some, however, are less conspicuous. This is of particular concern if you have allergies or are trying to avoid certain foods like meat.

Food additives can cause extreme allergic reactions such as anaphylactic shock, which causes breathing problems and loss of consciousness. Also associated with allergies to "real" foods like peanuts, anaphylactic shock can be fatal if it is not treated.

If you are unsure whether the listed ingredient on a package is or contains an allergen, contact the manufacturer.

An example of a vegetarian food made with or containing animal products is gelatin. It sounds innocent enough, but it is made from the bones, skins, and tendons of cows, pigs, and fish. It is used in making Jell-O and candies, two foods that would appear to be vegetarian.

In Your Kitchen

Conserving energy is a big part of reducing your impact on the planet. Microwaves heat food much more efficiently than standard ovens and stove tops. They don't require preheating nor do they take as long to cook food. There have been concerns regarding the way microwaves heat food, but there has been no proof that they damage food.

There is concern, however, with respect to the temperature of the food. Because microwaves heat unevenly, you can easily burn your mouth. Heating baby bottles in the microwave is not recommended for this reason.

Cooking plastic in the microwave may cause a chemical breakdown of the material and transfer of chemicals to food. Only use plastics for their intended method. Take-home Styrofoam should not be used to reheat any leftovers. If you really want to play it safe, do not use plastics in the microwave. Put your food on microwave-safe glass or ceramic dishes instead.

Other ways to conserve energy in the kitchen include using as small an oven as possible. The larger the oven, the more energy it takes to heat it to the proper temperature. Don't forget, ovens are made to keep heat inside, so you can turn off the oven before the timer goes off, and your food will continue to cook. Glass and ceramic retain heat better than metal; switching will reduce the temperature as much as 25 degrees. When using the stove, make sure the burner fits the pan; an uncovered burner wastes heat. Always use a lid when heating items on the stove for the same reason.

Eating Out Green

Patronizing green restaurants means supporting businesses that incorporate sustainable business practices in their operations; some green restaurants serve only organic or natural food as well. Restaurants use energy for cooking food and keeping it refrigerated. Dishwashers use a lot of resources, and thermostats are set to keep patrons happy. Many cities and towns work with small businesses, including restaurants, to help reduce their impact on the environment. For example, in California, the Green Business Program works with environmental agencies and utilities to recognize businesses with green operations. Restaurants with green operations conserve energy by using Energy Star appliances and low-flow spray nozzles and by reducing, reusing, and recycling materials like cardboard, plastics, and glass; they prevent pollution by making sure that grease traps are cleaned and that bio-degradable soaps are used for cleaning. The Green Restaurant Association certifies restaurants, coffee shops, and college and university cafeterias that operate in sustainable ways. Information on their certification process can be found at *www.dinegreen.com*.

Besides operating in environmentally friendly ways, more restaurants are offering organic and whole foods on their menus. The Bon Appétit Management Company owns 190 cafés in twenty-six states that serve organic, local, and sustainable fare. The company policy is to cook local food to avoid unnecessary food miles and environmental impacts. This policy has led to some creative cooking situations, leading chefs to boil seawater for salt and drive country lanes in search of wheat for flour. Local Harvest (*www.localharvest.org*) is an organization that keeps a directory of restaurants, farmers' markets, cooperatives, and farms that use sustainable practices and organic products. Their database covers the entire United States and includes products ranging from flowers to beef.

Consumers wield power with their wallets. When dining out, ask questions about the food. For example, many of the fish served at restaurants are not recommended for consumption either because of mercury concentrations or overfishing. The server may not likely know the answers to all the questions, but the management does. For larger chain restaurants, consider contacting members of the board with your concerns about the food they serve. Refer to Chapter 18 for successful ideas on how to get your point across with companies.

Chapter 7

Drinking Green

Some drinks start as fruits on trees, some as leafy plants on the ground, while others course through limestone below the ground. The Beverage Marketing Corporation estimates that the average American drinks about two liters of some form of liquid every day. That's about 192 gallons a year of soda, water, milk, coffee, tea, wine, and other assorted beverages. This chapter covers some of the green drinks out today and what makes some better choices than others when it comes to wetting your whistle.

It's in the Water

Without water, people have only days to live. It's a lubricant. It regulates metabolism and controls body temperature. It helps move joints and eases food through the digestive system. It's calorie-free and readily available at almost everyone's fingertips. And water is water, right? Not so fast. Some water really is more environmentally friendly than other water.

Bottle or Tap

Water bottles have become fashion accessories. No longer just for athletes, these days water bottles labeled with picturesque mountain streams and clear springs help hydrate everyone from business executives to school kids.

Bottling companies rarely put the source of the water on the bottle. That's because chances are it didn't come from the clear running stream shown on the bottle. The labels do include contact information for the company, so consumers can call to find out the source of their bottled water.

Unless you are traveling in an area where the water isn't safe to drink, there's no need to avoid the tap. Public water supplies are regulated and, by law, are required to be tested regularly. Bottled water, although it's been found to be safe, isn't required to meet the same criteria as public water supplies.

According to the Container Recycling Institute, if people recycled 70 percent of the bottles they purchased for one year, greenhouse gases could be reduced by 20,000 metric tons of carbon equivalent. It would also save the equivalent of 600,000 barrels of crude oil needing to be extracted and processed.

Water quality isn't an issue, but delivering millions of gallons of water in separate bottles is incredibly inefficient. Rather than taking advantage of existing treatment and distribution systems, bottlers individually package their water and ship it across the country. Plastic bottles are made from petroleum, and trucking them across country uses a lot of gas. The surge in bottled water has left mountains of plastic in its wake. Plastic bottles can be recycled for use in a variety of products, from other bottles to carpet, but most inevitably end up in landfills and incinerators all over the country.

Currently only eleven states have bottle bills that require refund systems for returning used water bottles. Companies that purchase recycled bottles for use in manufacturing prefer to buy plastics from states with bottle bills. The streams from these states contain only plastic bottles, making them much easier to use because additional sorting isn't necessary.

There has been quite a bit of debate lately over whether people should reuse single-use water bottles or toss them out. (Single-use bottles are the ones the water comes in from the store, not the sport bottles made to be reused over and over again.) The concern is twofold: whether the bottles can be adequately cleaned to remove bacteria, and whether the actual cleaning promotes the release of chemicals from the plastic.

Disposable bottles have narrow necks and can't be easily washed. This makes washing them nearly impossible. Bacteria from people's hands and mouths make their way into the bottles where they can make people sick.

The primary concern with releasing chemicals during the washing process is phthalates. Phthalates are added to some plastic to keep it flexible so it won't crack. Avoid water bottles with the recycle number three in the triangle on the bottom of the bottle. Water bottles with the recycle numbers one and two are considered safe.

QUESTION?

What's the best way to wash my water bottles?
After you've emptied it, clean your bottle with hot soapy water, making sure to get around the neck of the bottle. Let your bottle air-dry. To keep from contaminating your water bottle with germs, wash and dry your hands before you refill it—and make sure you're the only one using your water bottle.

Phthalates, the most common being di (2-ehtylhexyl) phthalate, are suspected of being endocrine disruptors that interfere with reproductive organs of both males and females.

The FDA has approved of phthalates in plastics that are used to produce food and drink containers, but other agencies like the National Institute of Environmental Health (NIEH) and the Centers for Disease Control (CDC) are concerned with the potential impacts of phthalates in plastic.

If you look further into this matter, you may find stories about dioxin being released into the water from plastic bottles. However, there are no dioxins in plastics, so this should not be one of the deciding factors when considering whether to reuse bottles.

Soda

The move to organics hasn't only affected food; it's made a difference in the beverage industry, too. Soda consumption has skyrocketed over the past five years, increasing 500 percent. Soft drinks make up approximately 28 percent of all drinks consumed. But soda may not be such a good choice when it comes to options regarding people or the planet.

FACT

One 20-ounce soda contains seventeen teaspoons of sugar and 250 calories. Just one soda a day will increase a child's potential to contract diabetes by 60 percent—and don't forget about tooth decay! Drinking soda is like soaking your teeth in a sugar bath.

If you need to have that fizz when it comes to drinks, there are some organic and healthy options to choose from. Blue Sky Beverage Company (*www.drinkbluesky.com*) offers a line of organic sodas made with all natural ingredients and no preservatives or artificial colors. Santa Cruz Natural (*www.scojuice.com*) makes organic fruit juice sodas in flavors like ginger ale, root beer, lemon lime, and vanilla crème. R.W. Knudsen (*www.knud senjuices.com*) makes fruit spritzers in flavors like black cherry, mango, and tangerine. You can also look to club soda or seltzer water. Seltzer water is filtered water that's been carbonated. Club soda is water that's had minerals and mineral salts added to it—just be careful to watch the sodium content where minerals have been added.

The Healthy Beverage Company (*www.steaz.com*), makers of Steaz Green Tea Soda, now offers Steaz Energy, the first energy drink that has been USDA organic and fair trade certified. It's made from tea that's Fair Trade Certified and includes a caffeine kick not just from green tea but from Guayaki yerba mate. The yerba mate tree is native to South American rain forests that have been heavily damaged by deforestation. It's hoped that conscientious farming of the yerba mate will help sustain the rain forest.

Even 7-Up now comes 100 percent natural. Along with removing artificial flavorings, the manufacturer removed almost half the sodium. What was behind the switch? Consumers asked for a healthier soda. But drinkers take note—all-natural doesn't necessarily mean organic.

Milk

It's poured over cereal, consumed with dinner, and used for dunking many a cookie. Of all the drinks consumed, milk comes in at third place, with over 10 percent of the beverage market. But milk is more controversial than most people realize.

Milk is a primary source for calcium and vitamin D. A one-cup serving—eight ounces—supplies 30 percent of the daily recommended amount of calcium and 25 percent of vitamin D. It also contains significant amounts of protein, potassium, vitamin A, vitamin B_{12}, riboflavin, niacin, and phosphorus.

Cows in large numbers are quite a burden on the planet. A satiated dairy cow can produce 120 pounds of manure a day, and cows account for 28 percent of global emissions of methane, a greenhouse gas. Two issues define the controversy over dairy cows: how the cows live and what the cows are fed.

Grazing Versus Confinement

Like most businesses, dairy farmers are under increased pressure to maintain a profit even when operational costs rise and the cost of milk stays level. Dairy farms generally operate in one of two ways, either using grazing or nongrazing methods to feed the cows. Research, studies, and evaluations abound regarding the profitability of both forms of farming. Both methods of dairy farming require daily milking of cows, and cows are slaughtered for meat when their milking days are over.

Grazing farms use pastureland and allow herds to forage with scheduled moves from paddock to paddock. Cows generally rely on pasture grass for food, with some forms of supplemental feed.

Nongrazing, or confinement or factory farms, limit cows' movement, keeping them close to the milking barn. Confined animal feeding operations (CAFOs) are popular ways of mass raising dairy cows. Since cows don't move in CAFOs, all of the food must be harvested elsewhere and transported to the cows. In warmer climates, cows need fans and misters to reduce the potential for heat stress and keep milk production up. With factory farms, a lot of money is spent on food and managing the cows' environment.

FACT

Cows living on factory farms expend little energy on anything other than producing milk. Their food is brought to them and they don't move much. The reason pasture cows make less milk than confined cows is that they spend energy walking from paddock to paddock and grazing. In short, pasture cows spend more time being cows.

Pasture cows tend to produce less milk on a daily basis than their confined counterparts, but they generally live longer. Also, grazing cows suffer less mastitis, an infection of the teats, and produce more conjugated linoleic acid (CLA), a potent anticarcinogen. When costs are tallied, the increased quantities of milk factory farms produce do not compensate for the high costs of running the farm. Grazing has been found to be the more cost-effective method of farming.

Antibiotics and Growth Hormones

Many dairy cows are given bovine growth hormones (BGH) to encourage milk production, and antibiotics to ward off infection. Organic milk has increased in popularity as people become more aware of the antibiotics and hormones given to cows. Horizon Organic (*www.horizonorganic.com*) has been in the organic dairy business since 1992. With animal welfare and healthful products in mind, the company refrains from giving antibiotics and hormones to its cows and from applying pesticides to its fields. Beyond running its own organic dairies, the company works with other farmers who want to make the move to organic farming.

Two New England farms that have made the switch to organic include Dean Foods and H. P. Hood. The two dairies started by eliminating the use of artificial growth hormones. It is hoped that this step will alleviate consumer concerns without dramatically increasing the cost of the milk. It's expected that the hormone-free milk will be offered at half the price of organic milk.

Many organic farmers do allow pasture grazing for their dairy. However, the USDA is working to define clearly what constitutes organic milk. Although the USDA understands that organic milk should come from cows that have not been subjected to growth hormones or antibiotics, the use of pasture or confinement farming has not been well defined.

Milk Alternatives

If you are planning to subtract dairy products from your diet, then soy, rice, or almond milk can be good replacements for cow's milk. These substitutes are extracted from natural ingredients that do not produce manure or methane, two environmental detriments for which cows are responsible. Like organic milk from cows, these alternatives also allow you to avoid hormones associated with the dairy industry. In addition, since a primary component of a cow's diet is plants, by drinking milk made from plants, you are bypassing the animals all together.

Soy, rice, and almond milk have a mild sweet taste and can be used instead of dairy milk in cooking. They work well in baked goods such as breads and muffins and in breakfast foods such as waffle and pancake mixes. But this sweetness doesn't make for a good substitute in cream sauces or mashed potatoes. Unsweetened soymilk works best in saltier dishes.

Soy and almond milk contain comparable amounts of protein when compared to dairy, with rice coming in slightly behind. Nutrients not present in dairy alternatives such as calcium, vitamin D, vitamin B_{12}, and riboflavin are usually added. Not all milk products taste the same so it may be worth trying a few different brands. Once relegated strictly to health-food stores, a variety of nondairy milk products can now be found in many chain grocery stores.

Coffee, Tea, and Juice

It seems you can't turn a corner without running into a coffee shop. Even elementary-age kids are well versed in all the coffees available, even swaggering up to the counter to order their own café latte or cappuccino. Tea shops are also cropping up around the country, and many watering holes offer both beverages in a variety of flavors.

Coffee

There are some things to think about as the coffee makes its way to the grinder, the brewer, and then into a cup. The environment suffers at the expense of coffee's popularity. Often, when land is cleared and coffee trees are planted, pesticides and fertilizers are needed to support an increasing demand. Some organizations combat this by encouraging shade-grown coffee, where trees are either planted within the existing forests, or other plants, like fruit trees, are incorporated into the planting. Fewer fertilizers and pesticides are needed with this method. The shade provided by the trees protects the plants from direct sun and rain and helps maintain soil quality. This means fewer weeds, reducing the need for fertilizers and herbicides. The shade also provides homes for birds that feed on insects, eliminating the need for pesticides. When the natural forest is left intact, migratory birds and other native species are impacted less.

"Green" Tea

Tea—real tea—comes from evergreen plants in India, China, Africa, Japan, and Sri Lanka. Its soothing flavor not only calms the soul but is reported to reduce cholesterol, improve immunity, and even fight cavities.

Tea leaves are picked by hand and then go through a series of steps before being steamed in cups of warm water. The leaves are spread out so they can dry, or wither, before being processed through a rolling machine where they are twisted. The rolls are then broken up and the tea is laid out on tile floors in cool damp rooms. Finally, the teas are dried.

Organizations such as the USDA and the Organic Trade Association encourage environmentally friendly methods of growing tea. Incorporating nature into the growing process can help avoid the need for pesticides, herbicides, and synthetic fertilizers. Using compost and natural organic matter can deter weeds. Crop rotation and mulching can encourage spider and earthworm populations that are helpful in destroying harmful insects and in optimizing soil quality.

Juice

Orange juice can be green. Before gulping down your juice on the way out the door, consider where it came from and how it got to the table.

Pesticides have been used to protect crops, but organic companies are leading the charge toward less pesticide use. Organic fruit juice generally relies on family farms to provide the needed fruits and vegetables. One example comes from Organic Valley, a cooperative that includes more than 700 farmers, roughly 10 percent of the organic farming community in the United States. The Roper family, a member of the co-op, has been farming orange groves in Florida for five generations. They turned to organic practices in 1995, and with the switch came the realization that without pesticides and other chemicals the oranges have more fruit solids and better taste.

Wine and Beer

When it comes to the environment, many wines have become or are working toward a certified organic designation. The National Organic Program (NOP) is part of the USDA and has set guidelines for whether items can carry the organic label. The NOP has determined levels of organic conditions and processing for the wines so consumers can choose how organic they want to go when it comes to raising a wineglass.

Sulfites are preservatives with strong antimicrobial powers. Although the complete health effects of sulfites are unknown, some people are sensitive to them. Any wine that claims to be sulfite-free must not have any detectable levels of sulfites. That doesn't mean it doesn't contain sulfites, only that the sulfites present must be below levels that can be detected through standard laboratory equipment and analyses.

For a wine to be labeled "100% organic," the grapes must have been grown in completely organic conditions and sulfites must not have been added. If a wine is made from 95 percent organic ingredients, it can post the "organic" label and cannot have added sulfites. Naturally occurring sulfites must not exceed a concentration of 100 parts per billion. Wines can also boast that they are made with organic ingredients. To do this, they must contain a minimum of 70 percent organic ingredients. To hold the title, the label must include a list of the organic ingredients. Organic wines are available at a variety of liquor stores and wine shops.

Frey Vineyards, one of the oldest and largest family-owned organic vineyards in the United States, is located in Redwood Valley, California. It carries a variety of organic and biodynamic wines. Biodynamic certifications are more strict than organic and account for complete sustainability with the environment and its surroundings. Frey wines are available across the country and are also sold to most states online at *www.freywine.com*. Biodynamic certification is not associated with the USDA organic certification process. Currently, Demeter, an international nonprofit organization, provides certification for biodynamic wines.

The organic beer label means that the barley, hops, and other ingredients are grown and processed without pesticides, fungicides, and fertilizers. Organic beer can be purchased at many stores, especially those catering to whole and organic foods. If you are looking for a local brewery, visit *www .beertown.org* and use the brewery locator.

Many local microbreweries and vintages make organic beers and wines. By buying locally, shoppers are reducing the travel miles associated with getting the drinks from farm to market. For those feeling particularly bold, home brewing and wine making are also options. Organic ingredients can be purchased at local farmers' markets and grocery stores. If you are interested in learning more about home brewing, check out the Seven Bridges Cooperative at *www.breworganic.com*. The Web site not only sells brewing equipment and organic ingredients but also provides a virtual brewing class.

Although a little bit harder to come by, organic spirits are also available. Organic vodka is made domestically and includes brands such as Rain Vodka of Kentucky, Colorado's Vodka 14, Idaho's Liquid Ice, Square One, and Vermont's Sunshine Vodka. Other organic liquor will require a little more postage. It's not made domestically and there are fewer labels. For tequila, there's Viva Mexico Tequila; for whiskey drinkers, there's Da Mhile straight from Scotland. Juniper Green Gin is made in London. There are a couple of organic rum choices as well: Brazil's Matraga Organic White Rum or Paraguay's Papagayo Organic Spiced Rum.

Chapter 8

Transportation

Daily commutes, errands, weekend trips—everyone has somewhere to go and needs some way to get there. Different methods of travel have varying degrees of impact on the environment. This chapter delves into the different energy-efficient and eco-friendly transportation alternatives that are becoming increasingly available and more popular. There are also tips on alternative ways to get around and to green the rides you already own.

Hybrids

A hybrid by definition is a combination of two separate things—in the case of automobiles, an engine and a motor. A hybrid car uses both an electric motor and a gasoline engine. Both the engine and motor have favorable and less savory qualities, but when working together they bring out the best in each other.

Cars that are strictly electric have to be recharged at regular intervals, and without the horses under the hood, they're not always good at high speeds. But electric cars do well at lower speeds and produce few or no emissions—a great benefit. Gasoline-powered cars have the pickup most drivers are accustomed to and they can be conveniently fueled. However, gasoline isn't the cleanest fuel. Producing it isn't good for the environment and neither is burning it. Gasoline combustion engines produce a host of contaminants such as volatile organic compounds, nitrogen oxides, carbon monoxide, and carbon dioxide. The United States consumes approximately 25 percent of all the oil used worldwide on any given day—20.8 million gallons. The Cambridge Energy Research Association estimates that in 2005 American drivers burned about 703 gallons that year, up 41 percent from twenty-five years earlier.

In hybrid vehicles, the electric and gasoline systems work together, utilizing each other's best aspects. The gas engine can charge the batteries. Hybrids capture the energy produced during braking, so they don't have to be plugged in to recharge their batteries. Because gasoline motors are so inefficient at low speeds, the electric motors kick in during stop-and-go traffic, significantly reducing the amount of fuel burned and emissions produced. For skeptics who are concerned that hybrid-car batteries are too expensive to replace and dispose of, rest assured. Ford, Honda, and Toyota claim that the batteries in their hybrids will last the life of the vehicle. When it comes to disposal, the batteries can be recycled just like any other car battery.

Hybrids, when compared to their gasoline-powered counterparts, get about 20 to 35 percent better gas mileage, but the improved fuel efficiency may not make up for the increased sticker price. For example, look at a side-by-side comparison of the 2007 models of Honda's Civic Hybrid sedan and its traditional Civic sedan. According to Honda, its Civic Hybrid gets 49 miles to the gallon in city driving and 51 miles to the gallon on the highway, averaging out to 50 miles to the gallon. The base price is $22,600. The 2007 Civic Hybrid may be eligible for a federal tax credit of as much as $2,100, and individual states may offer additional tax incentives. The hybrid's sibling, the gas-powered Civic sedan, gets an average of 35 miles to the gallon and has a base price of $15,010.

The EPA is arming consumers with more accurate information when it comes to fuel efficiency. It seems consumers weren't getting accurate mileage information, in part because driving patterns have changed since the testing protocols were developed in the early 1970s, so the EPA is devising better ways to determine accurate fuel efficiency that mimic realistic driving conditions. The new values are required to be used in 2008 models.

Taking the maximum federal tax credit for the hybrid into account, the difference in price between the two cars is $5,490. The hybrid will need to refuel less often, which will save its owner money, but the amount of time it will take to close the $5,490 price gap depends on the cost of gas and how often the tank needs to be refilled. A rough estimate: If the price of gas averages $3.25 per gallon (adjusted for inflation), and the cars are each driven 15,000 miles per year, the hybrid will take a little more than thirteen years to earn its higher price tag back. The Web site *www.fueleconomy.gov*, run by the Department of Energy and the EPA, allows browsers to do their own comparisons and view emissions statistics. The price of a hybrid might be higher, but it also includes the cost of developing new technology.

But the fuel efficiency and price of the car aren't the only things to consider when buying a greener car. Hybrids produce much fewer emissions than cars that run strictly on gasoline. According to the fuel economy Web site, the Honda Civic will produce about 5.5 tons per year of greenhouse gases, or carbon dioxide equivalents, while the Honda Civic Hybrid will produce 3.7 tons per year.

A side-by-side comparison can't be made on the first mass-produced and dominant hybrid on the market, the Toyota Prius, because there is no gas-powered version. In 2001, Toyota sold about 5,600 Prius models, and that number continued to rise until 2005, when it hit 108,000. In the first half of 2006, Prius sales accounted for nearly half of all hybrid purchases in the United States. By the end of the year, overall sales figures for the Prius were down slightly from the previous year, partially because Toyota introduced a hybrid model of its popular Camry in May.

QUESTION?

How much of the American auto market is driven by hybrid sales?
According to auto Web site ✐*www.edmunds.com*, sales in the hybrid market increased 2,200 percent between 2000 and 2006, although they still account for only one percent of the entire auto market.

Honda and Toyota were two of the first automakers to get into the hybrid market, but other companies are marketing hybrids. On either end of the pricing scale, Lexus and Saturn each offer cars and midsize SUVs. GM rolled out two truck hybrids, the Chevrolet Silverado and the GMC Sierra, that boast the same power as their nonhybrid counterparts with 10 to 15 percent better fuel efficiency. Auto companies anticipate unveiling even more new hybrid vehicles in the coming years.

Environmentally friendly cars have become such the rage that the 2006 Los Angeles Auto Show included not only hybrids and biodiesel hybrids but cars made from completely recycled material, too.

Biodiesel

Diesel fuel is produced as part of the process of refining regular gasoline. Diesel fuel gets better gas mileage than standard gasoline and produces less carbon dioxide. Unfortunately, diesel releases a lot of particulate matter that gets stuck in people's noses and lungs, even impacting the body's ability to transfer oxygen to the blood. The EPA estimates that 90 million people currently live in areas with elevated levels of particulate matter. The 2007 Heavy-Duty Highway Engine Rule looks to cut pollutants by 90 percent. That includes an annual reduction of 110,000 tons of particulate matter. While petroleum diesel is a fuel-efficient alternative to standard gasoline, it's still not very Earth friendly.

That's where biodiesel comes in. Made from renewable resources like vegetable oil, animal fats, even used cooking oil, biodiesel uses alcohol to separate nonfuel components from fat. Production ranges from full-scale facilities to home kits that can be built and operated in the backyard. By-products of the process include glycerol—the same ingredient that's used in making soap, toothpaste, food, and cosmetics—and seed meal that can be used in livestock feed.

FACT

The exhaust from biodiesel smells good. If the fuel is made from corn or feedstock, the exhaust can smell like popcorn or doughnuts.

Biodiesel can be mixed from ratios of B5 to B100. The numbers stand for how much of the mixture is biodiesel. For example, the B5 mixture is 5 percent biodiesel and 95 percent petroleum-based diesel. Significant benefits can be seen when using as low a mixture as B20. Substituting biodiesel doesn't reduce engine power, but it does burn cleaner, reducing both carbon monoxide and carbon dioxide emissions. Biodiesel does produce more nitrous oxide than traditional fuels, but the emissions can be controlled or offset using catalytic converters.

Other Alternatives

Hybrids may be the rage when it comes to mass-producing fuel-efficient cars, but there are still a lot of other alternatives. Tax incentives exist for people who purchase alternative-fuel cars.

Electric Cars

There's an ongoing debate about whether the electric car is really dead. After being promoted in the late 1990s, cars running strictly on electricity have been steered off the road and onto golf courses and tourist destinations.

Electric cars rely on batteries to provide electricity to an electric motor. The cars produce almost no pollution. However, many are charged from electricity produced from coal, which does produce pollution at the power plant where emissions can be heavily controlled and regulated. Electric cars have a range of only 50 to 100 miles and aren't known for their gusto. While this may limit long trips on busy roads, it can be a perfect fit for short trips on residential roads or places where speed isn't of the essence, but cleaner air is.

Many cities and even amusement parks use electric buses or shuttles for moving people around. Because buses work on set times and routes, the time needed to charge them is incorporated into their routine schedules.

Low-speed electric vehicles (LSVs) are gaining popularity in some planned neighborhoods, college and business campuses, and even tourist locations. In Key West, Florida, electric cars are available for rent alongside scooters. These cars allow families and groups to get around without adding noise and exhaust to the downtown air.

Flex-Fuel Vehicles

Flexible-fuel vehicles, or FFVs, are made to run on a mixture of gasoline and an alternate fuel such as ethanol or methanol. Standard gasoline engines can't operate using flex fuels, but FFVs can burn both—and that's what makes them so flexible. There are a variety of FFVs on the market, including sedans, trucks, and sport utility vehicles.

Ethanol—otherwise known as ethyl alcohol, grain alcohol, or moonshine—leads the way in replacing a portion of the gasoline. It's made by distilling a fermented brew of corn, yeast, sugar, and water. Other plants, such as switchgrass, are being considered as corn substitutes. It takes one bushel of corn to produce two and a half gallons of ethanol. There is concern that the environmental impact from growing plants to produce ethanol (i.e., from the use of fertilizers, pesticides, and transporting plants to processing facilities) outweighs the benefits of burning cleaner fuels.

The most common mixtures using ethanol are E10 and E85, where the number accounts for the percentage of ethanol in the mixture compared to gasoline. Gasoline is still needed because ethanol isn't volatile enough to ignite. E10, comprised of 10 percent ethanol, is used more for an octane enhancer, while E85 is considered a full-fledged alternative fuel. Ethanol burns cleaner, significantly reducing emissions.

Stations selling E85 are in short supply. Make sure when purchasing an FFV that you consider where you will be traveling and how that compares to where E85 stations are located. Also consider how your car will run on gasoline if you are ever in a situation where there is no alternative. Alternative fueling locations can be found at *www.afdc.doe.gov.*

There are a variety of ethanol-fueled cars available; Ford and General Motors are the major manufacturers. Ford offers the Crown Victoria, Mercury Grand Marquis, Lincoln Town Car, and F-150 pickup truck in E85 options. GM offers Suburbans and Yukons, along with a Chevy Police Tahoe. Because fueling stations are limited, FFVs can be better suited for public and private fleets where E85 can be supplied at a set location.

A less-popular fuel alternative is methanol or wood alcohol, which is made primarily from natural gas or methane. M85, the most common methanol additive, must be stored either as a compressed gas or a liquid. Significant amounts of electricity are needed to compress and liquefy the gas. Methanol had its day back in the late 1980s and 1990s when California led the charge in using this alternative fuel, although it was never really embraced by the country.

Alternative Fuel Vehicles

Where FFVs rely on ethanol and methanol as a fuel component, alternative fuel vehicles (AFVs) rely on a combination of gasoline and either compressed natural gas (CNG) or liquefied petroleum gas (LPG). As with other alternatives, fueling station locations are spotty across the United States. Most AFVs on the road were converted from standard gasoline-powered engines. Tax incentives encourage companies to convert their fleets and private individuals to convert their personal cars. Some states even allow drivers of certified AFVs to use high-occupancy lanes.

Motor Free

While cars may be the most popular mode of transportation, there are other alternatives. With environmental and health concerns as primary factors, more and more people are biking and walking to get around. Drivers take 1.1 billion trips every day. Based on information collected by the Bureau of Transportation Statistics, the majority of those trips, about 87 percent, are taken in personal vehicles. If each driver cut out one trip a day—or even a few a week—it would save up to 25 percent of the fossil fuels used for personal transportation.

Walking

Older generations lament their daily treks to school, walking uphill both ways in the snow. Today, fewer children walk to and from school, and when they do, it's rarely uphill both ways.

Walking usually takes more time than driving. As trip distances increased and busy schedules became the norm, most people turned to personal automobiles. Still, if you are looking to do the planet (and your body) a favor, you can walk to the grocery store for milk or to a friend's house for a visit.

When opting to walk instead of drive, there are a few things you can do to make it more comfortable. Quick-drying clothing means no more sweaty shirts, and carrying a water bottle will keep you hydrated. Lightweight daypacks are great for toting items that will be taken along or picked up on errands.

Consider safety when you choose to walk. Choose a route that's well lighted and pedestrian friendly, and take a cell phone. Even though you aren't driving, it's a good idea to take a driver's license or other form of identification.

Biking

Biking is good exercise—one trip on the bike saves one trip in a car. Many cities are not set up for safe biking, but improvements are being made. The city of Davis, California, boasts more bicycles than cars with wide streets and a network of bike paths. Davis's mild climate and gentle terrain encourages bike travel, which the city estimates makes up 20 to 25 percent of all trips.

FACT

There was no increase in the percentage of people riding bikes to work between 1990 and 2000. The U.S. Census in 2000 reported that 488,497 commuters, or 0.4 percent of the working population, rode their bikes to the office. This was the same percentage of biking commuters reported in 1990.

Legislation like the Bicycle Commuter Act, introduced in 2005, encourages employers to support bicycle commuting by offering tax incentives. The costs of bike commuting, like lights and bike repair and maintenance, would also be covered under this bill.

Bikers need to know the laws in their area and to be careful when sharing the road with cars. In many states, bicyclists can receive a ticket and points on their driver's license when breaking the law, such as failing to yield at a stop sign or peddling the wrong way down a one-way street. Another safety note: Bicycling under the influence is never a good idea.

Increasing Occupancy

Not everybody has to have a car. There are a lot of opportunities to share rides with one other person or with a whole bunch.

Mass Transit

Mass transit helps reduce the number of cars on the road. Numbers vary, but the Maryland Department of Transportation estimates that a full bus eliminates sixty cars on the road and that translates to reduced emissions to the air and runoff to streams and creeks. You can find out more about the bus service in your area by contacting the local transit authority or by looking online for schedules and routes.

Taking the bus allows riders time to read, listen to music, even catch up on sleep on the way to work or school. Bus rides can also be substitutes for long car trips. Greyhound and Trailways buses travel across the country, allowing riders to check out vistas along the way. Before making a trip, ask about meal stops and consider bringing along a pillow and snacks to make the trip more enjoyable.

FACT

According to the American Public Transportation Association, public transportation replaces personal cars and trips and reduces emissions. For every mile a passenger rides on public transportation instead of using his or her own vehicle, 95 percent less carbon monoxide, 90 percent fewer volatile organic compounds, and 50 percent less carbon dioxide and nitrogen oxides are produced.

In 1994, the city of Chattanooga, Tennessee, was determined to correct its choking air pollution and traffic congestion and started a free shuttle service utilizing electric buses. Over half a million passengers ride the 3.5-mile route every year. Parking revenues and leasing of commercial space in parking facilities pay the operating costs for the buses. The cost to operate the electric fleet is about the same as a diesel fleet. Tune-ups and oil changes are unnecessary and maintenance costs are lower. Since that time, more cities are utilizing alternatively fueled mass transit systems.

In many larger cities, trains and subways are a popular mode of transportation. Commuters in the suburbs can park near their homes and catch a train or subway all the way into the city.

Sharing Rides

If you live in an area where riding mass transit isn't feasible but still want to take a car or two off the road, consider carpooling. A number of Web sites match destinations and drivers looking to save money and vehicle use. Check out sites like *www.erideshare.com*, *www.carpoolconnect.com*, *www. icarpool.com*, and *www.rideshareonline.com*.

Not only does ridesharing offer companionship and a break from always having to be behind the wheel, many states have carpool lanes. These high-occupancy vehicle lanes allow cars to sidestep traffic for a less congested ride.

Depending on how long the commute is, riders may be spending a lot of time together, so it's best to set a few rules at the get-go:

- Where will drivers and riders meet? Will it be at someone's house or a common location like a parking lot?
- Will anyone be smoking? Some people may not mind being around smoke if it's in someone else's car while others may choose not to expose themselves to smoke at all.
- Is eating in the car okay?
- Are stops acceptable?
- Will there be a set wait time if someone is late?

Some Web sites allow rideshares to select criteria, filtering out certain elements. If everyone in the carpool drives equal miles, then the costs will be even. But if one person is the sole driver, the costs will need to be split. The American Automobile Association calculated in 2006 that every mile a person drives costs $0.52. This accounts for gas, insurance, and mainte-nance. So when one person drives more or is the only driver, it's fair to ask others sharing the ride to pony up.

Sharing Cars

Car sharing has increased as well, and there are a variety of programs available. Businesses like Zipcar (*www.zipcar.com*) and Flexcar (*www.flex car.com*) operate in numerous cities across the United States, including New York, Chicago, and Los Angeles. Cooperatives like City Carshare (*www.city carshare.org*) in San Francisco operate as nonprofits.

With car-sharing programs, members pay a monthly fee or hourly rates and have access to a variety of cars and trucks. You choose whatever vehicle suits your fancy, a truck for that trip to the lumber yard or a sedan for a night out with friends. Most programs offer a fleet of hybrid and low-emission vehicles, too.

Estimates for the number of personal vehicles taken off the road for each shared vehicle range from four to ten depending on how many people share the car. Car sharing encourages people to drive more efficiently because they're either limited to hours offered by their plan or paying for each hour. Costs of the program include gas and insurance (and sometimes perks like XM radio) and members don't have to bother with parking their own car or taking it in for repair work.

Scooters

Scooter sales are skyrocketing as people look for a break from high gas prices. Prices range anywhere from $1,000 to $10,000; fuel ratings for gas-powered scooters run 50 miles to the gallon or better. There's a true distinction in size and power; smaller scooters are slower and not as powerful. New larger scooters compare to motorcycles in price and power while still offering a low mileage alternative. Unlike motorcycles, scooters allow drivers to sit upright without throwing a leg over and straddling the seat.

Electric scooters range from the foldup push scooter to a full sit-down model. Unlike gas-powered scooters, electrics are allowed on mass transit, making a commute to the bus stop a little quicker. At a sticker price of $500 or less, they're much cheaper. Electric scooters require four to eight hours of charging and will take drivers about five miles. They travel at approximately 10 miles per hour and can be weak on hills. Depending on what riders need, scooters can be an excellent way to get across campus or to the train depot. When it comes to the environment, no exhaust means no air pollution. With proper maintenance and operation, battery life spans increase.

Smaller scooters fall under moped regulations, while the bigger scooters are legally considered motorcycles and require a special license endorsement. Drivers should always take care because although driving a scooter is fun, crashing is not. Proper shoes and a helmet should always be worn.

Hybrid scooters are new on the scene and operate using electric batteries and gasoline. Use of a battery reduces gas consumption, and the battery can charge while it's under gas power. The combination allows drivers to switch to electric and access buildings or covered areas where gasoline-powdered scooters aren't allowed. Because they have gas tanks and are larger than electric scooters, transporting them on mass transit isn't an option.

Improving Mileage and Reducing Emissions

For those times you do drive, you can take steps to increase mileage and even reduce emissions. Remember, the more gas a car uses, the more harmful emissions it's putting out.

ALERT!

The National Highway Traffic and Safety Administration calculated that the average mileage only increased 1.6 miles per gallon (mpg), from 23.1 mpg in 1980 to 24.7 mpg in 2004. The improvement could have been larger, but the huge successes of SUVs, relatively inexpensive gas, and more people idling in traffic brought down the mileage calculations (but did not decrease emissions).

Until zero-impact cars or fuels are invented, here's a list of things you can do to improve fuel efficiency:

- Aggressive driving, including rapid acceleration off the line and through traffic, wastes gas and increases emissions. Maintaining a smooth—and legal—pace will get you more miles to the gallon.
- Every car reaches its optimal fuel efficiency at a different speed, but it's generally around 60 miles per hour. According to the U.S. Department of Energy, for every 5 miles an hour you drive over 60 mph, it's like you are spending an extra twenty cents per gallon of gas.
- Carrying around heavy loads reduces a car's gas mileage. It makes more of a difference in smaller cars than larger ones because the weight carried is relative to the weight of the car.
- Idling, burning gas, and getting nowhere wastes gas. If you need another reason to avoid drive-through windows, consider this. Idling

for longer than a minute or two actually uses more gas than starting the car, except in the case of hybrids. If you just have to get that burger and fries, you can park and walk inside instead.

Properly maintained engines operate more efficiently and get better gas mileage. Air filters remove impurities from the air before they can reach the car's engine. Clogged filters can allow some impurities to get through and reduce gas mileage. Finally, properly inflated tires are not only safer to drive on, they improve mileage, too.

Chapter 9

Reduce, Reuse, and Recycle

Reduce, reuse, and recycle: the three Rs. They're the key to living a greener life and reducing the amount of waste you generate. Many people include recycling in their everyday affairs, taking glass, paper, and plastic to the curb or a recycling center. Reusing and reducing mean thinking about purchases and ways to minimize the impact of waste on the environment. How can you incorporate reducing, reusing, and recycling into your life? This chapter illustrates the importance of the three Rs and reveals the fate of waste that isn't reduced, reused, or recycled.

Are You Being a Good Consumer?

Spending has been encouraged for generations as a way to measure success and even to show affection. Being a good consumer is generally defined as being a buyer, pumping money into the economy. Your patronage generates a need for services and manufacturing, which creates jobs and benefits everyone. But there can be a downside to consumerism, too. Many products are not manufactured with environmental responsibility in mind. As production goes up, so does its impact on the environment. This can be especially true if keeping costs low is the greatest factor in producing anything, from sweatshirts to picture frames.

It used to be that people made purchases based on what they needed, not what they wanted. Items were harder to come by and were relatively expensive when compared with personal income. Today, however, shoppers tend to look beyond the necessities to what they want. Relatively low prices make this awfully tempting. But you can make a difference—by choosing to eliminate some purchases, you can cut down on the amount of waste generated. It's been said that the world today is a throwaway society. But as the green movement progresses, this may change.

When shopping, consider not just the quantity but the quality of what you buy. The cheapest product isn't always the best choice. Are you buying from conscientious companies? Were the products made from sustainable practices? Every purchase is a vote, and you as a consumer wield more power than you may think. Being a good consumer means thinking about the impact of what you buy, both economically and environmentally.

A Bit of Spending History

The Great Depression illustrated that society depended on the purchasing power of consumers. When people became unable to buy even the bare essentials, society collapsed. As part of the New Deal, citizens were encouraged to purchase and consume.

Following World War II, the U.S. market economy boomed. Even then, there were groups advocating more conservative financial restraint and concern for natural resources, but these small voices were engulfed by retail and manufacturing associations.

The Bureau of Labor Statistics calculated that purchasing power has tripled since 1901. Why and how did this happen? A change to a consumer goods–oriented economy combined with mass consumption brought about by the onslaught of advertising and the availability of credit.

While the economy has waxed and waned through the years, overall material wealth has exploded—and by all means, spending money isn't bad. You need a place to live, food to eat, and clothes on your back. Even non-essential items like computers, MP3 players, swimming pools, and kitchen gadgets not only make living easier, they bring pleasure to day-to-day life. Although there's no harm in enjoying life, it can be worthwhile to trim the excess in an effort to lead a greener life. Fossil fuels are an important ingredient in the production of just about anything, from forming the plastic to transporting the product to market, so cutting back even a little can have an impact.

Green Manufacturing

Conscientious manufacturers keep the environment in mind when designing products and deciding how to package and transport them. Businesses can also modify their products and methods for more sustainable production.

Sustainable business programs and practices are more prevalent in Europe and countries like Australia and New Zealand, but greener practices are starting to make headway in the United States as well. Sustainable, or green, businesses operate in ways that improve or minimize their damage to the environment. These companies work to integrate economic, environmental, and social considerations into the business network. Changes to business practices may have impacts as far-reaching as those of the Industrial Revolution.

Businesses may modify ingredients to ensure they are generated from sustainable practices, like using recycled steel in the manufacturing of new steel products. However, the energy used to transport, melt, and reprocess steel is not always the "greenest" solution. Environmental stewardship means revamping operations to consume fewer raw materials and produce less waste. One example is incorporating recycled colored plastics into new colored plastics; this reduces the amount of plastics being processed and disposed of and the amount of colorant needed to dye the plastics. In some cases, working toward sustainable business practices can save companies money while helping the planet.

Interface, Inc. and its founder Ray Anderson look to lead the way in setting the example for sustainable manufacturing. The flooring and fabric company incorporates green energy such as solar, wind, and biomass while recycling carpets and other petrochemical products for the manufacturing of new carpet. Anderson's goal for his company is to offset the negative effects Interface may have on the environment by the year 2020.

More and more university business programs are bringing sustainability into the classroom, teaching future business leaders the benefit of sustainable practices. Engineering curriculums have also accommodated more sustainable approaches. It's not enough to develop designs for manufacturing widgets; the process needs to account for minimizing raw ingredients and waste as well as adhering to all environmental laws and regulations.

The government is also involved, passing legislation to promote sustainability. There are federal and state regulations that require entities to purchase items with a certain percentage of recycled content. There are also laws that require a certain percentage of recycled material be incorporated into their product. The federal government initiated this with passage of Section 6002 of the Resource Conservation and Recovery Act, or RCRA, in 1996. This legislation related to procurement, requiring the federal government to purchase products with recycled content such as paper and paper products, lubricating oil, retread tires, building insulation, cement, and concrete. This action fostered markets for companies, encouraging their use of recycled materials. On a state level, Wisconsin, California, and Oregon have recycled packaging laws on their books. These states require that all rigid plastic containers sold contain 25 percent recycled content. This encourages manufacturers across the country to achieve the mandated content to avoid having to produce different packages for different states. Legislation levels the playing field for all types of businesses, making everyone play by the same rules. Successful regulations often set goals or standards, and programs are established to encourage companies to achieve or even go beyond compliance.

Reduce

Until manufacturing has conquered the obstacles to successful sustainability, it's up to consumers to make educated decisions when purchasing products. By reducing what you buy and therefore what is manufactured, you will help conserve natural resources.

Advertising makes products seem fun and necessary, regardless of whether they are. But before you embark on your next shopping trip, consider these tips to help reduce what you bring home:

- **Make a list and check it twice.** Whether you're shopping for groceries, school supplies, makeup, or home repair items, sticking with a list will avoid unnecessary or impulse purchases. Preparing an accurate list may take some time, but consider that time an investment in the future.

- **Avoid the just-in-case purchase.** If you aren't sure you need something, just assume you don't. Being organized at home can help you know what you have in stock.

- **Think about where the new purchase will go and what it will displace.** A new blender may be a wonderful treat, but if the old one still works, is it necessary to buy a new one? If a new one is in order, can the old one be donated or recycled?

- **Evaluate want versus need.** It can be worth the extra thought to consider if a purchase is for something you need or want. If it's just a desire, can it be quelled?

- **Beware of bargains.** Bargains are designed to move merchandise, not necessarily to save you money.

- **Beware of warehouses.** That twenty-five-pound bag of flour may seem like a good deal, but if it ends up getting thrown away, then it's not.

- **Walk to the store.** You'll buy only what you can comfortably carry.

None of these ideas are meant to make you feel so guilty that you forgo the comforts of life; they are meant only to help you put a little extra thought into your purchases.

Reuse

So many items have become or are made to be disposable that it's easy to forget that not everything has to be thrown away. Pack your peanut butter and jelly sandwich in a reusable container instead of that plastic wrap you'll discard immediately. Carry the drink of your choice in a plastic bottle instead of relying on multiple one-use cups throughout the day. Reusing not only avoids the production of new items, it also cuts down on the wasteful products you consume. It eliminates waste that will likely be disposed of in a landfill or incinerated.

There are a lot of other ways to reuse materials by taking small steps that can be incorporated into your life a little at a time. Here are a few for starters:

- **Reuse totes and bags.** When going to the grocery store or the mall, take along your own bags. This pairs reducing with recycling—you'll reduce the need for plastic bags and reuse the canvas or cloth bags you already have.
- **Swap it out.** Many cities today have networks to exchange one person's trash for someone else's treasure. This is also popular on the Internet—members post messages describing what they have available and other members post their interest. Members schedule a pickup, but no money trades hands. One dominant force in the swap arena is Freecycle. See *www.freecycle.org* for more information.
- **Make a charitable donation.** If you know of an organization in your area that's looking for household items, clothes, even cell phones, consider making a donation. Sometimes organizations offer to pick up the items, and donations are tax deductible.
- **Be creative.** There are a variety of ways to reuse items in your home. Printer paper has two sides and can be reused as scrap paper. Packaging materials can be used for arts and crafts projects. Sunday comics make colorful wrapping paper. Junk mail can be cut and used as note paper.

Some cities and counties have collection centers where reusable materials can be collected and stored. Items like paint and motor oil are shelved and available for free to other residents. Most communities have turned to online swapping, using sites such as *www.freecycle.org* and *www.freesharing.org*. These organizations allow items to be reused without having to maintain a storage unit. Members post what they have available, from paint to furniture to baby items, and other members ask for the items. The decision of who gets what is usually made based on the response time.

Recycle

Although it's the last of the three Rs, recycling has become a major industry in itself. Recycled materials have now become a part of the processing stream, taking the place of virgin materials in manufacturing. Manufacturing with recycled materials conserves raw materials and reduces energy consumption.

Energy savings add up. It takes 95 percent less energy to produce an aluminum can from recycled aluminum than from bauxite ore. Making a glass bottle from recycled glass uses 40 percent less energy than making one from sand, soda ash, and limestone. Recycled newsprint uses 40 percent less energy than making newsprint from trees, although paper mills get power from scrap wood while most recycling mills rely on conventional power sources.

Recycling cans and bottles started decades ago as container deposits. Before the onset of aluminum cans, people collected glass bottles, returned them to stores, and traded them in for a refund. The bottles would be washed and reused and put back on store shelves. In the 1960s, aluminum became more prevalent; with drink bottles no longer being returned for money, litter began cluttering the roadside. In an effort to reduce pollution, bottle bills were passed in select states to encourage the return of glass and plastic bottles as well as aluminum cans.

Eleven states have active bottle bills. Bottle bills provide an incentive to return bottles and cans rather than dispose of them.

The Container Recycling Institute estimated that in 2005, more than 50 million single-serve plastic bottles were used in the United States and that, of those, 40 million ended up in landfills, incinerators, or as roadside litter. The organization works to educate policymakers with information just like this in an effort to illustrate the environmental impact from plastic bottles and encourage recycling legislation.

The recycling loop includes three steps: collecting recyclable materials, physically recycling the materials, and purchasing items made from recycled materials. As a first step, many communities have set up curbside recycling programs in which materials like newspaper, plastic, and glass are collected in containers separate from waste. It is simple to recycle in your own home. Keep the recycling containers in a convenient location, possibly in or close to the kitchen. You may not be consistent early on, but eventually recycling will become a habit that you incorporate into everyday tasks.

Some towns and cities that don't offer curbside pickup have recycling facilities where residents can drop off recyclable materials free of charge. Separating the recyclables is one of the most important factors when it comes to making recycling economical. Many facilities require that paper and cardboard be separated, but others allow recyclables to be mixed. In this case, workers and equipment separate the glass, plastic, and metals. Bottles are poured onto a conveyor belt where machines sort materials based on different properties such as density or color, or employees can hand-sort, pulling out green, brown, and clear glass bottles. Magnets are used to pick out any steel. After everything is sorted, it's compacted and baled and ready for sale.

Know your recycled products. A lot of merchandise is made from recycled materials. Sometimes the information is stated on the product. If you're not sure, ask a salesperson if the product you're looking to purchase contains recycled materials. Common products with recycled content include paper towels, carpeting, egg cartons, and motor oil.

The Recycling Market

Today's recycling market is as sophisticated as any other business, with stocks traded and futures projected. Processes continue to evolve to provide better quality and more consistent sources of recycled materials, and manufacturing changes allow the use of recycled materials. As these trends continue, recycled products will become a viable and vital component of manufacturing. It's likely that with improved recycling processes and a consistent demand, recycled materials will become more economical. The three main recycled materials are plastics, metals, and paper, and each has its own markets and uses.

Plastics

Plastic bottles are everywhere from the refrigerator to the laundry room, each with an arrowed triangle and number stamped on the bottom.

The numbers associated with recycled plastic can be confusing, so here's the rundown:

- **No. 1 plastic** is polyethylene terephthalate, also known as PETE or PET. It's used for soda bottles and other food containers. PETE can be recycled into fiberfill for pillows and sleeping bags and other food and drink containers.
- **No. 2 plastic** is high-density polyethylene, or HPDE. Milk jugs are made from nonpigmented HPDE; laundry detergent bottles are manufactured using pigmented, or colored, HDPE. If separated well, these plastics can be recycled into the same color bottles and jugs.
- **No. 3 plastic** is polyvinyl chloride, or PVC. It's used to make PVC pipe and medical tubing. Orange traffic cones and garden hoses are also usually made out of recycled PVC.
- **No. 4 plastic** is low-density polyethylene, commonly known as LDPE. It's used to make squeeze bottles for condiments like jelly and ketchup. LDPE can be recycled into landscape timber and garbage-can liners.
- **No. 5 plastic** is polypropylene, or PP. It's used for storing food like yogurt and can be recycled into a variety of items from medicine bottles to battery cables.

- **No. 6 plastic** is polystyrene. It's used to make meat trays used by grocery stores along with plastic cups and plates. When recycled, polystyrene is turned into foam packing and license-plate frames.
- **No. 7 plastic** incorporates all other plastics not included in the first six categories. It's used to make large water bottles and plastic lumber.

Once sorted at the recycling facility, plastics are baled and sent out for processing. There the plastics are cleaned, possibly sorted by color, and converted to flakes and pellets. Then they're sold to manufacturers for use as feedstock.

Metals

Everything from aluminum soda cans to used engines can be recycled; it's just a matter of getting them sorted and to the right place. Currently, whole engines can be sent overseas to countries such as India and China where labor rates are low and it pays to break down engines manually into separate components like copper wiring and steel casing for recycling. The same shipping companies that bring merchandise from China and India to the United States take back our recyclables. It's a cycle.

Aluminum cans are one of the easiest items to recycle. From the time a can is turned in for recycling, it will take about sixty days for it to be sorted, cleaned, processed, filled, and back on a store shelf.

Aluminum is sorted by composition because it contains alloys such as iron, silicon, and zinc. It's then sent to a processor where it's melted and either cast, rolled, or extruded. A variety of aluminum products can be recycled including pots, pans, and even baseball bats. Once recycled, aluminum sheets and forged aluminum can be used to make drink cans, car parts, and construction materials. Aluminum can also be made into a powder and used for a variety of products like explosives and decorating materials.

Paper

Like other materials, paper is sorted and baled in the recycling facility. Bales of flattened cardboard and bales of mixed paper and newsprint are sold to mills for processing. Processing paper requires a progression of different treatments.

FACT

According the Paper Industry Association Council, 86 percent of Americans have access to curbside or drop-off paper-recycling programs. More than 50 percent of the paper used is recycled. That adds up— every ton of paper that is recycled saves 3.3 cubic yards of space in a landfill.

When paper comes to the mill, it is pulped into fine pieces and water is added to make slurry. The slurry is run through a screen so pieces of glue and other contaminants can be removed. From there, the soupy mixture is cleaned by spinning it around in a cone-shaped cylinder that causes heavy objects like staples to fall out. The pulp mixture is then de-inked, or brightened. During this process, sticky inks are removed. The mixture is then bleached to remove any remaining color. The end result is paper pulp that is ready to be used for processing. The bleaching process has many negative environmental impacts since it usually involves chlorine. In the water, chlorine can react with organics such as dead leaves to form trihalomethanes (THMs), which have been found to be carcinogens. New green alternative bleaching processes are being developed to eliminate these concerns.

E-Waste, the Garbage of the Future

One of the largest concerns of recycling today is managing electronic waste. E-waste includes cell phones, computers, televisions, VCRs, copiers, and fax machines—anything with a battery or a plug. While some of this equipment can be recycled or donated to a charity, much of it is obsolete or broken.

More than 3,000 tons of electronic equipment are discarded every day. Computers contain a multitude of parts, and some include enough lead and mercury to be considered hazardous.

When taken to a landfill for disposal, e-waste takes up valuable room. Worse, it has the potential to release metals such as mercury and lead into the environment, although placing e-waste in a landfill is healthier for the environment than incineration. When incinerated, the plastics release dioxins into the air. The only national legislation regarding e-waste applies to cathode ray tubes (CRT) from computer and television monitors. This legislation states that CRT will not be considered solid waste when processed for recycling. This act saves recyclers from having to abide by strict solid waste regulations and keeps the waste from being considered hazardous. But because it only affects one component of the volume of e-waste generated, it doesn't really help the e-waste recycling industry as a whole.

Some states have enacted legislation to address the growing problem of e-waste and e-waste recycling. California, for example, assesses an advance recovery fee when electronics are purchased. The amount of the fee varies from $6 to $10, depending on the size of the product, and goes into an account that's used to pay collectors and recyclers.

An important concern with the recycling of e-waste is that portions of waste that are generated in the United States are now shipped to China and India for recycling. This has huge transportation costs, financially and environmentally. However, as these countries become overburdened by waste and citizens rally for stronger environmental laws, it is expected that exporting e-waste from the United States will be limited.

A more malicious problem is e-waste that is shipped to developing countries under the guise of technological donations. As much as 75 percent of the "donated" products do not work, according to a speech by the executive director of the United Nations Environment Programme. The defunct products end up in landfills, where dangerous pollutants leak out and contaminate the soil and water.

Other items take up relatively small portions of the waste stream but should be recycled nonetheless:

- Single-use and rechargeable batteries are accepted by some radio electronics and office stores.
- Carpet and padding can be used to make other carpet and padding. Ask when you're buying new carpet if the old one will be recycled.
- Car parts such as batteries, used oil, and oil filters can usually be dropped off at local auto-part stores for no charge.
- Printer, fax, and inkjet cartridges can be recycled. There are many fundraising programs available for collecting and reimbursing for these recyclables. You can also send old cartridges back to the manufacturer; Hewlitt Packard provides a self-addressed pouch with its new cartridges for just that purpose.
- Cell phones can be returned to your service provider to be reused or recycled.
- Some electronics stores will take your old materials for recycling. Call local stores to find out whether they will allow you to drop off your old electronics for recycling. Best Buy boasts it helped its consumers contribute 20 million pounds of e-waste to recycling programs in 2006.
- For locations of other recycling organizations, see *www.earth911 .org* for a directory.

Trash: What a Waste

When items that are no longer needed aren't reused or recycled, chances are they will end up in the trash. Just a generation ago, it was common to toss trash into sinkholes or spent mining pits or quarries, but now garbage is disposed of in highly engineered landfills or burned in incinerators.

The EPA reports that over the past thirty-five years the amount of waste generated for each person has increased from 2.7 to 4.4 pounds per day. This adds up to over 236 million tons of municipal solid waste annually in the United States, double what was thrown away in 1980.

Federal legislation involving solid waste or garbage was initially enacted in 1966 and was born out of a need to protect human health more than the environment. Garbage was put in open dumps where pigs were allowed to scavenge and flies continued to breed. Much of the garbage was then burned with no real controls in place.

The Resource Conservation and Recovery Act was passed in 1976 and amended in 1984. States are now obligated to enforce either federal regulations or more stringent local laws for managing garbage. All solid waste facilities, both landfills and incinerators, are permitted by state or federal agencies and are required to be operated according to the applicable laws.

The Life of a Landfill

Most discarded waste is disposed of in landfills with strict guidelines for construction, operation, and closure when the landfill has reached its allowable height. The groundwater, surface water, and air around the facility must be monitored, even if it is no longer operating.

As waste decomposes in a landfill, it produces a liquid called leachate. The leachate drains through the waste and collects on a liner of plastic sheeting in the bottom of the landfill. Leachate is usually pumped to storage tanks at the landfill facility and is later either pumped or trucked to a wastewater treatment plant. Because little was known about what happened when waste degraded, older landfills were not required to have bottom liners, and the leachate was able to migrate into the ground where it contaminated groundwater or surface water.

Decomposition also produces methane, a dangerous greenhouse gas. Methane can be collected through piping and used to generate electricity; however, there is a limited time in landfill life when this is economically feasible as methane generation peaks and then decreases. Vents are constructed on top of landfills that go into the waste and allow the gas to either disperse into the air or be collected and burned. The size of the landfill and the volume of gas produced dictate how methane is handled.

Bioreactor landfills, a recent advance in solid waste, have piping and pumps that recirculate the leachate from the bottom of the landfill back to the top so it can again drain through the waste. This practice provides liquid that microorganisms need to degrade the waste, speeding up the process of decay and allowing the waste to settle or become more compact in less time. Because landfill height is one of the limiting factors for operation, compacting the waste allows for more garbage to be buried within the landfill.

The number of landfills has decreased over time, but their size has increased. Finding a place to construct a landfill is difficult because it doesn't make a pleasant neighbor. So rather than try to locate new landfills, municipalities are choosing to expand the landfills they already have. Instead of operating a landfill, many municipalities would rather send their waste to other counties or even to other states.

The Burning Issue of Incinerators

About 14 percent of collected solid waste goes to incinerators where it's burned at very high temperatures, which destroys bacteria and certain chemicals. However, incineration also produces air contaminants like nitrogen oxides, sulfur dioxides, mercury compounds, dioxins, and carbon dioxide. The composition of the waste incinerated affects the types and quantities of compounds emitted. Pollution equipment is required at all incinerators, but strict adherence to operations must be maintained for the incinerator and pollution equipment to work properly.

Backyard burning isn't such a great idea either. Depending on where you live, you may be able to burn waste in your own backyard in a barrel or a pit. Unless the waste is burned in an incinerator, the high temperatures needed to safely break down dangerous chemicals won't be reached, which could cause the release of chemicals like dioxin. For a safer alternative, try composting.

Ash is produced as part of the incineration process. Bottom ash, the remnants of the burned material, remains in the incinerator. Fly ash is lighter particulate matter that floats up the stack of the incinerator. Stacks are required to capture the fly ash before it escapes. Both types of ash are usually disposed of in landfills; this is a concern for workers and nearby residents because it can be difficult to manage the light material.

Contamination—namely, from metals and organics such as dioxins and furans—is also a concern because it can trickle from the ash into the leachate and potentially into the groundwater and surface water.

Waste-to-energy plants generate power from garbage that is incinerated and use the heat to generate steam and produce electricity. Construction of these plants is very expensive, but as the cost of energy continues to rise and the space for new landfills becomes harder to find, these facilities may become a more popular disposal approach.

Chapter 10

Earth-Friendly Clothes and Fashion

One of the largest manufacturing industries around, textiles is looking greener these days. There are more and more options available for choosing sustainable clothing that's environmentally responsible. Where Earth-friendly clothing was once mild in color and design, today's designs incorporate bright bold colors with professional and trendy styles that blend in with the other garments strutting down the catwalk. This chapter introduces readers to what makes clothing and accessories green—and what keeps them from being environmentally friendly, too.

What Goes into Clothes

Fashion magazines promote new styles for every season. Everybody needs clothes, but before you purchase that must-have sweater or perfect-fit pair of jeans, consider what goes into the manufacturing of those garments. Fashion can be a dirty business, but choosing clothes that are made with environmentally friendly materials ensures it doesn't have to be that way.

Clothing is a process that starts with either renewable or nonrenewable feedstock, which is treated and woven, dyed, and sewn to produce a piece of clothing. The clothing may have started out as a fossil fuel, or a cotton plant, with many workers and manufacturing and transportation processes along the way.

Most synthetic threads like polyester are made from petroleum, a nonrenewable resource that even during the refining process produces contaminants. Synthetic fabrics and clothing are durable and relatively nondestructible, which means they don't easily degrade. And when it comes to athletic clothing and sportswear, synthetic and synthetic blends that wick away moisture are hard to beat. Some companies such as Patagonia accept used synthetic clothing for reuse as feedstock in their new synthetic blend fabrics.

When choosing clothing, check the labels and consider limiting clothes that require dry cleaning. Also, as a substitute to dry cleaning, some fabrics can be hand-washed instead—but not all. Don't forget, the dry-cleaning process is hard on the fabric as well as on the environment.

Once clothes are in your closet, how you wash and care for them also impacts the environment. This is particularly true of dry cleaning. The traditional dry-cleaning process uses solvents with a little water to remove soil from dirty clothes. The solvent most often used by dry cleaners is perchloroethylene, known in the industry as perc. When spilled on the ground, perc leaches into groundwater. Because it is denser than water, it sinks in the aquifer, making remediation costly and complicated. Perc is also released into the air during the cleaning process and is a hazardous air pollutant at certain levels. There are many green alternatives to dry cleaning today, including using carbon dioxide, the same gas that makes soda fizzy, under high pressure to clean clothes. One alternative in particular is GreenEarth (GE) Cleaning. Because the cleaning system relies on biodegradable silicone-based solvents, harmful chemicals don't linger on your clothes or in the environment. GE facilities can be found at *www.greenearth cleaning.com.*

The Materials

When looking for clothing that reduces wear and tear on the earth, consider natural and organic cotton, hemp, wool, and even bamboo. Many people wonder why wearing organic clothing should be a concern since no one is going to ingest it. However, what people wear does impact the environment.

The Basics of Cotton

Cotton has been used to make clothing for thousands of years. It was first spun mechanically in England in 1730, and later that century Eli Whitney patented his cotton gin in the United States. Rumor has it that Whitney's was not the original cotton gin, but it was undoubtedly the most successful. As a result of the Industrial Revolution and the cotton gin, the cotton industry took off and is now one of the leading cash crops in the United States.

The Conventional Way

As with many other crops grown using conventional methods, pesticides are used to kill insects before they can cause damage. Large-scale agribusinesses now run the operations that depend on pesticides and fertilizers and include separating out the cotton fiber from the seed. The cotton fiber is used for clothing while the seeds take another route. Cottonseed oil is used in vegetable oil, salad dressings, and many processed foods like potato chips and snack crackers. Hulls are also used in cattle feed as high-protein fiber. The use of pesticides is fraught with environmental impact. Stormwater runoff from rain flowing across cotton fields brings with it the residue and contamination left over from the chemicals.

To avoid the problems with pesticides, researchers have genetically modified cotton plants to be pest-resistant. The most common transgenic cotton plant carries the *Bacillus thuringiensis* (Bt) gene. This gene kills caterpillars that feed on the cotton plant. The Bt gene kills the caterpillars, preventing any damage. Transgenic cotton has been used all over the world by leading exporters such as China and India to increase prosperity by increasing production. There are skeptics, however, who do not believe the increased production will last and that nature will find a way around the resistant cotton, eventually making stronger pesticides necessary.

FACT

It's estimated that cotton uses 53 million pounds of chemicals as pesticides, herbicides, and defoliants every year. More than 90 percent of the cotton grown today relies on chemicals, while 20 percent is grown from genetically modified seeds. Organic cotton represents only about 1 percent of the cotton grown worldwide.

The Organic Way

It is more expensive to grow cotton organically, but farmers are paid sufficiently to make up the difference. Organic cotton sells well, with extra money going back to the farmer. Large companies like Patagonia, Nike, and Timberland are supporting the growing trend of organic cotton by promoting and selling lines of products made with organic cotton.

Organic cotton requires farmers to forgo using genetically modified seeds, chemical pesticides, and fertilizers. By going organic, the farmers no longer have to pay for expensive pesticides and receive a higher dollar value for their crop, sometimes bringing in twice as much. Organic cotton is a win-win situation for both the environment and the farmer.

Clothing made from organic cotton often uses ladybugs and other natural enemies to combat pests. Pests are also handpicked from the plants. While this process takes much more time than applying chemicals, the farmers make up for it with the high prices they receive for their crops. Another important factor is that by eliminating pesticides from crops, workers are no longer exposed to dangerous chemicals. Studies have shown that the houses of farmworkers routinely contain pesticides brought home from the field, exposing the family members who live there.

QUESTION?

How large is the organic cotton market?

Organic cotton accounts for less than a tenth of a percent of all cotton harvested throughout the world, according to the USDA. However, demand for organic cotton is growing, and retailers are responding by incorporating more organic cotton into their clothing lines. For example, Nike hopes organic cotton will comprise at least 5 percent of every cotton-containing product by 2010. In 2006, Levi Strauss launched Levi's eco, a line that boasted its use of 100 percent organic cotton in its jeans.

The History and Uses of Hemp

Hemp, the nondrug form of cannabis, suffers from its association with marijuana. However, it is environmentally friendly. It does not require pesticides, and because the plants grow so densely, herbicides are not required either.

Over the centuries, hemp was commonly used to make sails on ships, leading experts to believe that the word *canvas* actually originated from the word *cannabis*, or *kannabis* as it was spelled then. From masts to sails, hemp was used to make clothing, shoes, and even the paper for maps. For decades it was a favorite of industry, and farmers were encouraged to grow the crop because it had so many uses. Recreational use of hemp didn't become popular until the early twentieth century.

The U.S. government didn't initially back the illegality of hemp and, in 1942, distributed 400,000 pounds of seed for farmers, including 4-H groups, to grow hemp in support of the war effort.

Even with legislation against its use, hemp never went away. Scientists who continued to study it found it to be lower in saturated fats than other vegetables oils. Still, growing the plant, even for industrial purposes, in the United States is unlawful. Hemp must be imported, usually from China, Romania, Hungary, and Poland, which is why it carries a higher price tag. It also doesn't benefit from the subsidies that other domestic textiles receive.

The hemp used in clothing is chemically different from the cannabis people smoke. The amount of the chemical responsible for making people high, THC, is much lower in industrial hemp. Hemp is available in a variety of clothing from T-shirts to sport jackets. It's even available for wedding apparel.

For more information on the history of hemp, check out *The Emperor Wears No Clothes* by Jack Herer. Published in 2000, this book gives readers a rundown on the politics of why hemp was outlawed and the powers that keep it out of out of reach. Experts agree Herer took hemp out of the closet and back on the table as a viable textile.

Wearing Wool

Wool is a renewable and sustainable fabric, but problems abound with conventionally grown wool. As with cows, when sheep are raised in small, overgrazed pastures, they become vulnerable to parasites. To combat the pests, the sheep are dipped, literally, in pesticides. These dipping vats are walk-through troughs placed in pastures. The pesticides are toxic to fish and amphibians and are suspected endocrine disruptors.

When chemicals escape the vats, they contaminate groundwater and surface water and are capable of bioaccumulating in wildlife. Workers responsible for dipping sheep have become sick and chemicals have been linked to nerve damage.

Alpacas are camel-like animals that are smaller than llamas. These gentle animals graze in herds in the Andes. The Suri alpaca grows long silky dreadlocks, a favorite of spinners. Alpaca wool contains no lanolin and is truly hypoallergenic. Alpacas come in over twenty different colors but are bred white for ease in dyeing.

Wool's chemical dependency continues with manufacturing. Wool is often washed and treated with formaldehydes and dioxins. Newer technologies even incorporate chlorine oxidation and silver backwashing to prevent shrinking.

Organically raised sheep live in pastures without pesticides and are not dipped. Healthy sheep are able to fend off parasites, making dipping unnecessary. Organic wool yarn is not chemically treated but washed using biodegradable soap. While some people may be allergic to lanolin, oil that naturally occurs in wool, wool in itself is nonallergenic. It's also naturally fire retardant, making it safer than treated clothing. Natural wool clothing is breathable but makes for a good insulator. It's durable and wrinkle resistant and can be dyed and spun into a variety of fabrics.

A Case for Bamboo

Bamboo is a quick-growing grass. Two of the more redeeming qualities include that it removes dangerous carbon dioxide from the air as part of photosynthesis and that it can be harvested relatively quickly, meaning smaller amounts of land are needed to grow it. Bamboo doesn't require fertilizers or pesticides and is hypoallergenic. And to date, there hasn't been any genetically modified bamboo used in the apparel process. The fiber produced from bamboo is moisture wicking and antimicrobial. Clothing made from bamboo is colorfast and can be washed as if it were cotton clothing.

The Skinny on Silk

Silk is a protein fiber spun by moth larvae. It can be considered a renewable resource and is biodegradable; however, traditional harvesting and processing methods don't comply with everyone's idea of planet friendly. The majority of silk seen in the United States comes from China, Korea, Japan, and India. The silk production process uses *Bombyx mori* caterpillars or larvae, which attach themselves to the leaves of mulberry trees and begin spinning. The cocoon is finished in about two days and contains one continuous silk strand that can measure thousands of feet long. If left alone, the larvae would continue through the pupa stage and then emerge from the cocoon as a moth, but it would break the silk strand in the process. To maintain the continuous thread, cocoons are usually steamed, boiled, or baked to kill the larvae inside. The cocoons are then opened and the silk unfurled. The thread is washed or degummed using alkaline washes. It takes an estimated 25,000 cocoons to produce one pound of silk thread. This harvesting process is highly labor intensive and commonly relies on low-wage workers.

There are a limited number of companies that offer silk while working to improve one or more aspects of the harvesting process. Both Peace Silk and Ahimsa Peace Silk allow the larvae to continue to grow inside the cocoons, requiring the threads broken by the moth's emergence to be spun back together. Christoph Fritzsch, a German company, offers organic silk and claims to use only silk from harvesters that employ good working conditions. The company also uses wind and other alternative power in its processing facility.

Turning Fiber into Fabric

Fibers from both natural and human-made materials are made into fabric at mills. Cooperatives like the Organic Exchange work with brands, retailers, and farmers to match organic fibers with mills and brands. To be certified organic, a mill must be cleaned of residues. If a farmer's crop is small, a mill won't stop work to clean the equipment, and independent farmers have difficulty finding a mill. By working with cooperatives, farmers are able to combine their volume, making it more profitable for the mills to process their cotton. The farmers then have a better chance of selling their crops. Also, more and more brands are incorporating organic fiber lines and working with organic farmers to purchase their feedstock.

Manufacturing

Clothing manufacturers can help the environment by implementing sustainable designs and operations. By working toward using renewable energy and increasing energy efficiency, achieving improved health and safety for employees and the public, and addressing waste disposal and reclamation within the manufacturing process, companies can positively impact their neighborhoods and surrounding communities.

The Institute for Market Transformation to Sustainability developed the Unified Sustainable Textile Standard specific to the garment industry for monitoring both social and environmental impacts through the life cycle of a garment. One area specifically addressed encourages manufacturers to reduce emissions. McDonough Braungart Design Chemistry and GreenBlue, for example, are working together to introduce sustainable design, manufacturing, and business methods. Their goals include encouraging businesses to address the cradle-to-grave aspects of the garment industry.

Clothes with a Message

Because clothes send a message, no one has to leave anything to interpretation. You can wear a slogan and support an eco-friendly lifestyle or let the world know how you feel about politics or the environment. Chances are shirts printed with an environmental message will come from organically grown cotton and will not have been made in a sweatshop. There are plenty of stores to check out online.

If you are the creative type, you can purchase your own T-shirts wholesale and have your own message printed. There are T-shirt manufacturers that have lines of organic T-shirts and will print slogans with little or no minimum order. Here's your chance to become an ecoentrepreneur or just give friends and family a gift with a conscience.

Reusing and Recycling

Donating clothes to a charity or selling them to a consignment shop ensures that your materials are not unnecessarily wasted in a landfill. More and more manufacturers are turning to reusable or recycled materials for their clothing.

Second-Chance Clothes

There's no better to way to save resources than to buy clothes someone else isn't wearing anymore. It saves natural resources both in creating the material and processing it. The work has been done and the energy spent. Consignment shops all over the country sell gently used clothing and accessories and can come in particularly handy when you need an outfit for a particular occasion that you may only wear once or twice.

It goes both ways, too. When you cull old clothes from your closet, you can donate them to charity or give them away through a swap group like Freecycle. If you wear a difficult-to-find size that is either shorter or taller than average, your swapped clothes can go to someone else who may find it hard to shop. There are few things more exciting than receiving a bag of clothes that are just the right size. Giving those clothes away is pretty rewarding, too. Goodwill Industries and the Salvation Army accept clothing donations for either resale or to give to those in need. If you want to bring in some cold hard cash for your clothes, sell them to a consignment shop or through the newspaper. This works well for specific sizes or styles and expensive items like wedding dresses and formal gowns. Even Halloween costumes can make their way to another closet through classified ads.

Recycled Fabrics

Rather than recycling the whole garment, many items can be recycled for parts. An old pair of jeans can be sacrificed for parts to save another pair, a patch here, a pocket there. Denim and other fabrics can also be kept for other homemade projects like purses, pillows, and blankets. Old T-shirts from concerts or sport teams can be patched together to make a memorable quilt. Before tossing that shrunken T-shirt or those threadbare jeans, consider whether they could be reincarnated in a different form.

A number of designers are incorporating used clothing into their designs. Material is used as-is and isn't reprocessed. It may be cut and stitched and incorporated into a design with other recycled fabrics. This industry is still in its infancy, with limited retail lines.

Manufacturers are also incorporating recycling activities, using clothing that is no longer used, postconsumer waste, and material waste from processing, also known as postindustrial waste. Postconsumer waste is material that would more than likely end up in a landfill or at the incinerator. Removing it from the waste stream saves landfill space, air quality, and other degradation caused by common disposal practices. Recycling postindustrial waste is beneficial to the economy and the environment.

Using recycled material saves energy because incorporating recycled material into feedstock reduces the energy needed for manufacturing. The energy needed to obtain and transport raw materials is reduced as well. In addition, fewer natural resources are needed when recycled material is incorporated.

If you're looking to purchase recycled clothing, see what companies like Florida-based Clothes Made From Scrap, Inc. (⊘*www.clothesmade fromscrap.com*) have to offer. The company uses recycled plastic bottles and 100 percent cotton to create a 50/50 cotton/poly blend. The fabric is used to make T-shirts, caps, and visors. Clothing and hats can be purchased plain or screened with predesigned eco-friendly messages.

Clothes brought into a mill for recycling are sorted into material types with different end uses. Pants and skirts can be shredded and used for fillers in car insulation and furniture padding. Wool clothing can be reclaimed to make yarn or fabric. Cotton and silk can be recycled to make cloth rags and even paper. Denim can be recycled into insulation for buildings to improve energy efficiency.

Shoes and Accessories

Now that basic clothing has been covered, it's time to look at rounding out the perfect eco-friendly ensemble. There are innovative ways to help the environment and look stylish at the same time.

What's on Your Feet?

Just as you have choices in buying clothing, you face similar decisions when it comes to purchasing shoes. Shoe manufacturing is heavily dependent on dyes, glues, chemically tanned leather, and rubber. The industry as a whole has been slow to incorporate more sustainable practices and improve environmental welfare.

In 1993, Nike developed the Re-Use a Shoe program, which collects used athletic shoes and defective products. The shoes are accepted all over the world (locations are posted on their Web site at *www.nike.com*) and processed at recycling centers in China, Indonesia, and Vietnam. Shoes are separated into components and ground up to make what's called Nike Grind. The upper fabric is used for padding underneath hardwood basketball courts. The midsole foam is turned into tennis courts and playground surfaces. The outside sole is used to make running tracks and weight-room flooring. However, the transportation costs can slightly reduce the "green" factor for these efforts.

FACT

Throughout the ages, left and right shoes were identical. In 1928, a Philadelphia shoemaker realized a duplicating lathe could be used to make soles that were mirror images of each other. But Phil Gilbert's Shoe Parlor in Vicksburg, Mississippi, was the first to sell left and right shoes as a pair in a box.

Hemp is used to make a variety of shoes from sandals and clogs to dress shoes and sneakers. It's durable and it breathes, giving feet fresh air. Recycled rubber is also used to make flip-flops and soles for sneakers.

While cotton and other natural fibers can be grown organically, rubber can be obtained from sustainable practices. To produce rubber, tree sap is turned into solid latex that's strong and water resistant. Under routine conditions, the process includes a step known as vulcanization, which was patented by Charles Goodyear in 1844. Processing rubber is extensive and includes compounding and mixing, milling and calendering, extruding, coating, cooling and cutting, building, vulcanizing, and grinding. Each step in the process generates emissions, wastewater, and solid waste material. Heavy metals are a primary chemical component and waste product of making rubber. Sustainable practices take into account healthy harvesting of the trees and proper handling of wastes. As efficient processing methods expand, using recycled or reprocessed rubber is also becoming more common.

Leather is largely garnered from factory farming of cows and pigs. The process used to transform the animals' skin into the leather seen in the stores depends largely on a mix of harmful chemicals. After cows are slaughtered, salt is used to cure and preserve the skin. This is usually done at the meat-processing facility, and then the cured skin is shipped out for tanning. Any remaining flesh and hair are removed using a lime solution. The liming chemicals are then removed by neutralizing them with an acidic rinse. The process use to tan the leather depends on the leather's end use. Softer leather for purses and shoes uses a mineral or chrome tanning wash. Stiffer leather for luggage or furniture uses a vegetable tanning process. Shoppers looking to purchase leather products can consider fair trade organizations that rely on free-range cattle and good working conditions for those processing the hides. The life of shoes can be extended by having them repaired rather than replaced. Not only does this support a local business, it saves natural resources.

The Final Touch

The purse, the wallet, the belt, the jewelry—all of these can help make your outfit. As with other leather items, take advantage of leather's longevity. Many purses incorporate organic and recycled materials. Take into consideration the fact that big-name manufacturers generally control much of the market without encouraging sustainable practices.

While diamonds may be a girl's best friend, they are no friend to the environment that is damaged in the process. In order to mine diamonds, the land surface is scraped clean and a pit is dug to access the diamond deposits. Waste is generated as trees and cover materials are hoisted aside, dirt and rocks are excavated, and mine tailings are generated. Depending on the environmental laws in the area, the mine *may* be reclaimed after the diamonds are gone, but it is impossible to restore it to natural conditions.

Consider purchasing eco-friendly jewelry. Organizations like Global Exchange carry jewelry made of silver and other bright gemstones made by small organizations in an effort to promote sustainability. Another group, greenKarat, promotes the use of recycled gold.

Chapter 11

Personal Care

The move to more natural personal-care products has grown in leaps and bounds recently, giving conscientious consumers more products to choose from. From natural to organic, there is a lot to consider when selecting products for a daily regimen. In addition, don't forget trying to avoid excess or inefficient product packaging. It is possible to choose products that aren't harmful to the environment and still bring out your natural beauty. This chapter gives information on skin- and hair-care products along with makeup and other beauty regimens, and it identifies what the green issues are and how to choose them.

Chemical Concerns

If you are interested in more environmentally friendly lotions, shampoos, makeup, and soap, you may want to look at the common chemicals in the products you use everyday. The Environmental Working Group (EWG) is a watchdog agency comprised of scientists, engineers, and policy experts who sift through scientific data in search of potential risks to people and the environment. The group works in a variety of different consumer- and environmental-protection areas, including the beauty industry. The EWG maintains *Skin Deep*, a report on the chemical ingredients of thousands of personal-care products.

ALERT!

The scientific community is considering potential problems with personal care products that wash down the drain and potentially settle in rivers and streams. Wastewater treatment plants and septic systems are not designed to handle many of the chemicals used in products today. As a result, many chemicals may escape into nature.

Skin Deep

The *Skin Deep* report can be found online at *www.ewg.org/reports/skindeep2*. Here is a list of ten things you can do when it comes to picking out safer personal-care alternatives:

1. Read the fine print on the labels.
2. When it comes to soap, go mild. Strong soaps can remove natural moisturizers.
3. Cut back on the fragrance to avoid allergic reactions.
4. Don't go for dark hair dyes. They may contain coal tar ingredients.
5. Avoid baby powder. It's not healthy for babies to breathe it.
6. Avoid giving children under six fluoridated toothpaste.
7. Lay off the nail polish to avoid exposure to toluene and acetone. If polish is used, make sure the area's well ventilated.

8. Lighten up with the cologne. Many fragrances contain phthalates (endocrine disruptors) and parabens (chemicals linked to breast cancer).
9. Try to cut back on the number of products used.
10. And of course, use the lists on Skin Deep to find personal-care products with minimal amounts of chemicals.

Animal Testing

When looking for cruelty-free cosmetics, look for the leaping bunny logo. The leaping-bunny symbol is awarded by the Coalition for Consumer Information on Cosmetics, an organization made up of eight national animal rights groups. The coalition works with companies to promote nonanimal testing and is making progress in the United States and overseas. The shopping guide is available online at *www.leapingbunny.org/shopping_guide .htm*. You can either print it from the Web site or request a pocket guide to take with you when looking for cruelty-free products.

Although efforts have been made to reduce and eliminate animal testing, it is still the primary method of providing data on most cosmetics. Its continued use is partly based on the familiarity with the protocols and data analysis. Testing is performed on both finished products and individual ingredients.

Tests for cosmetics are usually performed on rabbits, rats, mice, guinea pigs, and dogs. Advances in technology have allowed companies to use computer models, in-vitro testing, and other methods to test their products, but animal testing continues to be a contentious topic.

Packaging

The way a product is packaged matters to the environment. Packaging is designed not only to protect products but to be eye-catching and attractive too. Efficient packaging promotes a healthy environment by ensuring everything remains safe during shipping and nothing is wasted. You can look for products that use recycled content in their packaging, and you can also recycle some packaging material. Conscientious companies are making efforts to cut down on the nonrecyclable materials they use and reduce the toxicity of the nonrecyclable materials they cannot avoid.

If you would like one of your favorite products to come with less packaging or recycled packaging, call the manufacturer. Generally, products have a toll-free customer service telephone number printed on the outside of the package, and that is what the number is for. If one of the company's competitors offers less packaging, make sure to mention that, too.

Skin Care

Natural and organic labels are everywhere, from face cleansers to face masks and everything in between. But the labels may not tell the whole story. Products that are used in natural skin care usually include botanical extracts and essential oils, but that doesn't mean all the ingredients are natural. The USDA certifies organic food but not personal-care items. That gives companies some leeway when it comes to labeling, making it difficult for consumers to know whether a product is natural or organic. Following is a list of some organic skin-care lines that contain organic ingredients:

- **Dr. Hauschka Skin Care** (*www.drhauschka.com*) offers the customer a holistic approach to skin care that relies on plant extracts to bring out a person's essential beauty. If you don't know what products are best for your skin type, you can answer a series of questions on the Web site and be directed to a line of skin-care products, or if you need personal service an aesthetician will answer any questions.
- **Juice Beauty** (*www.juicebeauty.com*) carries a line of cleansers, toners, exfoliants, and moisturizers made from freshly squeezed organic juices. The company uses USDA-certified organic growers for the juice, honey, and aloe vera in their skin care products. Because the USDA doesn't certify personal-care products, the Juice Beauty designs their own organic labels indicating their discrete purchasing practices.

- **Kiss My Face** (*www.kissmyface.com*) was started in an old New York farmhouse by a vegetarian duo back in the 1980s. The company now carries a line of 150 all-natural products that have eliminated the use of unnecessary chemicals. The pair believes personal care need not be sacrificed when it comes to protecting the environment.
- **Nature's Gate** (*www.natures-gate.com*) provides personal-care products that are environmentally friendly, developed using natural botanicals. Not only that, the company sells all its products in recycled packaging.
- **Noah's Naturals** (*www.noahsnaturals.com*) is a product line sold exclusively by Wal-Mart. Their products are made from organic herbs, essential oils, plant oils, and emollients.

Just because skin-care products are made with organic ingredients doesn't mean they'll be compatible with your skin. Even though a product is organic or natural doesn't mean it won't cause an allergic reaction.

Common products that are labeled as hypoallergenic may still cause allergic reactions. Labels such as hypoallergenic and allergy tested are up to the manufacturer's discretion and don't have to meet specific regulatory criteria. It's up to consumers to determine what's really hypoallergenic.

Finding the perfect match may not come the first time around. If you have a particular concern, such as reddish or very sensitive skin, you can call the company to consult on the best choices to make. Sometimes this information is available on the Web sites, providing recommendations based on skin type. Beyond eliminating the production and use of chemicals, purchasing organic products supports organic farming, which is better for the environment.

Hair Care

Many companies that produce organic skin-care products also carry hair-care products. A benefit of organic shampoos and hair care products is the absence of synthetic surfactants. These chemicals can persist through wastewater treatment plants and septic systems to end up in ground and surface water.

Here are a few companies that sell their own lines of environmentally friendly hair care products:

- **Terressentials** (*www.terressentials.com*) was selected as a top product in 2004 by *The Green Guide*. Their products are 100 percent natural and chemical-free. There's no detergent or synthetic fragrances in these shampoos.
- **J. P. Durga** (*www.jpdurga.com*) offers all-natural, chemical- and petroleum-free hair-care products. Their message is "healing humanity one body at a time." The company is careful to maintain proper temperatures while they're making their products to ensure that natural ingredients are able to maintain their benefits.
- **Aubrey Organics** (*www.aubrey-organics.com*) was started more than forty years ago when Aubrey Hampton developed his natural hair-care product line. After finding success in Manhattan salons, Aubrey expanded the line. Aubrey Organics also includes hair spray and other styling products to help perfect a manageable do.
- **California Baby** (*www.californiababy.com*) offers a selection of natural and organic hair-care and other products for babies, kids, and adults with sensitive skin. The business was started by Jessica Iclisoy, who was concerned about putting chemicals on her baby boy's noggin.

Prices for organic and all-natural hair-care products may be a little higher than for traditional products, but they are comparable to products sold in hair salons. Look for organic and natural hair-care products at the grocery store or the local whole-food grocer.

Makeup

Like hair care and other organic products, makeup may cost a little more than at a conventional store, but costs are comparable to other specialty lines. Some natural or organic makeup might be found in health-food stores or whole-food grocers, but a larger variety is available online. Many of the natural makeup lines rely on powder foundations as opposed to liquid to avoid ingredients that are more likely to cause irritation. Here's a sampling of Web sites that carry organic and natural makeup that are cruelty free: ·

- **Burt's Bees** (*www.burtsbees.com*) is a name that's common at retail counters with lip balm and hand crèmes, but the company also produces makeup. The company was started by two friends looking for a good use for the besswax one of the friends (Burt). The company now makes a variety of Earth-friendly products. Better yet, the packaging is Earth friendly as well.
- **The Alchemist's Apprentice** (*www.alchemistsapprentice.com*) carries makeup that was developed especially for sensitive skin. It contains no fillers or oils so it doesn't clog pores, and it's anti-inflammatory too.
- **Canary Cosmetics** (*www.canarycosmetics.com*) carries a variety of makeup designed for sensitive skin. Ingredients include mica, zinc oxide, titanium dioxide, and refined iron oxides. As with other skin-sensitive recipes, Canary products don't include any oils, fragrances, or preservatives.
- **The Organic Make-Up Company** (*www.organicmakeup.ca*) is a Canadian company whose makeup is not only organic but vegan too. There are no genetically modified ingredients, synthetic chemicals, or animal by-products, not even beeswax. Organic Make-Up's concern for the planet extends from the products they sell to the packaging used.

There are also shops like Bath & Body Works and Sephora that carry lines of organic and natural makeup. Check on your favorite brand to see if it carries a line of organic and natural products.

Many consumers are used to makeup with a sun-protection factor, or SPF, rating. But obtaining an SPF factor can be expensive, and some of the smaller makeup companies have yet to do it. If this is of concern to you, wear sun block underneath your makeup. Also, the oxides used in many powder formulas do assist in blocking out the sun's rays.

Aerosols

Much of the concern about using aerosols in products like deodorants and hairsprays comes from the use of chlorofluorocarbons, or CFCs. First developed in the late 1920s, CFCs became widely used as coolants for refrigerators and air conditioners, cleaning agents for electronics, and propellants for aerosols. CFCs had many advantages: they had low toxicity levels, they were nonflammable, and they did not react with other chemicals or decay. Their longevity would prove to be damaging to the environment, however. In the 1970s, scientists discovered that CFCs were eating away at the ozone layer, damaging its ability to protect Earth from the sun's harmful rays. CFCs also trap heat in the atmosphere and contribute to global warming. Because of these concerns, the EPA banned the use of CFCs in aerosols in 1978.

CFCs are being phased out under the Montreal Protocol, administered by the United Nations Environment Programme (UNEP). As part of the agreement, industrialized nations were required to stop using CFCs by January 1, 1996, with developing nations following suit by the year 2010. Today, 191 nations abide by the Montreal Protocol. The UNEP lists five nations that have yet to ratify the treaty: Iraq and Timor-Leste in Asia, and Andoro, San Marino, and the Holy See, otherwise known as Vatican City, in Europe.

The protocol does afford exemptions for the use of CFCs in metered-dose inhalers, for use in the Space Shuttle and Titan Rocket programs, and for use in laboratories.

If you are concerned with the chemicals present in your favorite product, you can check out the material-safety data sheets (MSDS) at *www.householdproducts.nlm.nih.gov.*

FACT

The MSDS for hair spray and other aerosols list that these items should be disposed of as hazardous waste because of their RCRA D001 designation. This designation simply means that the products are ignitable. There have been reports of aerosol cans exploding so violently inside hot cars that they became embedded in car seats and broke car windows.

Aerosols do produce a mist of fine particulate matter; that's one of the qualities that allows an even and light distribution on your hair or under your arm. Studies performed on hair stylists have not indicated any propensity to life-threatening diseases, but they were susceptible to skin irritations and minor breathing problems. Aerosols should be used in well-ventilated areas to avoid any health risks.

Aerosol cans are made of steel that can be recycled. They should be emptied before they are placed in the recycle bin to avoid explosion.

Just for Women

Once a month, women of childbearing age menstruate, necessitating the use of boxes and boxes of tampons and sanitary napkins. Disposable tampons that are flushed down the toilet are removed from the wastewater as it enters the bar screen. There, tampons and other larger items are removed and taken to a landfill for disposal. Sanitary napkins thrown in the trash are either taken to a landfill or incinerated. Either way, feminine hygiene products create waste.

If your green living takes you on an outdoor adventure, you probably don't have the option of scheduling it around your menstrual cycle. There is no conclusive evidence that menstruating women are more likely to be attacked by a bear or shark. Just to be on the safe side, park rangers recommend that, when hiking, women wear tampons and double-bag their waste.

If you are particularly concerned with the waste produced as part of having a period and are willing to add to your laundry load, consider trying reusable sanitary pads. There are a variety of pads on the market that have other benefits besides reducing waste. The reusable pads are made from 100 percent cotton and do not include any irritating fragrances, deodorants, or other chemicals. They come in a variety of sizes and over time can save money when compared to single-use tampons and pads. Other options include the Keeper, made from latex, and the Moon Cup, made from silicone; these menstrual cups can hold up to one ounce of flow for up to twelve hours. If you are interested, check out these and other reusable menstrual options at sites like *www.natural-woman.com*, *www.pandorapads .com*, and *www.feminineoptions.com*.

Chapter 12

Raising a Green Family

Being a parent is a great opportunity to set a good example for future generations. What children learn growing up will stay with them the rest of their lives. This chapter explores the different aspects of parenting that can be made more environmentally friendly. Whether you are a parent, thinking about taking the plunge, or an important player in a child's life, there are ways you can leave a positive and lasting impression on a child and on the environment, too.

Babies

The number, type, and variety of baby products available have increased exponentially over the last few generations. Along with new clothes, gear, and utensils, books on raising babies and magazines chock-full of informative articles now line the shelves. This onslaught of information and alternatives comes at a time when parents may already feel overwhelmed. Trying to lead a greener life doesn't have to happen overnight. Parents can take a deep breath, tackle items or concerns one by one, and then get ready to improvise.

Bottle or Breast

Many parents anguish over whether their baby should be fed mother's milk or formula. Breastmilk gives a baby the nutrition nature intended along with important antibodies, but many mothers either don't have the option or don't choose to breastfeed for the twelve months recommended by the American Academy of Pediatrics. The Centers for Disease Control reports that 20 percent of U.S. infants were breastfeeding at twelve months of age in 2005.

ALERT!

The Human Milk Bank Association of North America (HMBANA) provides guidelines for milk-banking facilities. Milk banks store and distribute milk donated by wet nurses who have been screened to ensure the quality of their milk. Mothers who cannot provide sufficient milk for their babies can get breastmilk from participating hospitals with a doctor's prescription.

In any case, breastmilk is more environmentally friendly than formula. The production of formula depends on concentrated animal-feeding operations (CAFO) of dairy cows and miles and miles of petrochemically based transportation. Some formulas are dairy-free and are based on dairy substitutes like soy. While this eliminates the dependency on CAFOs, it's still a highly industrialized process. There are also concerns that soy may not provide all of the nutritional requirements needed by growing babies.

Moving to Solids

After six months, babies may be ready for some solid food. The first food babies usually get their lips around is cereal. Some parents may choose to make their own baby food rather than rely on store-bought baby food.

Cereal either can be purchased in a box or made at home. Generally, when cereal is purchased, all that's required is adding a little milk, formula, or water. Homemade cereal is a little more time-consuming, but it can be made in batches and frozen for easy use later. Ice cube trays can be used for freezing baby food; each cube measures out to be a serving size of approximately one ounce. There are also commercially available baby food freezing trays that are compartmentalized with lids. When making rice or oat cereal at home, the grains must be ground and cooked, unlike commercially made cereal that's already cooked and dehydrated before it's purchased.

If you are looking for baby-food recipes and don't know where to turn, check out ✎*www.wholesomebabyfood.com*. This Web site contains recipes for your baby's beginning cereal and even more recipes for different stages up to one year. The site also has help articles on other food-related issues and answers to frequently asked questions.

From cereal and oats, parents can move on to feeding baby other foods like vegetables, fruit, and yogurt. Some foods, like bananas, can be mashed with a fork, while other foods, like sweet potatoes, may need to be ground in a food processor or a baby-food grinder. Vegetables will need to be cooked before you grind them. As with cereal, foods can be made ahead of time in batches and frozen as individual servings in reusable trays. Making baby food at home eliminates the single-serve containers used to sell baby food and the environmental impacts from manufacturing and transporting all those little jars.

The Diaper Dilemma

Which kinds of nappies are best for babies and the environment? Some children are allergic to the dyes and fragrances in disposable diapers. Others may be sensitive to cloth diapers if they aren't changed quickly after they're soiled or if they're not washed well between uses. Diapers washed using a diaper service can reduce the potential for diaper rash when compared to home-washed nappies because services tend to use extremely hot water over chemical disinfectants.

FACT

Marion Donovan was more than a mother to her children—she was a mother of invention. While staying home to raise her children, Donovan developed the prototype for the disposable diaper. In 1946, she made the "Boater," which included a shower-curtain covering lined with a cloth diaper insert. She patented the product, but it still took decades for the disposal diaper to gain popularity.

Disposable diapers are made from cellulose and plastic. It's estimated that in the United States the manufacturing of disposable diapers uses up to 80,000 pounds of plastic and more than 200,000 trees every year. It's a highly industrialized process that results in the discharge of wastewater into rivers and streams and the release of dioxin into the air.

Dirty diapers make up about 1.3 percent of all the solid waste going into landfills today, and they're full of human waste that contains germs and viruses. When cloth diapers are washed, the solids are flushed down the toilet and treated with other waste at a proper wastewater facility. Landfills are not designed specifically to handle biological waste; however, when operated correctly, all liquid draining from a landfill is collected and disposed of at a wastewater treatment plant. More than the contents of the diapers, the volume of diapers and the ability to reduce any component of the waste stream going into a landfill is the concern. If diapers are incinerated, the chlorine bleach they contain is converted to dioxin, another mark in the negative column for disposables.

But then again, cloth diapers have to be washed and dried, which uses a lot of water and electricity. While the amount of water needed to wash one dirty diaper can be considered negligible, its impact on water use and waste-water discharge can be significant when large quantities of diapers are taken into account. Diaper services enjoy water savings because large numbers of diapers are washed together, requiring less water per diaper. Where you live impacts the cost of a diaper service. In areas where there is a high population of people who use a diaper service, the cost will be lower. In remote and more rural locations, the cost will likely be higher because delivery trucks will have to travel longer distances. In some areas, the cost of using a diaper service is lower than using disposable diapers; in other areas, it's more expensive. Diaper services have suffered from the rise in disposable diapers and negative advertising from the disposable diaper manufacturers, and as a result there are fewer services. However, as more parents become concerned with the environment, diaper services are back on the rise.

Many parents compromise when it comes to diapering, using cloth diapers at home but opting for disposables when traveling and at night. Parents can opt for biodegradable and even flushable disposable diapers and inserts that draw urine away from the baby and make dumping solids much easier. Some biodegradable diapers are made with chlorine-free absorbent materials that don't contribute to the production of dioxin. Check the packaging for more information.

Cloth diapers have come a long way over the years. Pins can be used but are no longer necessary. Parents or caregivers can opt to use form-fitting covers with Velcro straps or all-in-one diapers that have Velcro straps right on the diapers. Parents can even choose between organic cotton and hemp. Diaper covers come in cool designs, making cloth a fashion statement. For additional information on cloth diapers and other accessories, check out *www.clothdiaper.com*, *www.cottonbabies.com*, *www.mother-ease.com*, and *www.softclothbunz.com*.

Bedding and Blankets

The same environmental standards that apply to adult mattresses also apply to crib mattresses. Most commercial mattresses today include fire-retardant chemicals that have been linked to health issues. While most studies indicate that the safety afforded by treating the fabric with fire retardants outweighs the concerns of chemical exposure, there have been no long-term tests supporting this statement. For an environmentally friendly option, consider a natural and organic mattress. Not only are beds made from these materials better for the environment, they can be better for babies when it comes to what they breathe and how well they sleep.

Natural and organic bedding is made from natural rubber or latex and organic cotton or wool. Natural latex is harvested from rubber trees in a manner that allows the sap to regenerate and the trees to heal in between tappings. It's used as the core of the mattress and is antimicrobial, hypoallergenic, and resistant to dust mites.

Organic cotton and wool are used to cover the natural latex, making the mattress more comfortable. Organic wool is sheared from sheep that are raised without pesticides or hormones, and the sheep are allowed to forage for at least one-third of their food rather than spending their days in a feedlot. Wool is an excellent temperature regulator. As babies sweat, the perspiration is wicked away so they don't get damp; this allows the sweat to do its job and help cool babies. If it's cold, wool has air pockets that hold in warmed air and insulate babies. Wool has its own fire retardants as well. No additional chemicals are required to ensure that proper safety regulations are met.

FACT

U.S. law required stuffed items such as mattresses and pillows be labeled to describe the fabric and stuffing material. In an effort to protect consumers from used goods, the products were sold with tags declaring it illegal to remove the labels. This warning led many consumers to believe they could be arrested for removing the labels. The confusing labels have since been changed to state that consumers, as opposed to retailers, may remove the labels.

Beyond the mattress, organic cotton makes for great sheets and blankets. For some parents, going organic may be the best way to ensure that no chemicals were used in growing the cotton or manufacturing the sheets. If parents are concerned about babies breathing in fumes like formaldehyde while they're sleeping, they may want to avoid using permanent-press commercial sheets. Wool is naturally hypoallergenic, making breathing problems less likely.

Strollers and Slings

There are plenty of options when it comes to carrying babies. Some people prefer using strollers to roll about town, while others prefer carrying babies up close in a sling or carrier. It's really personal preference. Concerns with strollers are that are that they are made using plastic and soft polyvinyl chloride (PVC) coverings. Not only is this a concern with babies chewing on the materials, other issues arise from the environmental impact of the manufacturing process. Although no studies specifically addressing strollers have been done, studies on toys show that babies don't chew on the toys long enough to absorb chemicals. Parents who are bothered by the idea of buying a stroller and supporting the petrochemical industry can consider purchasing a secondhand stroller. Many strollers are made to last through multiple children; a used stroller will be less expensive than a new model.

Slings and baby carriers come in all shapes, sizes, and patterns and allow parents to keep babies close while keeping their hands free. Some slings snuggle the baby right up to Mom or Dad's chest while others, usually those for older infants, are worn on the hips. There are also styles that are worn on the parent's back. If you are interested in looking for different designs and more information on slings and carriers, check out these Web sites: *www.theslingstation.com*, *www.peppermint.com*, *www.onehotmama.com*, and *www.ergobaby.com*.

Friendly and Safe Toys

Kids nuzzle everything, rubbing it on their faces and putting it in their mouths. Parents want to make sure their toys are as safe as can be. Safety regulations for toys sold in the United States are governed by the Federal Hazardous Substance Act and respective amendments, along with the 1969 Child Protection and Toy Safety Act. Regulations are enforced by the

Consumer Product Safety Commission (CPSC) and include testing requirements for the following:

- Paint and other surface coatings
- Pacifiers and rattles
- Noise levels
- Electric or thermal toys
- Chemistry sets
- Sharp edges and points
- Small parts or choking hazards
- Flammability
- Hazardous substances

There has been a lot of concern over the materials used to make children's toys, particularly PVC plastics. Chemicals added to plastic to soften it include phthalates, which are considered carcinogens by the EPA. Phthalates are also suspected as endocrine disrupters that can affect hormonal activities in laboratory animals. There is concern that children could absorb phthalates contained in the toys when chewing on them; however, as mentioned, studies have shown that the children do not chew the toys long enough for the chemicals to be absorbed. Other countries consider the levels of phthalates allowed in U.S. toys too high; the European Union has banned six specific phthalates.

Kids

Teaching children about the environment can be just as much fun for adults as it is for kids. It gives parents a chance to learn something they may have been interested in or share some of their knowledge. There are a lot of different ways for parents to help their children appreciate the world around them. Many schools incorporate some aspect of environmental awareness in their curriculum, but parents play the most important role in leading their children toward environmental stewardship.

Field Trips

Field trips can be a great way to expose kids to the wonders of the environment firsthand. To get the most out of the excursion, the location and length of a visit should be age-appropriate. Consider taking children to a science museum, particularly one that's geared at least partially toward a child's interest. Here children are allowed to see, touch, and even crawl on or climb through nature exhibits. The Florida Museum of Natural History (*www.flmnh.ufl.edu*) on the campus of the University of Florida is home to a life-size limestone cave. Children and parents can walk through it, looking at geologic formations and searching for bats and other animals. The museum also has a screened-in Butterfly Rainforest that houses subtropical and tropical trees and plants that support hundreds of free-flying butterflies. Many museums also offer docents who will lead a tour, telling stories and providing information.

Or if you are looking for the real thing, take a trip to a park, experience nature firsthand on a nature walk looking for bugs and other wildlife. Some parks are home to rocks and formations that offer their own learning experience. Some parks regularly offer ranger-led walks, or one can be scheduled ahead of time, that will point out what the park has to offer. What better way to learn about the environment than seeing it firsthand with a professional?

Hands-on activities can really pique a child's interest. Exploring a park can lead to picking up litter and checking for animal footprints as well as discussions on recycling and protecting animal habitats.

Local farms offer another outing. Taking children out to pick local fruit can show them how food is grown and harvested. They will learn what grows in their region with respect to the seasons. Even a trip to the grocery store can be a learning experience if you point out the labels and talk about where the fruits and vegetables were grown.

Some zoos offer children's camps, where kids can be zookeepers for the day and learn about the animals, their environments, and the threats they face. Parents can also take advantage of open houses offered at local animal rehabilitation centers and vet schools to give children a little more insight into the environment.

Green Reads

Reading is a big part of most children's lives, and books and magazines are a good way to interest children in the environment. Books that help nurture naturalists can range from warm and fuzzy stories from authors like Eve Bunting and James Herriot to more informative nature book series such as DK Eyewitness Books, Owlet Books, and Real Kids Real Science Books. Childsake offers lists of environmental and nature books for children, organizing them by category (*www.childsake.com*). Your local librarian may also have some suggestions.

Magazines introduce kids to environmental topics in quick gulps. *Ranger Rick*, *Kids Discover*, and *National Geographic Kids* give children the opportunity to learn about all different aspects of the natural world around them and ways to take care of it.

The Internet also offers an array of sites that teach environmental lessons. Many state and local regulatory agencies have pages expressly for children. The EPA sponsors the Environmental Kids Club at *www.epa.gov*. Nonprofit organizations also offer information designed for children. The Natural Resources Defense Council (NRDC) created The Green Squad for kids to learn about different ways they might impact or help the environment (*www.nrdc.org*). Audubon Adventure Kids (*www.audubon.org*) provides lessons for kids in kindergarten through twelfth grade that can be incorporated into classroom activities.

Teens

Teenagers may be ready to learn about the environment more independently than younger kids, but parents can still be involved by providing suggestions, directions, and limitations. Parents may also lend a hand in creating and directing different opportunities for teens. Becoming involved with certain groups can help improve teenagers' self-esteem and introduce them to other teens with similar interests. Some opportunities may offer insight to future careers, while others may help students accrue volunteer hours needed for grade school or college.

Teens can do environmental research for a science-fair project. Many students are required to do a science-fair project either for extra credit or as part of their grade. Topics can include burying waste to determine how long it takes to degrade, or watering plants with acidic liquid to determine the effect of acid rain. By performing the research and the experiment, students can learn environmental lessons firsthand.

If teenagers want to experience the outdoors and learn about the environment, they can participate in a parks program. Some programs include helping maintain facilities or teaching and leading children, while others focus on adventure. The Yosemite National Institutes offer teens from eighth through twelfth grade sleep-away camps at different parks. At the Olympic Park Institute in Washington, students can participate in the Elwha River Project that includes five days of exploring the ecosystem. The Yosemite Institute in California offers twelve days of backpacking, rafting, and rock climbing. Campers also perform research that could lead to college credit. More information on these programs is available online at *www.yni.org*.

The Teen Environmental Media Network, founded by Jerry Kay, gives high school students in Marin County, California, experience in learning and reporting on the environment. The teens perform research and learn how to interview, write, and edit their articles. Stories appear in community newspapers and on local and national radio programs. More on this program can be found at *www.eecom.net*.

Rather than sit on the sidelines listening to adults, teens can be active participants in environmental, humanitarian, and animal causes. Teens can join organizations geared toward their age group or they can mix it up with other ages. Organizations such as the Humane Society have a special branch just for teens called Humane Teen. This organization provides teens with information on organizing projects that can help animals in their own town. The Web site *www.humaneteen.org* also has information on becoming involved in larger issues like factory farms and fur labeling.

Snack Options and Brown Bags

Snacks now come in helpfully portion-controlled packages. Many teachers even request that group snacks be provided to the classroom already prepackaged and individually wrapped. Not only do single-portion packages cost a lot, they produce an excessive amount of waste as all of the single wrappers are tossed in the trash. So while grabbing a snack out of the pantry and heading out the door may be convenient, there are more environmentally friendly alternatives.

You can buy snacks in bulk, or at least more than a single-serving container, and pack individual servings in reusable containers yourself. You can also make snacks at home and pack them in lunches or take them to the park. The same goes for drinks. There's no need to buy juice boxes or bottled water. Use washable bottles and fill them with 100 percent juice or tap water to wash down your snacks.

If you're looking for suggestions for packing a healthy lunch for younger kids, check out *www.laptoplunches.com*. The company Obentec was started by two California moms looking for ways to provide nutritional lunches while reducing waste. They came up with colorful and innovative lunchboxes and containers and offer menu support from their Web site.

Many children take lunches that are completely prepackaged from drink to desert. They produce a hefty amount of trash because nothing is reusable and much of the lunch often goes uneaten. Moreover, these lunches contain very little nutrition and a lot of fat and preservatives. When packing a child's lunch, take advantage of reusable containers and only pack what you think your child will eat. This will set a precedent so that when kids begin packing their own lunches, they'll go for the reusables and portion-control automatically.

Parents can also invest in plastic lunchboxes or reusable bags for their child's lunch. Reusing brown paper bags and recycling them when they get too ratty is another option.

Arts and Crafts

Arts and crafts allow children to express themselves, create gifts, and work their little fingers. It seems there is an endless supply of materials available, from nontoxic glue to paint, glitter, feathers, and paper. But parents can use homemade and more environmentally friendly arts and crafts materials that are just as fun as the glitzy products. Arts and crafts projects can be a perfect opportunity to experience and learn from nature while spending time together.

For example, homemade play dough can be made from ingredients common in any home. Just combine the following ingredients:

3 cups flour
½ cup salt
3 tablespoons oil
1 cup water

This mixture can be divided and tinted with food coloring. By making it at home, parents save a trip to the store. Homemade dough can also be used to make other crafts like furniture for a dough-filled dollhouse or game pieces.

Other more nature-oriented crafts include using treasures found in the yard or garden to make a collage or decorate a picture frame. Make a tape bracelet with the sticky side out and let your children inspect the yard for odds and ends they can stick to their wristband. It's a perfect opportunity learn about seeds, plants, and leaves.

QUESTION?

What items are good for arts and crafts projects?
Cereal boxes can be used for a number of projects. They can be cut up and used to make picture frames or blocks. Children can decorate boxes with recycled items like milk-jug tops and scraps of paper. With a little ingenuity, wheels can be added to a box to make it a car—biodiesel or hybrid, of course.

Papier-mâché can be used to make bowls, plates, and even animals. It can also be crafted into personalized desktop accessories like pencil and notepaper holders or jewelry and trinket boxes. Just mix flour and water to form pasty glue, and use it to attach strips of newspaper over a model dish, balloon, or balled-up newspaper. It's likely more appropriate for older children with more patience, because it takes days to get to a point where the piece can be painted and decorated. It's a perfect project for long summer vacations or other breaks.

There are lot of activities in books and on the Internet that allow parents, teachers, and other caretakers to save money and the environment. *EcoArt!* by Laurie Carlson includes different art projects for kids three to nine years old and includes crafts made from nature. MaryAnn Kohl's *Good Earth Art: Environmental Art for Kids* also gives parents and children ideas about how to incorporate nature into art projects.

Getting Educated on Health-Care Alternatives

A pediatrician is an important figure when it comes to raising a child. Parents rely on the pediatrician to provide accurate answers to their questions. But medicine, like other practices, has different methods and approaches, so when you are choosing a pediatrician select one who shares your beliefs. Pediatricians should be patient in answering your questions as well as validating your concerns, and while doctors may be experts in their field, the parent-doctor relationship should be a partnership.

Like other doctors, there are pediatricians who practice holistic medicine. These doctors have received medical degrees and have continued their education with holistic coursework. Holistic doctors use conventional medicines and immunizations, but they also consider the whole child and how he or she fits in the environment. Doctors who practice holistic or complementary medicine encourage patients and families to include lifestyle as part of the healing process and encourage prevention over treatment if possible.

FACT

Many mainstream doctors are trying to decrease the amount of drugs they prescribe, especially when it comes to cases of mild depression. Studies have found that exercise or even joining a club helps alleviate symptoms. This is particularly promising when it comes to medicating children.

Complementary medical practitioners may also include positive visualization, chiropractic, and probiotics as part of their regimen. They work with parents on other alternative treatments for chronic illnesses to help alleviate the cause rather than the symptoms. Often, there are natural and herbal remedies that can relieve a baby's discomfort, from diaper rash to colic. Ask your doctor or visit your local health-food store to see what remedies they can suggest.

Another option to traditional medicine is seeking the services of a doctor of osteopathy (DO). DOs obtain education similar to traditional medical doctors and can perform the same duties. The difference lies in their approach to medicine—much like a holistic practitioner, a DO tends to take a step back when diagnosing a problem to look at the big picture. They tend to become general-care practitioners, focusing on preventive medicine and psychological and social factors relating to their patients.

Chapter 13

Vacations and Travel

There's no better way to appreciate the planet and all it has to offer than by going out and experiencing it firsthand. Increasing numbers of opportunities allow vacationers to help the environment while having fun. This chapter explores the different travel options, from visiting exotic lands and locales to checking out what's right around the corner or in the backyard.

Ecotourism

Ecotourism is a hot buzzword in the tourism industry. What makes a trip ecological, environmental, or green? The general rule of thumb is that ecotourism meets three goals. It helps sustain the environment, the economy, and the culture of the area visited. Unless those three criteria are met, it may not be considered full-fledge ecotourism.

ALERT!

Don't be taken in by the Green Globe logo. This circular award is given, or sold, by the American Society of Travel Agents to those travel destinations that agree to work toward more environmentally sound practices. Note that they agree to work toward sound practices; they don't have to achieve them. It's marketing at its greenest.

Tourism has become a global industry. Its popularity is such that even the United Nations has become involved with the Convention on Biological Diversity (CBD), which works to develop guidelines on biodiversity and sustainable tourism. Many locals who earn their living through tourism believe that global initiatives aren't necessary since the indigenous people have more at stake in maintaining their own environment. There is also concern that large organizations and corporations will develop areas for sustainable tourism while economically overpowering smaller local businesses.

Ecotourism comes in many shapes and sizes, from adventure trips for the highly skilled and proficiently athletic to the more relaxing, softer trips for those looking to experience nature without breaking a sweat.

The Terms and What They Mean

There are a variety of terms used in the ecotravel industry that may be confusing. Not all types of travel afford the same kind of environmental benefits to local people that true ecotourism does. Here's a rundown of the most common terms used:

- **Adventure tourism** is usually nature-oriented and involves some amount of risk, but not all trips require a specialized skill or the desire to rough it. Some tours are considered hard adventure, meaning participants are required to either paddle or hike in difficult conditions and for durations well beyond novice level. Soft tours allow travelers greater comfort and are not quite as challenging.

- **Geotourism** usually centers on the geographic nature of the environment. Tourism helps to enhance the environment along with culture and overall well-being of local residents. This could include a hiking tour of Auckland, New Zealand's urban volcanoes, or archaeology trips through the Shetland Islands.

- **Nature-based tourism** relies on the natural environment or settings to entice travelers. This could include jungle lodges as well as whale-watching cruise ships. These may or may not be environmentally friendly.

- **Sustainable tourism** protects the environment, meaning that travel will continue in the area without destruction of any habitat or damage to resources. The area's integrity will be maintained for future travelers. Is trophy hunting in southern Namibia a good example of sustainable tourism? Not so much.

The Benefits

When done right, ecotourism can help preserve or even remediate a locale. Not only does tourism raise money, it increases awareness of native cultures and the environment, bringing to life images from magazines or television, adding touch, smell, and taste. It gives tourists a reason to protect an environment or a culture because they've seen it firsthand.

Ecotourists generally are on the upper end of the earning scale and have income readily available for spending. Whether buying goods or purchasing services, the money spent usually goes at least in part to the local economy that supports indigenous cultures.

FACT

Although it hasn't been called an official success yet, tourism has managed to offer hope to the population of mountain gorillas in Rwanda's Volcanoes National Park. Some years have seen in excess of 10,000 visitors. The income derived from tourists supports the conservation efforts, which have allowed the population of gorillas to increase 9 percent over the last thirteen years.

When it comes to money, villages and communities rely on tourism so they don't have to turn to other sources of income like mining, drilling, and foresting that degrade their resources. Properly run lodges and low-impact tours can support an economy, proving an alternative for inhabitants to earn a living. Tourists can't visit the rain forests of Costa Rica if the trees have been cut down for lumber, and the leather craftsmen can't survive without tourists visiting the Otavalo Market of the Andes Highlands and purchasing their wares.

The Pitfalls

Because of the increase in ecotourism, some unscrupulous guides, agents, or establishments will use the label for tourism that really doesn't meet the eco-criteria. This not only takes away from those promoting and relying on ecotourism, but not all adventure vacations, sustainable tours, or nature trips are 100 percent beneficial to the environment, and the term could be used as a marketing ploy to generate ticket sales. First, almost all travel involves the use of cars, planes, cruise ships, or other vehicles that depend on fossil fuels. Although tourists would be hard-pressed to avoid any degrading practices, minimizing them is possible. Also, while large crowds may spend a lot of money, they have negative impacts that must be considered. Crowds can inhibit certain animal behavior such as breeding, and trash generated from tourists can be costly if handled properly or dangerous to the environment if not.

Following the Rules

When abiding by the true spirit of ecotravel, there are rules tourists can live by to make sure they are promoting the conservation of cultures, economics, and the environment. Treat locations as you would your home. While you may not live there, others do.

Study Up

To get the most out of travel, prepare for your trip before you ever leave home. Learn about your destination. If you are traveling to a non-English-speaking country, learn a handful of words in the local language. Trying to communicate in someone else's native language relays a strong message.

Spend Locally

Whether for a tour guide, transportation, food, or souvenirs, purchases help the local community. By choosing local merchants, there is more opportunity to impact the economy and learn the culture. A local guide or scout can provide a wealth of knowledge, making the most of side trips. Take advantage of their knowledge by asking about other local places of interest. There's nothing like local advice to find the best restaurant and neighborhood hangout.

Take Nothing but Pictures

Everyone's heard it before. It is posted at park entrances and in guide books, but it bears repeating. "Take nothing but pictures; leave nothing but footprints." One small stone or shell may not seem like much, but repeated over and over again could leave a shore or stream barren. Leaving discards only means someone else will have to follow behind, picking up trash—or worse, it stays put.

Conserve Natural Resources

Don't be wasteful of a community's resources. Their water may be hard to come by, so use it sparingly. Other resources like wood and gasoline may be harder to get than you might think. Green hotels or smaller inns may create less environmental impact than a larger commercial lodge.

Be Respectful

Tourists are visitors. Be respectful of the people who call your travel destinations home. Consider the clothes you wear and how you speak in public, even going one step further and learning about local culture, traditions, and customs.

How to Go

There are many ways to travel—alone or in groups, with friends or family. No matter what kind of trip you plan, do some research. Not only will you be able to make better use of your time and resources, it's always more enjoyable to be familiar with your surroundings—not to mention that learning ahead of time makes for a great game of, "did you know?"

Going It Alone

You may be a planner ready to prepare your own green vacation, possibly going with a group of friends or family or alone. Thanks to the Internet and local libraries, there are plenty of resources available to help plan a trip. Ask others who have visited the area what they liked most or what they would change if they traveled there again. See if they have any recommendations for must-do side trips. Also, consider contacting local guides or outfitters and asking questions. Using local businesses not only supports their economy, it often gives you the best information.

Many more people, especially women, are traveling alone these days. When traveling solo, take precautions. It's a good idea to leave an itinerary of where you are staying and to know ahead of time where you are headed. Solo travelers may want to hold off announcing to strangers that they are traveling alone.

The International Ecotourism Society (TIES) works with the Rainforest Alliance, helping both tourists and tour operators with sustainable travel. The organizations provide information to travelers on how to be a green tourist and on the different travel opportunities available. Check out bulletin boards online where travelers can share information on different trips they have made. One example is Ecotravel.com.

Using a Travel Agent

Because ecotravel has become so popular, many travel agents include it in the gamut of trips they offer. Certain travel agents may specialize solely in ecotravel. Some agents may not understand the difference between ecotravel and adventure travel, leaving it up to the traveler to make the distinction. The Center on Ecotourism and Sustainable Development (*www.ecotourismcesd.org*) recommends the following online companies to find an eco-friendly travel agent:

- Solimar Travel, *www.solimartravel.com*
- Preferred Adventures Ltd., *www.preferredadventures.com*
- Eco-Resorts, *www.eco-resorts.com*
- Adventure Life, *www.adventurelife.com*
- GAP Adventures, *www.gapadventures.com*

Humanitarian and Working Vacations

If you are not one to kick back and relax, even during vacation, you may want to consider a working vacation. These vacations allow people to volunteer their time while experiencing another culture or environment. These trips could range from blazing trails and patrolling forests in national parks to recording whale migration patterns. They could be organized or sponsored by local churches, humanitarian groups, or volunteer networks that give those looking for the opportunity a chance to volunteer away from home.

The American Hiking Society organizes vacations where volunteers help rebuild paths, cabins, and shelters in parks in thirty different states. Vacation assignments cost members $100; nonmembers pay $130. Volunteers sleep at camp and hike to the work site every morning. Find more information at their Web site, *www.americanhiking.org*.

Even though travelers are working during their vacation, payment usually comes in the form of feeling rewarded. The cost of working or volunteer vacations is comparable to other vacations. Some Web sites offer tips on how to raise money to pay for humanitarian or working trips, and chances are that friends and family may be willing to contribute, too. Because of the volunteer nature of the trip and the work performed, the costs of working vacations are usually tax-deductible.

Environmental Group Trips

If you aren't up to planning your own trip and would like to take advantage of having an expert on hand, consider booking a trip with an environmental group. Groups like the Sierra Club and Nature Conservancy arrange trips all over the world. Trips usually include hiking, kayaking, horseback riding, and other activities and are led by an expert guide who shares information on the local environment and wildlife.

Like any other group activity, there may not be a lot of extra room in the schedule or flexibility for deviation or side trips, but travelers, especially those new to the locale, benefit by being led by a professional who knows the area and how to get around. Combining all the travelers into one group eliminates the need for personal vehicles, which allows passengers to see the sites and get to know each other rather than navigate unknown territory.

Retreats

If you are looking for a relaxing vacation, a retreat may fit the bill. Retreats are usually located in secluded areas. They can focus on themes such as all-women, yoga and meditation, or vegetarian cooking and (better yet) eating. They usually include workshops and educational classes. Some include menus and classes to body detoxification, to cleanse the toxins and stress from everyday life. Retreats like this might include fasting and fitness workouts as well as massage. These vacations tend to cater more toward relaxation and rejuvenation rather than ecological or sustainable travel.

Parks

National, state, and local parks abound in the United States. A study done in 2000 by the U.S. Forest Service and the National Oceanic and Atmospheric Administration (NOAA) concluded that one in five people will visit a park for outdoor adventure. Parks have a lot to offer—from overnight stays to hiking, biking, and even riding trails. They give individuals and families a chance to reconnect with each other and nature, with access to outdoor activities that are sometimes just a few yards away.

Many parks offer educational programs and ranger-led tours. Some of the programs may have a fee, while many of the tours and fire-ring sessions, where rangers gather visitors around a campfire and tell stories or give information about the park and its inhabitants, are free. Joining a tour or program allows visitors to learn more about the park and have a chance to meet other vacationers as well.

The National Park Service

The National Park Service (NPS) comprises over 400 natural, cultural, and recreational areas set aside for people to enjoy. The NPS is operated by the Department of Interior and was created by President Woodrow Wilson in 1916. Formation of the park service actually came after establishment of the first national park; Yellowstone National Park was established in 1872 by President Ulysses S. Grant.

ALERT!

When visiting a national park, it's important not to feed the wild animals. Animals that are fed not only lose their fear of humans but may act more aggressively around them. To avoid an altercation, keep food stored where it won't be tempting to the animals.

National parks not only allow visitors to witness some of the country's natural wonders, they also protect watersheds and vital elements in biodiversity. Designation as a national park means that no mining or hunting can take place, and timber cannot be removed. The area is protected as a resource, which also makes it a popular destination spot. There are areas protected within the NPS that are not duplicated anywhere else.

Park areas may get overcrowded, especially during July and August. When crowds aren't handled well, parks end up with traffic jams, noise pollution, and poor air quality. Yosemite National Park, which hosts over 3 million visitors a year, became the first park system to actively pursue a reduction in personal cars. In 2005, the park began operating eighteen 40-foot diesel-electric hybrid buses, encouraging visitors to use the free bus system instead of their own vehicles. As a result, the Environmental and Energy Study Institute reported a 60 percent reduction in nitrogen oxide, a 90 percent reduction in particulate matter, a 70 percent reduction in noise—and an estimated 12,500 gallons of gas saved.

Yosemite isn't alone. Many other parks are taking the initiative to ameliorate damages to the environment brought on by their popularity. Years ago, it was thought that increased numbers of visitors meant more exposure, awareness, and enjoyment. This philosophy is being reconsidered as managers try to handle increased visitor numbers with decreased funding.

If you decide to visit a national park, consider going when it's not peak season, or even avoiding peak weekend traffic. There are also a number of beautiful and solitary parks whose only fault is that they are relatively unknown. In any case, you can purchase a national park pass to cover the entrance fee to all national parks; additional fees for camping, parking, or tours are not included. Check out *www.nps.gov* for more information.

State Parks

State parks are run by various departments within each state. They offer a variety of camping, hiking, and water activities. Often, you can purchase a state pass that allows access to all the parks within a certain state without paying an entrance fee.

State parks provide an intriguing alternative to other traditional vacation spots like amusement parks. Not only are nature parks less expensive than amusement parks, they offer the opportunity to see a little of your own—or someone else's—backyard. Many state parks offer guided tours and even overnight outings. If you'd like to try a new activity but are wary of doing it alone, you may find that joining a tour is the best approach. Experts will be on hand and you will share the company of like-minded folks. Funds generated from these outings usually go back to the park to help with maintenance and maybe even the building of new facilities.

Many state parks have online reservations available that allow visitors to pick their site and pay online. Schedule and program information are usually available online, so visitors can plan their stay to take advantage of all the park has to offer. To find parks in your state or a state you plan to visit, go to the state's Web site and run a search.

The CCC Impact

The next time you visit a state or national park, take an extra look at the trails and structures. Chances are they were made by the Civilian Conservation Corp (CCC). The CCC was started by Franklin D. Roosevelt in 1933 as a means to address unemployment problems resulting from the Great Depression. Young men were paid $1 a day to build shelters and steps and clear trails. They lived in camps and after a long day working would kick back and unwind around a campfire.

FACT

The Appalachian Trail runs from Springer Mountain in Georgia to Katahdin, Maine. The trail is 2,175 miles long and it takes approximately 5 million footsteps to complete it. Parts of the trail were cleared and a portion of the structures along the trail were built by CCC workers.

By 1935, there were more than 2,650 CCC camps all over the country with over half a million workers. The CCC was not permanent and was disbanded in 1942. In the nine years of activity, workers built 97,000 miles of roads and erected 3,470 fire towers. To fight erosion and save soil, workers planted more than 2 million trees. They fought fires and floods and even saved stranded sheep during a Utah blizzard in 1936 and 1937. When the effects of the Depression started to wane and young men enlisted to fight in World War II, the CCC came to an end. But many of the structures still stand and their legacy continues today.

Souvenirs and Where They Come From

Before picking out a little souvenir to take home, consider how it was made and where it came from. Some traditional tourist locations sell trinkets made from coral, bone, shell, reptile skin, teeth, and even large animals' fur. If an animal product or natural resource was used to make the item, then it's better left on the shelf. The knickknack of interest may not even be from that area. Oftimes, shells sold at beaches in the United States are imported from places with less strict environmental laws.

Don't pick your own souvenirs from the sea or land either. Sand dollars and conchs may be beautiful when they are at home on the beach, but packed up in luggage they may stink. It's likely they'll end up being thrown away far from their home, so it's best that they're left at the beach. Exotic animals sold to tourists have usually been taken from the wild. Tourists are often not privy to the truth that taking animals from the wild frequently costs many of them their lives. Another concern is the law. Shells and animals can be legally protected, and being in possession of one may cause problems with the authorities.

Pass as well when it comes to the animal photo op because many animals used for photo opportunities were captured in the wild and may not be well treated when the cameras are gone. While it's tempting to support the local economies, forgo the photos. Choose other gifts to take home, such as crafts made by local artisans.

Take in a Festival or Expo

When planning to travel, check out everything the destinations have to offer. Many cities, especially the larger ones, sponsor green festivals and expos. Exhibitors staffing booths will be able to answer questions and provide advice and firsthand information on building, construction materials, home design, transportation, gardening, home energy, and other interesting green topics. Most expos also offer classes or workshops on topics like food choices and how the environment is affected by what people eat.

Festivals will be similar to expos but may have more entertainment. They will likely have movies and political presentations along with a concert or party. Travelers may even get to see an environmental celebrity promoting a cause.

When planning your vacation, be sure to check out festivals and expos at *www.greenfestivals.org* and *www.livinggreen.org*. These Web sites offer schedules and programs for green events all over the country. Also visit the online version of the local newspaper to see what events are scheduled.

The Backyard Adventure

Not that Dorothy in the *Wizard of Oz* was promoting a greener lifestyle, but her claim that "there's no place like home" often rings true. When green time is needed but time or funds don't allow a full-fledged ecotrip to exotic lands, investigate your own backyard. Local extension offices have information on what kinds of insects or birds you might find nearby. Check out books with a lot of pictures and try to match them with what you see. Some community colleges or outfitters offer classes on local flora and fauna.

Staying close to home gives you the opportunity to get to know the animals that share your yard. If you like them, you can take steps to attract them. Find out what plants grow in your area that will attract birds and butterflies. To attract even more animals, plant a garden and see who comes to visit. Putting up a bird feeder and birdbath will attract feathered friends that are either local to the area or just passing through. Bird counts are a way for residents to watch and tally the different birds that frequent their backyards. If there's a locally organized bird count, enthusiasts can learn even more about the birds in the area throughout the seasons. Outdoor fans may be surprised to find out what kind of endangered species inhabit nearby areas. You can work to help sustain the animal populations. Even if long trips aren't possible, shorter ones may provide just as much fun and excitement.

How do you discourage visits from backyard pests like skunks?
Skunks are saddled with an unfortunate reputation, but they can help you out, too. Yellow jackets eat harmful garden pests, but they can become a problem if they nest too close to your house or if you are allergic to stings. Skunks have an appetite for yellow jackets. Sprinkle some honey near the nest to invite them in. If the skunks bother you, try putting out some ammonia-soaked rags; they don't like the odor.

Nearby city parks can also provide an opportunity to get closer to nature. Parks provide open space for locals to get fresh air and for children to run around and work out their wiggles. Trees help clean the air and provide habitat for birds and squirrels. They offer not just physical relief but visual respite too. Green spaces break up the monotony of structures and roads and offer people a chance to take a breather. There's a chance that local parks and recreation departments are in need of volunteers. By helping park professionals, volunteers are able to learn a lot about their surroundings and the issues they face, from funding to encroachment.

Chapter 14

Pets

Pets are an important part of many families. In the United States, the American Pet Association estimates that the number of pet dogs and cats alone is almost 140 million. Pets fill roles as devoted friends, surrogate children, personal assistants, even therapists. As a pet owner, there are choices people can make to take pet ownership to a greener level and give back to their pet. This chapter offers information on ways you can choose and raise pets while helping the environment.

14

A Place for Pets

Domesticated animals play an important role in the lives of most people. They provide an opportunity for children and adults to learn the skills of caring, nurturing, and responsibility. People bring them into their homes, sometimes even making them a member of the family.

Making a fuss over pets isn't a new trend. Pets have been catered to for thousands of years, even having their own private servants.

FACT

Walking the dog can be an important part of a weight-loss program. Maybe out of obligation or just plain pleasure, dieters tend to stick to with dog walking. Most will opt to pick up a leash, not a snack. People are not the only ones who benefit from exercise; it can extend a dog's life and burn off extra energy, making them more relaxed.

Pets don't always have it so well. Some are mistreated, even abused, and laws have been enacted to protect them. Two large organizations, the American Society for the Prevention of Cruelty to Animals (ASPCA) and the Humane Society of the United States (HSUS), have a long history of working to protect animals. There are many other groups; some focus on particular species like dogs or horses, some act locally, and others focus on specific concerns such as unscrupulous breeders or farm animal rights. These local and national animal protection organizations work to educate people and help alleviate animal suffering.

Hurricanes and natural disasters over the last several years have brought to light issues of animal safety during mass evacuations. Recently, the Pets Evacuation and Transportation Standards (PETS) Act was signed into law, requiring states to prepare pet evacuation plans. These plans must be given to the Federal Emergency Management Agency (FEMA) before funding is received. The act also authorizes money to create pet-friendly shelters. Now those in the midst of a disaster do not have to choose between their own safety and that of their pets.

Picking One Out

It's important for both you and your potential pet that you choose an animal that's right for you, your family, and your lifestyle. Consider not just how cute it is, but how it will fit into your family and home.

Exotic Pets Aren't So Green

If you have your heart set on an exotic pet, there are some very important issues you need to think about. Some exotics are becoming more common and have been bred in captivity, like the ferret. But others, like parrots, are frequently captured in the wild. Methods used to catch and transport animals from the wild are harsh and often end up killing the animals. This is especially true with birds and reptiles. Some breeds are taken from the wild to the point of endangering the native population.

Another consideration when looking at exotics is whether they are legal and how big and dangerous the animal may become as it grows. Even relatively small animals can pose dangers to humans, especially children. Because of their dangerous nature, some captive animals are de-clawed and de-fanged to make them safer. Rather than taking an animal from the wild, consider pets that have already been domesticated and are looking for loving homes.

Animals need medical care, too. Access to a veterinarian who is familiar with exotics needs to be considered. If there isn't a vet nearby who can deal with the animal, proper care will be more difficult and costly, especially if the pet gets sick and needs immediate attention. Another consideration is the potential for exotics to spread disease to native populations and people.

As much as owners want to properly care for their pet, some exotics do not adapt well to domesticated life. While a home offers security against predators, it cannot mimic the environment of a South American rain forest or an African plain or provide the social community of similar animals.

Spay and Neuter

Spaying or neutering a pet is one of the greenest decisions you can make. There is an overpopulation of pets, both pure and mixed breed, and millions of animals are euthanized every year.

FACT

Operation Catnip humanely traps feral cats so they can be sterilized and then returns them to the wild. The organization operates with volunteers who capture and release the animals, and veterinarians who donate time and resources to perform the surgeries. They have organizations in Raleigh, North Carolina; Gainesville, Florida; and Richmond, Virginia; and can process up to 100 cats in a matter of hours.

There are many programs available to assist with the cost of neutering or spaying a pet. There are also programs to spay and neuter cats that have been abandoned or are strays. These feral cats are wary of people and congregate in groups for protection and food. By releasing them back to their environment, the cats are allowed to say together without multiplying.

Pet Food and Treats

Owners love their pets and want to make sure they are feeding them well. Common pet food for sale in the grocery or discount store is inexpensive and convenient to purchase; more than likely, natural pet foods require a special trip and are usually more expensive. Is there really a difference? Well, yes.

Conventional Versus Natural Pet Food

The differences involve the quality of the ingredients and the degree of processing. Pet food contains protein from various sources. The protein comes primarily from the ground remains of animal processing such as the heads, feet, and intestines—the discards of the human food industry. This practice allows farmers to gain added revenue rather than having to pay to get rid of waste, and it provides the pet-food industry with a low-cost protein supply. Preservatives are also added to pet food to ensure that it lasts for months, in the grocery store and at home. Many commercial pet foods include grains that are not digestible by dogs and cats. Even though grains contribute relatively small amounts of protein compared to meat, this is done so that the label will reflect a certain concentration of protein.

The meat processed into by-product meal or meat and bone meal may be from sick or healthy animals. The meat products are processed through an extruder that steams the material under high pressure to form food nuggets. This processing destroys the nutritional value, requiring manufacturers to put nutrients and minerals back into the product.

Hold off the sweets—or at least keep them far away from your pet's paws. A sweetener called xylitol, which is used in chewing gum, candy, and some baked goods, can be dangerous for pets. It causes a sudden drop in blood sugar that can result in depression, loss of coordination, and seizures. Large doses can bring on symptoms quickly, while symptoms from smaller doses may not show up for twelve hours.

The FDA is responsible for regulating the pet-food industry but does not require premarket approval before a pet food can be sold. Instead, its responsibilities lie with ensuring that the ingredients are safe and necessary and that the food is labeled correctly with the manufacturer's name and contact information along with all of the ingredients.

The Association of American Feed Control Officials (AAFCO) is made up of federal and state regulators. The group has no regulatory authority, but it is involved in developing model laws and regulations, uniform feed ingredient definitions, and appropriate labeling.

When choosing a pet food, it's important to pick a brand that has an AAFCO guarantee and cites feeding tests or feeding profiles, not just nutrient profiles. Many natural recipes will include higher quality protein without by-products. Look for labels that include identified meat like chicken, lamb, or beef as the first ingredient, not just the word *meat*. Natural pet food will most likely not use chemical preservatives but will rely on vitamins C and E to partially or fully preserve food. As an added bonus, some natural foods are sold in recycled packaging.

If you want to change your pet's diet, don't try it all at once. Although owners may prefer a change to more natural food, a sudden change may upset a healthy pet's digestive system. A small portion of the new food can be mixed with a larger portion of the old food to slowly introduce more and more of the new food. When changing pet foods, watch your companion for any warning signs, such as changes in coat, body weight, or odor, that mean the new food may not be agreeing with them.

Homemade Pet Food

One sure way to know your pets are getting a balanced and natural diet is to make their food at home. This may also prove successful if your animal companion suffers from reactions to commercial food. If planning to make homemade pet food, it's important to meet the animal's nutritional requirements. You can consult a veterinarian or a veterinary nutritionist on the appropriate breakdown of protein, vegetables, and grain and any other vitamins or minerals that need to be added. When planning your pet's meals, be sure to know what foods your pet shouldn't eat, such as milk and onions. You don't need to spend hours slaving over a dinner for your pet, either. Some animals, like dogs, can handle eating raw meat without problems. If you would like to switch your pet to a homemade diet, do it gradually, just as if you were changing commercial pet foods.

Bedding and Other Gear

Bedding can be made from organic cotton or hemp stuffed with recycled polyester. Beds need to be washed, not just to clean up the dirt and hair but to help with flea control. Toys made from organic and recycled materials are also on the market. Cat trees are now made from reclaimed untreated wood, giving indoor cats a real tree to perch on.

Training agents can be environmentally friendly, too. Grannick's Bitter Apple manufactures products to keep dogs, cats, birds, ferrets, horses, and small animals from chewing on things they shouldn't—from your furniture to themselves. The Bitter Apple product line is nontoxic and biodegradable. It works by giving a bitter taste to the items you use it on, thus discouraging your pet from chewing. Clean up after your pet with odor- and stain-control solutions that use natural ingredients. To disperse pet odors, Earth Care markets its Clear the Air product, which does just that.

Is it safe to use human shampoo on animals?
There are shampoos made specifically for pets, but using a mild or baby shampoo on your pet may work just as well as fancy products just for pets. Consult with your veterinarian or a groomer; they'll know best. In any case, your pet does not need to bathe nearly as often as you do. Washing your pet too frequently will dry its skin, resulting in an itchy and miserable companion.

There are organic shampoos and skin treatments available that use organic, biodegradable ingredients. The popularity of the green movement along with the desire to pamper pets has led to a market for organic grooming products.

The Scoop on Poop

Poop management for domesticated animals is more of an issue with dogs and cats than others. That being said, bird owners and small animal owners can take advantage of biodegradable bedding and poop-remover sprays.

What to Do with Doggie Doo

Many cities have laws requiring dog owners to pick up after their pets when walking in someone else's yard or in a public place. This reduces the possibility of stepping in something unpleasant; more important, the laws help control levels of bacteria in the ground and water.

Droppings left on the roads or sidewalks can be washed directly into storm sewers that drain into lakes and ponds. When pet waste washes into a body of water, it causes an increase in fecal bacteria, which is a health threat to humans and animals and also sets in motion a potentially dangerous chain reaction. Nutrients like nitrogen released from fecal bacteria encourage weed and algae growth. The excessive growth limits the amount of sunlight able to penetrate the surface, which kills aquatic vegetation below. Those plants provide dissolved oxygen to the environment and serve as nurseries to fish populations. Without them, the ecosystem can be thrown into disarray.

The best solution for picking up an animal's droppings is to use a biodegradable bag. That way, when it's disposed, the bag will degrade along with the droppings. You can find them at pet stores and at many gathering spots like doggie parks and campgrounds.

Small backyard dog waste digesters like Doggie Dooley—✎*www.dog giedooley.com*—have been developed as alternative solutions for disposing of animal waste.

Some cities, like San Francisco, are developing ways to make the most of dog feces by converting it into methane that can be used for fuel. The city partnered with Norcal Waste Systems to collect waste from a dog park in San Francisco for a pilot program in 2006. Norcal fed the feces into a methane digester. Some dairy operations use similar digesters, feeding cow dung into the digester to convert it into methane to supply electricity.

What's in the Box?

Along with building a better mousetrap, people are always trying to come up with a better litter box. Even when cleaned regularly, they can smell and are usually surrounded by litter that's been tossed about by kitty. Manufacturers churn out new and improved litter boxes to reduce the hassle of cleaning up after your cat, but not all of the newest fads are really good, especially for kittens. Clumping kitty litter does make cleaning easier, but it will expand if ingested. Because of their curiosity, kittens nibble the litter, making them particularly vulnerable. This can cause vomiting or blockage of their digestive systems.

Most kitty litters are made from clay that is mined, and any mining operations are hard on the earth. Regardless of the reclamation performed, the land can never be returned to pristine conditions once the mining is complete. Mining operations disrupt the land surface by removing all the trees and the topsoil, rerouting storm water onto and off of the site. They generate waste, which can include the release of metal contamination into the groundwater. Silica dust is produced during mining and in the litter box. Silica from the clay litter has been known to cause silicosis, a chronic and sometimes fatal lung disease.

Alternatives for filling the cat box include biodegradable litter. Green options include litter made from recycled paper or reclaimed wood. Not only do these litters avoid mining operations, they utilize postconsumer waste that would otherwise be sent to a landfill. If you are planning to switch your kitty to biodegradable or recycled litter, you may need to do it gradually, adding a little at a time so as not to confuse the cat.

If you want a break from the box, tackle toilet training for your cat. The switch begins with moving the litter box next to the toilet, gradually raising it using books or boxes until it's the same height as the toilet. Eventually move the litter box, or a modified version of it, into the toilet. Then take the litter box away and voilà!

Health Care

Just as with human doctors, it's important to make sure you see eye to eye with your veterinarian. Some pet owners are very happy with traditional vets while others seek the extended services of a holistic practitioner. Holistic vets have degrees in traditional veterinary medicine but take additional course work in more natural approaches to healing and helping animals.

Holistic medicine is generally used to treat chronic conditions, not traumatic injuries. Vets that use holistic methods still employ traditional approaches such as vaccinations, x-rays, and pharmaceuticals. But they also look at the whole animal and consider other treatments when healing or improving the condition of a patient, including diet and emotional well-being. Holistic vets also look at alternative medicines such as the following:

- Acupuncture
- Behavior modification

- Chiropractic therapy
- Herbal remedies
- Homeopathy
- Nutritional therapy

When it comes to other aspects of pet care such as flea control, owners should make sure they are on the same page as their vet in looking for solutions that everyone feels comfortable with.

Options for Flea Control

If you bring home a dog or a cat, there will have to be decisions on flea control, for everyone's sake. Fleas can irritate a pet's skin, which can result in open sores and hair loss. Battling fleas and flea bites makes life hard on pets and their owners.

Adult fleas feed on the blood of pets—and possibly on people living in the house as well. They're strong and gravity has little impact on them; they're able to jump sideways as far as five feet and straight up as high as nine inches.

There are a plethora of synthetic chemicals on the market to help owners wage war on fleas. These dips, sprays, and topical ointments all contain pesticides that are absorbed into a pet's body through their skin. Fleas are able to build up a resistance to these chemicals, requiring new formulas to be produced. While these flea treatments work very well in most cases, they can pose a danger to the pet and possibly even others in the house. Potential risks of flea treatment can be researched on the EPA Web site (*www. epa.gov/pesticides/factsheets/flea-tick.htm*), which contains fact sheets for a variety of active ingredients.

There are organic pesticides available to control fleas. Even though they are derived naturally, they may still pose a threat and not be acceptable to some. Pyrethrin derivatives are made from chrysanthemums and are used to make dips and sprays. According to the EPA, they are the least toxic pesticide to mammals. There was some concern that they may cause cancer, but so far there is no data to support this idea. However, they have been shown to cause skin and breathing problems in some cases. While they do break down in nature, they are highly toxic to fish.

Diatomaceous earth is fossilized algae that have turned to dust. Used in powder form, the sharp edges of the fine particles cut into the flea's exoskeleton, causing it to dehydrate and die. Because of the fine particles, take care to keep both people and pets from breathing in the dust. This powder can be used directly on the pet, as well as on bedding and furniture.

You can set flea traps by placing a soapy dish of water under a light. The fleas will be attracted to the warmth and will drown in the soapy water. Also, when combing out pets, keep a cup of soapy water handy. Pull fleas off the comb and drop them into the water; the soap makes it difficult or impossible for the fleas to escape, leaving the tiny biters in a watery grave.

Letting Them Go

Animals that have been domesticated, even if they were born in the wild, may not fare well on their own. Domesticated animals exist in a world without predators and with a constant food supply. Putting them out on their own leaves them at risk. Without care, many released animals will likely starve, fall prey to predators, be hit by cars, or die from disease.

Released animals that survive can wreak havoc on their new surroundings. The introduction of a new species upsets the local balance already in place between animals and the environment. In south Florida, the wild Burmese python population has exploded. Growing upward of 20 feet and weighing in at 200 pounds, these reptiles now rival the alligator for the top spot in the Everglades food chain and may be vying for food and territory with the eastern indigo snake, a threatened species.

FACT

In October 2005 wildlife officials in the Everglades National Park found a 13-foot-long python that bit off more than he could handle when he tried to down a 6-foot alligator. The python's girth wasn't big enough and it literally burst at the seams. Neither the alligator nor the python survived.

The same goes for aquatics that are released from their fish tanks into wild waters. One of the most threatening is the snakehead. Snakeheads are non-native air-breathing freshwater fish that are making homes in lakes all over the United States. This fish is very aggressive, particularly when protecting its young. As a species, it is predatory and capable of eating other fish, birds, and mammals. It also carries diseases to which native fish have no built-in resistance. Its ability to breathe air makes it capable of surviving for days out of water or buried in the mud.

If a new home is needed for a pet companion, owners should work to find one. Vets and local rescue organizations can sometimes help find pets new homes.

Chapter 15

Green and Jolly Holidays and Celebrations

Holidays give people the chance to express gratitude, share each other's company, eat well, and occasionally take time off from work or school. No matter what the holiday, it's likely to come with pressures to shop, decorate, give gifts, and feed friends and family. But before getting caught up in the holiday hype, take a step back and think about what the occasion really means—and how you can celebrate without doing too much damage to the planet.

The Planet's Very Own Holiday

Hundreds and thousands of years ago, holidays and celebrations were defined by the time of year. Autumn was a time to celebrate the changing of the seasons, the bounty of the fall harvest, and the potential discomfort of a long, dark, and cold winter. Holidays noted pinnacle times and transitions. Spring brought with it a release from winter chill in exchange for brighter and longer days and the start of planting.

The 1970s saw the advent of a new holiday that helped solidify the environmental movement. The annual planetary celebration was dubbed Earth Day. Gaylord Nelson, a Democratic senator from Wisconsin, started the holiday. Growing up in northwestern Wisconsin, Nelson enjoyed exploring the outdoors, and as a senator, one of his speaking points was the environment. Nelson strongly believed that the environment—and the impact people had on it—was not receiving the attention it deserved. He worked with President John F. Kennedy, who shared his belief, even doing a conservation tour in 1963. Still unable to get a foothold in the political movement, environmental concerns were perpetually relegated to the backseat as other pressing issues gained recognition.

During the summer of 1969, Nelson was speaking about conservation and witnessed the energy of antiwar-demonstration teach-ins. He knew then that if he could harness similar enthusiasm for the environment, his battle to protect the planet would be successful. He organized a day of observance for environmental issues—April 22, 1970. In preparing for the event, the media and other politicians clamored to be involved, helping to make it a day like no other and striking the match that would fuel the environmental movement.

Today Earth Day is celebrated in a variety of ways, from community events and parades to political gatherings. Many use the day to promote environmental issues such as sustainable living and global climate change. The Earth Day Network (*www.earthday.net*) includes a list of celebrations and some great ideas for organizing an event.

Greening Your Holidays

One trait many holidays have in common is the pressure exerted by marketers and manufacturers to shop until you drop. People are encouraged to show caring by spending money on friends and family. Not only is money not analogous with love and care, it can be wasteful to your wallet and the environment. There are ways to enjoy the season—no matter what's being celebrated—and reduce the environmental impact, too.

The Holiday Season

The holiday season conjures up images of blinking lights, crowded shopping malls, and lots and lots of presents. The term usually refers to that stretch on the calendar between Thanksgiving and New Year's Day that includes a variety of different celebrations. It's a time of year that marks the viability of the economy. Forecasts for holiday shopping start in the fall, and data on how much shoppers spent ring in the New Year. But are shopping and spending really such a good idea?

ALERT!

According to *42 Ways to Trim Your Holiday Wasteline*, written by Robert Lilienfield and Dr. William Rathje, the authors of the *ULS Report* (✎*www.use-less-stuff.com*), 25 percent more trash is tossed during the holiday and shopping season than at any other time of year. When it comes to season's greetings, 2.65 million holiday cards are sold each year. That's enough to fill a football stadium ten stories tall. It's not humbug to practice conservation and reduce your mailing list.

The holidays bring families and friends together, but there is a lot of stress over excess spending, hectic schedules, and the potential to overindulge on just about everything. The holidays also generate a lot of waste. If you want to scale back, you don't need to change years of tradition, but a little cutting equals less environmental impact.

When looking at ways to simplify, consider starting with decorations. If your family purchases a Christmas tree, a living tree might be a good choice.

Living trees can be purchased and planted when the holidays are over. Buying an artificial tree means it can be used over and over again. If you don't have a place to plant a living tree but want the authenticity of a real tree, make sure to recycle your cut tree.

When you put up ornaments, let the tree show. If some needles show after all the ornaments are hung, that's okay. Not every branch needs to be glittering and sparkly. If you need more ornaments, consider making them from recycled materials. There are tons of Web sites and library books with great ideas for ornaments, and if you remember to date your new ornaments, you can look back and reminisce every year.

QUESTION?

How do I change traditions?
Changes to your family's customs and traditions don't have to happen all at once. Little changes add up over time. Make sure to explain what you'd like to do and why. Include your family and ask for their suggestions, too. You can use one suggestion from each member.

When lighting up inside or out, lower-wattage lights can bring about the same glitter and gleam without the expense. Not only do smaller lights burn less electricity, they produce less heat, making them safer. Light-emitting diode (LED) holiday lights are new on the scene. They cost about $8 more than a standard strand but will last up to ten years and use less electricity. Remember to put your lights on a timer so they automatically shut off. Here's where a little procrastination can pay off—the later you wait to put them up, the less time they'll be using extra energy.

When it comes to partying, consider swapping cookies instead of gifts. If you plan a cookie exchange, have guests share stories about their recipes. Was it a hand-me-down from a beloved aunt or a brand-new recipe from an easy-cooking guide? Some hosts ask guests to bring a dozen cookies for each guest, but you can adjust the numbers as you like. Your flexibility and creativity as a host will foster a festive atmosphere for everyone.

Once the last present is unwrapped and the last guest leaves, it's time to clean up. Make sure to keep the reusable items like decorations and table settings. Pack them with newspaper and shredded junk mail. Keep any cards that can be used next year.

Halloween

It's a scary time of year filled with costumes and candy. The costume market has exploded as children and grownups dress like their favorite movie and television characters. But before splurging on a costume that may only be worn once, consider what's in the closet. See if there is anything that can be modified and mixed up to be used as a costume. Leftover 1980s clothes or an old sport coat can be the beginning of a retro-theme costume. Overalls and a plaid shirt can be the basis for a farm or scarecrow costume. A common theme for teens is dead anything—from a dead prom queen to a dead baseball player. All it takes is an old dress or uniform and some scissors and makeup. If your closets aren't serving up any costume ideas, visit a local consignment shop.

Whatever costume you use, however, be sure to keep it when the trick-or-treating is over. For kids, old costumes can be kept in dress-up bins and trunks. Grownups can mix and match or even swap costumes down the road.

Scary jack-o'-lanterns yield a lot of waste. Don't throw your pumpkin's guts away after you're done carving. Use the meat to make muffins or a pie; the seeds are delicious baked and salted for snacks. When the jack-o'-lantern has seen his last day, you can also toss him on the compost pile instead of throwing him to the curb.

This may sound cheap, but don't go overboard giving out candy. It's rare for kids to go home without candy spilling out of their buckets and bags. More candy given out means more candy bought, and the more candy bought means the more candy made and the more waste produced. Depending on how much trick-or-treating traffic you have, you may be stuck with leftovers. Consider donating candy to a shelter or keep it for another holiday down the road. If sealed well or frozen, candy can keep for months.

Greeting Cards

It's more of a tradition with winter holidays, but that doesn't stop stationers from promoting more and more special-occasion cards. Forgo the Halloween and St. Patrick's Day cards altogether if you're seeking to be greener, or consider sending e-cards to friends and family.

Holiday cards don't have to be thrown as away as soon the occasion passes. They can be made into a variety of useful items. Fronts can be reused to make new cards, bookmarks, gift tags, and lace-up toys.

If sending cards or holiday letters just isn't a tradition you are willing to give up, consider sending only a letter. Use hand stamps to make it festive. Another alternative is to purchase cards from your favorite charity. Choose an organization that sends a message you support and uses recycled materials.

Gifts

Gifts are integral to most holidays and special occasions, but take a minute to think before you purchase. Don't buy a token gift that will soon be forgotten just because you feel obligated. Think about what resources it took to make and package the gift and what will become of it after the special day. It's not that you should feel guilty when making a purchase, but it is worth considering where it came from, where it will go, and how it fits into the whole scheme of things.

To Buy or Not to Buy

Gifts made with love can be particularly sweet. Knowing someone made homemade soap or jewelry really adds a personal touch to the holiday or occasion. When shopping, eliminate or reduce the number of plastic bags you bring home. Take along your own bags or double up your purchases by putting them in bags you already have from other stores.

Consider gifts of entertainment or endowment. Tickets to a stage show, sporting event, or a movie don't require excess packaging or wrapping. An evening out might be the perfect gift. Donations to a favorite charity are something to think about, too. A commemorative brick or the care and feeding of a sea bird may be a very special gift for someone who has everything.

When buying a gift, shop green. Look for items that encourage conservation and sustainable living. There are plenty of Web sites promoting sustainable products. Consider buying friends and family canvas bags to take shopping or items made from recycled materials like street signs or old album covers. Chances are there won't be any awkward duplicates with unique recycled gifts.

Do a good deed. Instead of buying a gift for neighbors or relatives, do something nice. Rake their lawn, shovel their sidewalk, or take on another chore. This is particularly nice if they really don't want anything. Some people would rather not be given gifts that they must find a place for or figure out what to do with. This is the perfect opportunity to make frozen meals, put together an emergency kit, give a gift certificate for a nearby grocery store, or make a gift basket of essentials like stamps, envelopes, and pens. Don't forget about photos—put them in a small book or on a magnet or mug.

Look around you. Is there something you have that you know someone would enjoy receiving? Give a decorative bowl from your own hutch or a book from your bookshelf to make a nice gift. This makes for a great opportunity to re-gift too. If you can't return a gift, leave it boxed up and go shopping in your closet the next time you need a gift (no wallet required).

It's a Wrap

You've picked out the perfect gift. Now what? Consider a reusable bag or box to wrap the present. For paper options, try comics, maps, coloring pages, or wrapping made from recycled paper. Use scarves to secure a gift. The wrapping can even be part of the gift, using containers like flower pots and dishes. For gift tags, cut up used greeting or holiday cards so the art on the card serves as the front of the gift tag and write a message on the back. If there is writing on the back, just glue a piece of paper with your message over it.

Wrapping presents has been a custom since the Chinese invented paper making in A.D. 105 In the United States, tissue paper was routinely used to wrap presents. In 1917, the Hall brothers ran out of the traditional tissue paper and sold decorative envelope liners for wrapping presents instead. The idea obviously caught on.

When sending gifts, try to reuse shipping materials like padded envelopes, cartons, and peanuts, and think about how the gift will be sent when you're shopping for it. Smaller and lighter may be easier and greener to package and send. If the gift is staying local, avoid wrapping altogether. Hide the gift and send the recipient on a scavenger hunt to retrieve it.

Entertaining

Entertaining can vary from an extended visit from out-of-town friends and family to a fancy one-night shindig. If the evening requires entertaining a large group of people, turn the heat down before your guests arrive. Lots of people in the house create a lot of body heat.

Depending on the theme, consider whether decorating is necessary. If you do need some zing, make your decorations. Create banners from recycled newsprint. Homemade banners are much more personal than mass-produced ones, and large rolls of recycled newsprint can be used for the banner and then reused as drawing paper throughout the year. One way to make birthday-party decorations more special is to make a photo collage of the birthday celebrant.

Conservative Cooking

It might be difficult to think of ways to conserve when planning a party. No one wants to look like a Scrooge or a tightfisted host. Consider cutting behind-the-scenes corners that will conserve energy, natural resources, and money.

Don't overcook. Meals should be planned according to the guest list. Consider who will eat what and what portions are appropriate. Don't feel obligated to offer guests every potential appetizer or entrée under the sun. There's no need to overfeed guests either. The holiday season is a time most people struggle with temptations and add extra pounds, so eliminating enticements may not be such a bad idea.

The *ULS Report* includes serving recommendations for traditional holiday dinners. A twelve- to fourteen-pound turkey should serve up to ten people. Each person is likely to eat a quarter-pound of stuffing, green beans, and sweet potato casserole, but don't expect them to eat any more than three tablespoons of cranberry relish.

Don't throw leftovers away. Send them home with guests, pack them into your own refrigerator or freezer, or donate them to a shelter. Turkey carcasses and ham bones make for great soup. If there is a whole pie or untouched leftover, donate it to a local food bank. If leftovers outlive their useful life in the fridge, add them to the compost bin. However, meat and processed foods are not good for a compost bin if it is not rat proof.

Dishing It Out

It may mean extra work for you, but think about hosting the event with reusable dishes instead of disposable dishes. If it's a particularly formal event, borrow or rent dishes rather than buy them. When washing up after the affair, fully load the dishwasher to get the most out of the hot water. Put out separate bins for recyclables and label them so guests know where to toss their glass, plastic, and aluminum.

Chapter 16

Green Learning and Working

Working full-time, people put in about 2,000 hours a year at their jobs. With that amount of time, some people believe it is important to have a job that is rewarding to them and to the environment. The U.S. Department of Labor projects that the growth of careers in the environmental field, particularly hydrology and environmental engineering, will increase over the next decade and salaries will be competitive with other careers. More and more universities and colleges offer courses and degrees in environmental fields. This chapter gives a rundown on different green careers and educational paths.

Green Fields of Study

The variety of jobs available in the environmental field range from those requiring bachelor's degrees and above to those that provide on-the-job training. Environmental careers can involve highly technical desk jobs or active work out in the field. When looking for a job, consider what you want to do and how you want to spend your time. Do you want to interact with the public or to be outside? Is designing environmental systems for landfills, water-treatment plants, or even manufacturing facilities more up your alley? The field is awash with job opportunities—so much so that deciding on a career will likely be more difficult than landing a job.

Choosing a Major

Choosing a major goes hand in hand with choosing a career. Although some students may decide on a major without a thorough understanding of the jobs available, others will decide what job they want and determine what degree is needed to get there. Some professions can be achieved with a variety of degrees, but others require very specific degrees and training. For example, conservation specialists may have a degree in biology or environmental science. On the other hand, an engineer needs to have a degree in engineering. Also, some degrees provide stepping stones to other careers. A person with an engineering degree can work as a regulator, and that may lead to a career in politics down the road. Not everyone entering a university knows exactly what career path he or she will follow, but students can analyze their interests, passions, and talents to decide on a career path.

Picking a University

Choosing a university to attend should be based on the area of study. When considering a university or college, look at all the programs the school offers and what kind of jobs graduates find. If you plan on earning a master's or doctorate, take into account how well the undergraduate program has prepared past graduates. Make sure the program is accredited; this may directly impact your job opportunities, advanced degrees, and any certification or licensure you need.

The Environmental Education Directory at *www.enviroeducation.com* has a searchable database for numerous fields of environmental study. The database includes a list of learning institutions from colleges and universities to more specialized centers such as the Audubon Expedition Institute run through Lesley University. If you are interested in graduate school, look at *www.gradschools.com* for lists of programs and universities leading to advanced degrees in environmental fields.

College or university degrees aren't the only way to get started in the environmental field. The Wilderness Awareness School in Duvall, Washington, provides courses of study in nature awareness, tracking and mammal studies, and even wilderness survival. Many colleges and other institutions offer classes on campus and through distance learning.

Beyond obtaining a degree, you may want to consider how the university or learning institution you plan to attend operates when it comes to environmental responsibility. Universities and colleges function as microcosms of larger communities, with planning departments that must consider the same issues as cities and towns. A benefit for universities is that they have access to researchers and professionals in innovative fields that can influence campuses to test and utilize environmentally friendly and sustainable practices.

FACT

The EPA works with universities and other organizations to purchase electricity from sustainable resources as part of its Green Power Partnership. In January 2007, the EPA reported that New York University, the University of California at Santa Cruz, Western Washington University, and the University of Central Oklahoma each purchased 100 percent of their electricity from sustainable resources.

Universities and colleges rely on master plans that identify different operations—including transportation, waste generation and handling, and heating and cooling—and specify how they will be implemented. By incorporating environmental stewardship in preparing a master plan, these schools not only set examples but provide hands-on experience for students to take with them after they graduate.

Master plans may incorporate sustainable considerations as the university ages and expands, constructing new buildings and refurbishing older ones. When building new facilities, does the school administration encourage energy-efficient design? Is the equipment used by the administration, faculty, staff, and students energy-efficient?

You may want to find out how waste is handled at the universities that interest you and if recycling programs are in place. Many schools of higher learning maintain their own incinerators, particularly if biomedical wastes are generated. If this is the case, ask if the university operates the incinerator as a cogeneration plan, providing electricity and hot water for the campus, and if the air emissions meet required standards.

QUESTION?

How can I determine how environmentally friendly colleges and universities are?

If you are interested in a particular institution, go to its Web site and search for information on its environmental stewardship. If you don't have any one college or university in mind, check out Princeton Review's *Colleges with a Conscience*, a broad reference book that highlights select institutions for their social awareness, including their commitment to the environment.

Another aspect you may want to consider is transportation. Many campuses provide shuttle services from off-campus locations. Switching to hybrid or biodiesel can increase the benefits of these shuttle services. Also, universities purchase many cars to be used by faculty and staff. When buying cars, does the university consider energy efficiency? Universities should purchase fuel-efficient or hybrid cars and discourage excessive driving.

Environmental Professions

There are a variety of jobs that revolve around the environment. Many involve ensuring compliance with environmental regulations and laws through proper design, operation, or enforcement. Others are more involved in specifically protecting and improving the environment.

While some occupations are inherently environmental, other careers—such as engineering, science, writing, public administration, and law—can have an environmental facet. Some jobs, like park rangers or camp counselors, allow workers to spend time outside and possibly educate others in learning about the environment, while other positions require most of the work to be done in the office with little interaction with nature.

Don't confuse the terms *environmental* and *environmentalist*. Many jobs that involve working with or for the environment do not frequently endorse ardent environmentalism. Environmental jobs usually require a balance between politics, people, costs, and the environment and do not strictly advocate environmental protection or even conservation. Before choosing a career, talk to someone in the field to make sure the job is what you think it is.

A big part of deciding what career path to follow is what the job will entail. Here are just a few of the different environmental professions out there.

- **Environmental engineers** design and permit all different types of environmental operations, including water treatment plants, wastewater treatment plants, solid waste facilities, and water and wastewater collection and distribution systems. Engineers can also design remediation systems to clean contaminated soil and groundwater. Engineers can work for federal, state, or local regulators overseeing operations in their district. They can also work in the private sector for consulting firms whose clients include cities and counties with environmental projects and operations.

- **Environmental journalists** research and write on environmental topics. They can work for nonprofit groups or media outlets as media consultants or correspondents. It is their responsibility as environmental journalists to be objective and present facts, not simply to promote propaganda or someone else's agenda. This requires an understanding of the topic, and the journalist must interview various professionals with different perspectives.

- **Geologists and hydrologists** work for industries and regulatory agencies independently as consultants. They use their knowledge of the subsurface to evaluate groundwater quality and availability. In areas where groundwater is the primary source of drinking water, geologists and hydrologists determine impacts from overpumping and look to alternative supplies. In industry, they often work with mining and oil corporations. When groundwater has been contaminated, geologists and hydrologists assess the degree and extent of contamination.

- **Ecologists** often advise groups that want to construct projects for potential environmental effects of the development. They survey areas, determining what species of flora and fauna exist and what impacts a project would have on the populations. They can work to eliminate negative impacts and suggest alternate approaches or supplemental work to enhance a project.

- **Toxicologists** work to protect the public from environmental impacts. Many circumstances arise where chemicals are released, exposing the public. It's the job of a toxicologist to evaluate the impact of those releases. Often, this is performed through a risk assessment through which the toxicologist calculates the possibility that a given contaminant at a given concentration will cause a disease. Toxicologists often work in the chemical and pharmaceutical industries and for regulatory agencies.

- **Conservation scientists** work to protect natural resources like soil, rangeland, and water. They develop plans and make recommendations to allow use of the natural resources with the least amount of environmental impact. With respect to soil, a conservation scientist might recommend ways to reduce erosion. With water, the scientist evaluates how to protect quality while providing drinking water to the public.

- **Foresters** usually work with private timber companies or landowners, making sure that regulations are met when wood is harvested. They also work to encourage the healthy growth of forests and make recommendations when alternative operations or equipment should be considered.

- **Environmental lawyers** work for regulators, private industry, and activist organizations to interpret the meaning and applicability of environmental laws. It is not uncommon to see environmental lawyers on either side of a dispute, representing clients charged with polluting the environment and regulators that want the situation corrected. In working with activist organizations, lawyers often press the government to enhance enforcement actions or pass stricter legislation.

- **Urban and regional planners** work to balance the needs of a community. They must take into account growth and expanded infrastructure, such as water and wastewater facilities. Most planners work for local government agencies and are required to attend public meetings.

- **Wildlife biologists** study how animals live in either human-made or natural environments. Their roles may be similar to or overlap with ecologists. Wildlife biologists can be employed to determine what animals exist in a certain area and how changes may impact their populations. This is of particular importance in areas where endangered or threatened species exist.

- **Solid waste managers** work for cities and counties and handle issues with garbage collection and disposal. They usually work with outside consultants to help design transfer stations, landfills, and incinerators while making sure regulations are met. Solid waste managers educate the public in matters of disposal practices and recycling and can be key players in determining economical ways to recycle and discourage waste.

- **Wastewater treatment plant operators** run facilities that treat sewage. Sewage is processed through a plant where waste is collected and removed. The end result is treated water and sludge, a mud-like material that requires proper disposal. Properly run wastewater treatment plants abide by federal and state regulations. Treated water is often discharged to bays or rivers, while sludge is taken to a landfill or—depending on contaminant concentrations—used as fertilizer for farming operations.

- **Park rangers** operate parks, ensuring that the environment and wildlife are in good condition, and they also work to educate the public. They maintain facilities and make sure they are safe for animals as well as the people who visit. Some rangers with wildlife rehabilitation facilities provide a place for rehabilitating and releasing injured animals.

The Internet offers a variety of Web sites that provide information on different environmental careers and job openings. Check out Green Dream Jobs at *www.sustainablebusiness.com* or the Environmental Career Center at *www.environmentalcareer.com*.

Environmental Regulators

Environmental protection starts with the government, which oversees programs on the federal, state, and local levels. Regulators enforce environmental laws and supervise operations and situations to determine how the environment is being impacted, to what extent, and what remedial actions are needed.

The EPA employs scientists, engineers, policy analysts, and lawyers. Not only does this agency help to enact and enforce environmental laws, it performs research and prepares policy. The EPA is responsible for protecting human health and the environment by supporting laws and defending and maintaining the quality of the air, water, and land.

The U.S. Fish and Wildlife Service monitors and enforces illegal trade, habitat destruction, and environmental contamination of wildlife habitats. Through its office of law enforcement, it works to protect endangered and threatened species by monitoring trade routes and breaking up illegal trade rings; using forensic technologies to investigate crimes involving wildlife; training other federal, state, and local agencies; and distributing information to educate the public. It also works to combat invasive species and restore native habitats.

FACT

Many federal government employers categorize positions by General Schedule (GS) levels. Job openings are identified by GS level, so when applying for a position, you may be asked to supply your GS level. If you've never been employed by the federal government, you won't have a GS level and will have to estimate your own level based on categorical information provided by the agency.

The U.S. Department of State heads the Office of Environmental Policy, which works on a global level to institute policy geared toward worldwide impacts on air quality, toxic chemicals and pesticides, hazardous waste, conversion of critical habitat, and invasive species. This multilateral department works with organizations such as the United Nations and World Bank to develop policies that will protect the environment and afford sustainability for all cultures. While not an enforcement agency, the State Department works with other nations to ensure that the environment is protected by following agreed-upon policies.

Other departments and agencies that dabble in the environment include the U.S. Department of Energy and the Office of Energy Efficiency and Renewable Energy (*www.eere.energy.gov*). These offices administer alternative energy programs and provide information to consumers and businesses on solar, biomass, and other renewable options.

States operate their own environmental programs if their laws meet or exceed federal legislation. Many states have their own environmental protection division, public health department, and wildlife commission.

Working for state or even local agencies includes inspecting facilities for environmental compliance, reviewing permit applications and issuing permits, and even educating the public on environmentally sound practices. Facilities likely to be permitted and inspected include water treatment plants, landfills and incinerators, and industries.

Environmental Research

The federal government employs environmental researchers in many areas. These workers do not enforce environmental laws or regulations but work to collect, analyze, and maintain data for regulators and the public, as well as invent greener chemicals and materials. There are a variety of organizations and agencies within the government that perform research used to promote and protect the environment.

The U.S. Centers for Disease Control and Prevention (CDC) work to protect the public from environmental impacts. The CDC address health concerns regarding air and water quality as well as exposure to toxic chemicals. The National Center for Environmental Health (NCEH) is a program within the CDC that works to eliminate illness, disease, and death from environmental impacts.

Different departments operate independently, but government jobs generally provide excellent benefits. While the pay may not be as high as in the private sector, the benefits may just make up for the disparity in wages.

The National Oceanic and Atmospheric Administration (NOAA) carries out research to better understand the oceans and coasts and promote ecosystem-based management of natural resources. The organization conducts experiments to research natural processes, develops models to predict environmental outcomes, determines methods to collect and analyze data, prepares assessments for the public, and assists the government with policy management. NOAA is a key player in predicting the dangers of global climate change and evaluating corrective measures needed to slow and reverse the trend.

Even the U.S. Department of Transportation, an agency that may not spring to mind when considering environmental opportunities, operates the

Federal Highway Administration (FHWA), which works in part to encourage nonmotorized means of transportation. The FHWA is currently working on a nonmotorized transportation pilot program in four communities: Columbia, Missouri; Marin County, California; Minneapolis-St. Paul, Minnesota; and Sheboygan County, Wisconsin. The program aims to encourage biking and walking by building sidewalks and bicycle paths to and from highly trafficked areas such as transit stations, workplaces, schools, residential areas, and community centers. The information gathered during the program will be used to provide state and local agencies with means to increase nonmotorized transportation.

Working for a Nonprofit

There are nongovernmental organizations that work to address environmental issues, largely when they feel that the government is not doing enough or that their hands are tied. Although their relationships with governmental agencies may sometimes be adversarial, nonprofits also provide important information to the government to direct policy.

FACT

The Career Center at Action Without Borders collects information on nonprofit employment opportunities all over the world. You can visit their Web site at ✑*www.idealist.org* and check out employment and internship opportunities with nonprofits. The site also includes links to salary surveys and nonprofit career fairs.

Earth Share is an umbrella network that includes leading environmental and conservation groups across the United States. Charity Navigator (*www.charitynavigator.org*) awarded Earth Share four stars, the highest rating for a charitable organization. Not all charities that fall under the auspices of Earth Share have received four-star ratings, so do background work on the ones that interest you.

Here are a few of the charities included under the Earth Share umbrella:

- **Natural Resources Defense Council** utilizes skilled lawyers and scientists to promote activism and evaluate political policies and legislation.
- **Clean Water Fund** investigates and reports on water quality issues. A report prepared by the group in 2006 titled *Are We Still Wading in Waste?* documented how wastewater treatment plants report spills into waterways.
- **Union of Concerned** Scientists works to protect the environment and public health by promoting the use of valid and accurate science.
- **Nature Conservancy** uses a planned methodology to select important environmental properties and works with landowners to purchase them for protection. The organization also provides funds for areas to be studied to determine the environmental impact from different operations.
- **Rainforest Alliance** works with companies, cooperatives, and landowners to protect ecosystems and the people and animals that depend on them.

There are vast numbers of nonprofits out there. Some nonprofits offer unpaid internships that enable students to receive college credit and gain valuable experience.

Local Environmental Programs

Many communities or community colleges offer courses in ecology, energy efficiency, waste management, and other topics that impact your life. You can take advantage of these opportunities to learn how the different systems coexist and what impacts them the most.

Learn It

Many communities offer programs for their citizens to learn about different aspects of services provided in their area. You can take tours of solid waste facilities, water and wastewater treatment plants, and even power sub-stations. Participating in these programs will enlighten you about how your city or town operates. It's likely that the tour guide may also interject some insight into funding and operational issues, providing you with some background on the politics involved as well. If your community does not offer these informal classes, consider suggesting it. Speak with city or county commissioners or even the mayor.

If you want to learn about both sides of an issue, consider taking a field trip to the wastewater treatment plant to learn where its water is discharged and the problems it faces to ensure quality. Then kayak or canoe down the same river with an environmental group and learn the impacts from the wastewater discharge.

Local parks, outfitters, environmental groups, and community colleges also offer environmental courses and programs. These can range from exploring the different ecosystems in the area, such as tidal communities, to hiking through a nature preserve to observe the wildlife in local hardwood forests.

Teach It

If you have experience in promoting the environment, you can use it to teach others. Share your knowledge and passion with others and introduce them to topics they may not have known about.

If you operate a manufacturing facility that incorporates recycling, give a tour and let the public know. Not only will it educate the public on the importance of recycling, it can serve as an advertisement, too. If you are a skilled outdoors person, give a lecture or lead an expedition. It doesn't have to be complicated or dangerous, just down-to-earth and sufficient for a layperson to enjoy and learn more.

Chapter 17

The Green Office

Whether you're the sole employee of a business run out of your own home or operate a corporation employing hundreds of workers, you can take actions to make your place of business more environmentally friendly. Not only will walking on the green side likely save money, it is a business practice that can be used to promote your company to customers and potential employees. This chapter will give you a rundown on how your business can lessen the impact it has on the planet.

Your Company, Your Image

No matter what kind of business you operate, you can run it more efficiently and look for ways to green things up a bit. Any changes you intend to implement will more than likely require a formal plan or program or, at a minimum, a memo (preferably an electronic one to keep the use of paper to a minimum). Although some programs may have a cost associated with getting them up and running, once started they will most likely save energy or the environment and wind up reducing operating costs as well. In addition, businesses can promote their green actions to potential customers and future employees.

There are ways to make the service you provide or the product you make greener. If you are constructing a new building or renovating an older one, look at the Green Building Council's (GBC's) Leadership in Energy and Environmental Design (LEED) rating system. Your project may be certified in at least one of five areas, allowing building owners to display their certification and possibly receive incentives. If you manufacture a product, consider revising operations to meet the criteria for fair or organic trade. Pacific Natural Foods—an Oregon-based company whose product line includes soups, broths, beverages, and ready-made meals—shows its commitment to environmental responsibility in its procurement and packaging efforts. Although Pacific Natural Foods are sold throughout the United States, the company tries to get its ingredients from local farms to reduce the amount of fossil fuels required to ship the food. The company also works diligently with manufacturers to reduce waste and design the most efficient and environmentally friendly packaging.

FACT

The federal government began constructing LEED-certified buildings in the 1990s; the private sector soon followed. Proper and efficient lighting is one of the LEED design goals, and it makes good business sense, too. A 1999 report prepared by Pacific Gas & Electric showed that stores with skylights report a 40 percent increase in sales, and employees who work in buildings with increased lighting control are 7 percent more productive.

Not only does certification let others know that business owners care about the environment, it sets an example for other businesses. Apply for any awards that might be available locally or statewide. Consider joining or starting a recycling or green organization in the community where people can share information they have learned while improving their office operations. Submit articles on your efforts to local newspapers and magazines. To raise the bar in your area of business, go green and watch the others follow.

It's important to communicate your intentions with clients and employees so the purpose is understood. If cutbacks and reductions are not explained to employees or if clients see that they are receiving used materials or that a company is cutting back on production, there may be suspicions that the company is in dire financial straights. To avoid any misconceptions, let people know the changes are all focused toward meeting environmental goals.

Employee Buy-In

If you expect to successfully make changes at work, it's best to get your employees to buy in to the concept. Employees will probably be administering the programs, and they may have some inventive ideas. Employees who came from a university environment or a former employer where sustainable living was promoted may have worked with campus or workplace programs. They may also have experience in their personal lives, at their homes, or in their communities.

Employees who feel they've been included in a plan or program are more likely to cooperate. Be sure to let them know that the goal for improving the operations and making the business more environmentally friendly is not strictly to save money and that any savings will be used to initiate more programs or improvements for the environment or the employees who helped with the success.

Sometimes all it takes is acknowledging the cost and environmental impact for employees to look at operations just a little differently. Think about rewarding employees who offer suggestions on ways to save or implement programs in their own departments. Make good examples of those advocating greener operations.

Reducing Waste in the Office

One of the first steps in tailoring office operations in a greener fashion is to take a look at waste. This may mean actually dumping out a trash bin and looking at the contents. See what's being thrown away and consider what kind of reductions can be made. This will give you a good idea of how much money and resources are lost every day.

Then take a step back and come up with a plan. Itemize the different components of the waste stream and determine what can realistically be reduced. Appoint one person to conduct the survey and evaluate the options.

Here are some common ways to reduce waste in the office:

- **Go paperless.** Encourage employees to use electronic means to work and communicate. You will inevitably have to use some paper, so start a recycling program. If your company does not generate enough recycling for your municipality to pick it up, set out boxes yourself and take them home for recycling. Make double-sided copies for handouts at meetings to conserve the amount of paper you use.
- **Choose your printer inks and toners carefully.** Reuse and refill toners; recycle ink cartridges.

- **Reuse office equipment.** If you choose to upgrade your computer system, you'll be left with fully functioning machines that still have a lot of life in them. Donate them to charities or give them back to your supplier instead of throwing them away.
- **Cut down on disposable products.** If your business has a kitchen, a cafeteria, or a coffee machine, encourage employees to bring their own mugs and silverware.
- **Reuse boxes** and other shipping and packaging materials.
- **Reuse old envelopes** for interoffice mail.

These simple suggestions can be accomplished relatively painlessly. Tailor them to your company's needs to make them more effective.

Energy Audit

A first step in the direction of reducing the company's impact on the environment is to have an energy audit done for the facility. By cutting back the electricity demands from the business, you can reduce the need to burn coal or other nonrenewable power sources. You'll also be cutting back on the pollution generated as part of the power to electricity process.

The local power company may offer to perform an audit for a modest fee or possibly for free, but you may have to contract with an energy expert. You may spend money in the beginning, but you'll save some in the end.

When hiring a contractor to perform an energy audit, make sure you know what you are signing up for. A preliminary audit includes just a walk-through with recommendations. A general audit goes further and includes a review of expenses. An investment audit will calculate the return on investment that can be expected, allowing businesses to budget building and operation renovations.

Before bringing in someone else, you can do your own energy walk-through, taking note of the following things:

- Is natural lighting utilized as much as possible?
- What kind of lighting is used?
- Can lights be replaced with compact fluorescent lamps or halogen lamps?
- Can green power be purchased from the local utility?
- Is the office equipment (i.e., computers, printers, fax machines) Energy Star rated?
- Are computers set to go to sleep?
- Are employees encouraged to turn off their computers, printers, and lights at the end of the day or if they will be gone for a few hours?
- Are outdoor windows and doors kept closed? If windows are not low-e, have they been treated for energy efficiency?
- Is a comfortable temperature maintained for most employees? It's understood that some employees may occasionally need to don a sweater to warm up and use a fan to cool off.

A professional energy auditor will have more recommendations than one from a utility and will mostly include construction or material suggestions. After the audit, you will have to decide which and when improvements can be made or schedule them into the capital-improvement budget.

Reducing Paper and Ink

Since the onset of personal computers, the amount of paper generated has skyrocketed. Not only is paper a waste product, it's expensive to buy and diminishes natural resources. By reducing the amount of paper used in the office, you can reduce the amount of paper needed to be stored and delivered. Come up with milestone goals for the percentage reduction in paper used.

Encourage employees to think first before printing and make sure all documents are spell-checked and formatted correctly. When making copies, double-side the documents. If you are producing handouts for a meeting, consider whether they are really necessary. When audiovisuals are used, paper handouts are usually superfluous. If handouts are a must, consider printing double pages on a single side of paper.

On average, Americans use 700 pounds of paper each year; that amount has doubled since 1960. The environmental impacts from using so much paper start with getting the fiber to the mill, manufacturing the paper from the fiber, and handling the paper after it's been used.

Encourage employees to use electronic mail rather than printing memos. Maintain electronic copies of company directories, manuals, and other material rather than printing hard copies for each person to shelve. Determine what activities can be accomplished through online programs rather than generating a paper trail. Office supplies can be ordered, conference or training requests submitted, even time sheets and expense reports can be completed online. Not only does this save time, eliminating the need to shuttle paper from one desk to another, it saves resources, too.

Other ways to cut back while maintaining a professional appearance include minimizing margins, decreasing font size, and eliminating double-spacing. These minor changes will add up over time, especially when printing large documents.

When looking at how your company can reduce paper, check in the recycle bins and trash cans. Is paper being thrown away that could be placed in the recycling bins? Is paper being tossed in the recycling bins that could be used for printing draft documents or for scrap paper? Are blank pages inserted as holding places in documents and then tossed into the bin with other scrap paper?

Give paper a second life. Beyond recycling, consider what else can be done with scrap paper. Can employees use it for notes, or can local schools use it in their classrooms? Can employees take it home to use in their computers and printers or for their children to use for coloring? Additionally, paper left over from shredders can be used as packing materials for shipping fragile items.

Printers may be inexpensive, but cartridges are not. Ink can be a costly part of any office operation. There are a number of ways to reduce its use. When printing a document that is not final, print it in draft mode. There is also software available that allows more control over the amount of ink a printer uses. Inksaver allows the user to choose the percentage of ink that is used when printing. The draft mode on your printer uses approximately 50 percent of the ink used in normal print mode, so although using the software may not save as much ink as printing in draft mode, it does offer some in-between options.

Cutting Back on Travel

Even with the advent of online meetings and teleconferencing, people are still flying and driving an extensive amount. If a trip out of the office is necessary, consider more fuel-efficient ways of traveling or combining trips to nearby locales or with other meetings. Sometimes, juggling a schedule can reduce travel from two trips to one.

QUESTION?

How do I encourage my employees to carpool?
Employers can provide special parking spots for those who carpool. This is particularly valuable if the office is large or parking is scarce. Carpooling must be defined to employees and may include stipulations that at least two people must share the commute at least over half the distance.

When it comes to getting employees to and from work, encourage the use of mass transit. Employers can provide tax-advantage spending accounts for employees to cover the cost of riding the bus or taking the train or subway. These programs allow employees to pay for mass transit with pre-tax dollars using a convenient pass or card that's ordered online. Companies like WageWorks, Inc. institute programs like these. WageWorks also maintains a database of transportation services available across the country.

Choose energy-efficient vehicles or hybrids as your company cars or fleet vehicles. Companies will feel the savings on multiple cars more than individuals. Not only will this save money, it sets an example of conservation and environmental protection at a corporate level.

Telecommuting has also become popular and saves on more than transportation costs. Some companies are strictly set up for telecommuting using field representatives or contractors who work out of their houses. When compared to going in to the office, there are other benefits in working from home. Depending on the company dress code, allowing employees to work from home can decrease the cost and environmental impact from dry cleaning.

Buying and Operating Green

When it comes to making purchases for the company, buy green. Almost any office supply is available in recycled or organic versions, from sticky notes to calendars. Large office-supply retailers carry a variety of recycled-content paper products including folders and pencils. Other more specialized stores such as Green Earth Office Supply raise the bar for environmentally friendly supplies and equipment. They carry everything from hole punches made from recycled steel to hemp planners.

Make sure that the paper purchased is made from either 100 percent recycled fibers or at least a percentage of recycled fibers. Make sure that all of the office equipment is energy efficient with the Energy Star emblem. Take a little time when the next orders are placed to check out the environmental alternatives.

If you want to calculate the benefits of using recycled paper, use the Paper Calculator program designed by the U.S. Office of the Federal Environmental Executive at *www.ofee.gov*. Input information includes the amount of paper used and the percentage of recycled material. Output includes the energy consumed and the sulfur dioxide emitted for the lifecycle of the paper.

Allow equipment to be shared, such as printers, when it's realistic and won't hinder performance. Like society in general, many employers and employees see new office furniture and accessories as status symbols and a way to reward performance. If this is an attitude you want to discourage, it's even more important to communicate well with workers and make sure everyone is on the same page.

Consider all the different processes that make up the day-to-day operations of the company and you will realize that little steps add up. When sending out mailings that need to be returned, use reusable envelopes. If possible, reuse envelopes you receive. If giving out promotional gifts, make sure they are usable, rather than just a trinket that will be thrown away, and are made out of recycled material. Review everyday practices for mailings and cut out any waste in the process. Can packages going to different people at the same address be combined? Can packages from different departments be shipped together? It may take some additional communication, but with support that travels all the way up the corporate ladder, savings can be seen in this area.

Starting a Recycling Program

There are so many options and venues for recycling at the office that it's a good idea to appoint one person as the recycling coordinator. This could be the same person who conducted the waste assessment or audit, but depending on the size of the business, this doesn't necessarily need to be his or her only responsibility. This coordinator should be someone who is enthusiastic about recycling and either is already familiar with the company's waste management practices or is willing to jump right in—so to speak. Explain that he or she will be responsible for preparing a plan, educating coworkers, and determining a method for evaluating performance.

It's better to start off recycling only a few items and then adding to the list. Other aspects to consider when preparing a recycling plan are the haulers in your area. Some may come by to collect materials while others may require that you deliver the items to them. Also, the recycling coordinator will need to decide if it's best to separate the recyclables or comingle them; both methods have their pros and cons.

Among antirecycling myths is the fiction that recycling is expensive. But there are factors that naysayers don't take into account. Any recycling fees must be compared to disposal costs. Markets for recycling materials (i.e., paper, plastic, and metal) vary, so recycling costs or earnings must be evaluated as a whole, not as individual components.

If the office does not generate a lot of one particular kind of recyclable, it might work best to combine efforts with other offices in the area. Also look into participating in a cooperative that could not only get better prices in purchasing recycling equipment but be the difference between paying to have your recyclables picked up and making money from them. Smaller haulers may also be available at better rates than larger haulers for taking away materials. If a business is located in a rural area, there may not be an option to benefit from joining a co-op or using a mom-and-pop hauler. In this case, secondhand hauling could be used. When office supplies or another item is delivered to the office, the hauler may be able to take the recyclables to a recycling facility for you. This works best if the truck is usually empty on return trips, allowing the driver room to haul and the potential to make a little extra money.

Some common office items that can be recycled include the following:

- Aluminum cans
- Batteries (if rechargeable batteries aren't used)
- Cardboard boxes
- Computers
- Ink cartridges
- Magazines
- Paper
- Plastics and glass

With a successful recycling program under way, it's important to revisit new solid waste practices. Some companies may be able to decrease the size of their Dumpster or the frequency of disposal because of the reduction in the amount of material thrown away.

FACT

The Charleston Place Hotel found out firsthand how much money recycling could save. In 2001, this luxury travel destination in South Carolina saved $58,000 through its recycling efforts. In addition, recycling won't just stay at the office or the hotel. Many business owners report that they and their employees practice recycling at home.

As the recycling program continues, make sure to solicit ideas and suggestions from the other employees as to how they think it's working out. Share the problems and successes experienced with the program with them as well. Let employees know if contaminants are making their way into the waste stream and what the impacts from those contaminants are. The quantities of recycling being performed should be shared along with any revenue generated. Consider donating the revenue to an employee program, such as a scholarship, or to a local charity.

Chapter 18

Making the "Green" in Your Wallet Count

Money is a powerful thing. Without it, businesses wouldn't exist and charities wouldn't thrive. You can make your dollars count in very tangible ways when you choose to spend or invest your hard-earned cash in ways that support the environment and other causes. Where you decide to spend or invest your money makes a difference, and this chapter offers some options and thoughts to consider the next time you pull out your wallet or open your checkbook.

Corporations Get Greener

Many corporations are starting to see the green in being green. Whether out of social and environmental concern or to cut costs and increase profits, more companies are looking to improve the construction and operation of their facilities and businesses. It's up to you as a consumer to let these environmentally minded companies know you approve of their actions by doing business with them.

Big companies, including big box retailers, are moving to more sustainable construction and operation. One of the most notable companies, simply because of its sheer size and reputation as a low-price retailer, is Wal-Mart. This company illustrated its green effort with the construction of the McKinney, Texas, retail outlet. The store was designed and constructed in accordance with the Leadership in Energy and Environmental Design (LEED) guidelines and included wind turbines and used cooking and motor oil for providing energy for the building. The company also vowed to increase fuel efficiency in fleet vehicles, reduce energy in its outlet stores, cut solid waste production, and reduce the production of greenhouse gases. A second LEED building was constructed in Aurora, Colorado. It is hoped that with the experience of these two stores, Wal-Mart will be able to create a set design applicable to its other locations and set a green example for other retailers to follow.

Courses focusing on sustainable development and environmental responsibility are showing up in business programs all over the country. The Center for Sustainable Enterprise at the University of North Carolina is one place where today's students are learning to be tomorrow's responsible leaders by understanding the impacts of social and environmental changes.

Many smaller companies operate with the environment in mind. However, as large corporations build more efficient and environmentally friendly buildings, perhaps the process will become part of the mainstream and more businesses will be encouraged to follow suit. Sustainable development has the potential to streamline the design and construction processes and possibly lower the cost of green construction, making it more viable for other companies that might not have been able to afford it.

Government Grading

Sometimes it can be difficult deciding which companies to support in their environmental endeavors. There are organizations that rate different companies on a variety of issues and provide information that can help consumers make the most responsible choice.

The EPA evaluates companies on their environmental performance using the National Environmental Performance Track, a program that was started in 2000 to recognize public and private institutions that go above and beyond the minimum environmental requirements. Interested parties apply for the program by implementing an independently prepared environmental management program. They must also maintain a record of compliance with environmental laws, commit to achieving quantifiable goals, and provide information to the community on their practices.

QUESTION?

How could I find out what companies are evaluated by the EPA?
The EPA's Web site (✐*www.epa.gov/performancetrack/*) lists companies involved in the performance track program. Lists are broken down by the ways they improve the environment; for example, companies that work best with commuters, or businesses that work toward preventing pollution.

Beyond recognition, organizations that are required by law to submit environmental reports may benefit from a reduction in reporting and inspection requirements. That is why this program lends itself primarily to organizations that utilize or impact resources that require permitting from the EPA or other environmental regulatory agencies, such as water, wastewater, and solid waste. The EPA estimates that since its inception the program's members have made great strides, including the following:

- Reduced water use by 1.9 billion gallons
- Reduced solid waste generated by almost 600,000 tons
- Increased use of recycled materials by 20,000 tons
- Set aside more than 1,000 acres for land conservation

Companies involved in the program manufacture anything from pesticides to auto parts, and they are trying to run at least portions of their operations in a more environmentally conducive way.

Spending with Environmentally Friendly Companies

There are other private organizations that rate companies, allowing consumers to decide which businesses operate in ways that are most important to them. Organizations such as IdealsWork, Inc. classify different companies according to how they perform environmentally and socially. The organization was started by two friends with a drive to make the world a better place by giving consumers useful information to make informed decisions about their purchases.

If you are planning to go shopping but are concerned about where to spend your money, you can visit *www.idealswork.com*. There you can select from the pull-down menu. You'll be given the option to check the criteria that are important to you, such as the environment, human rights, or animal rights, and then you'll be given a listing of companies and how they rate.

The Green Guide, now published by National Geographic, also offers information on sustainable companies that make organic and fair trade products. The guide has a directory that includes a variety of companies that range from sustainable bamboo surfboards to video games with humanitarian themes.

The result is a database of companies that manufacture products and businesses that provide services. Businesses are divided by type of operation and are ranked based on research performed by the Investor Responsibility Research Center.

The Co-op American Foundation publishes the National Green Pages, which includes companies that have demonstrated that they use their business for positive social change, exercise environmental sustainability practices, operate their offices or plants in ways that improve social and environmental responsibility, and are determined to incorporate practices that go above and beyond when it comes to benefiting their workers, the community, their customers, and the environment.

Appendix A includes a list of organizations and companies that work in ways to promote sustainability and protect the environment while supplying commonly used goods and services. The list is growing every day as companies learn that protecting the environment doesn't have to be expensive and can actually increase profits.

Social Investing

Planning for your financial future can take into account the future of the planet, too. Many investors today understand that earnings don't have to be made at the expense of the environment, social justice, or public health.

FACT

Green investing is good investing. Socially responsible investing does well, with assets growing 4 percent faster than other managed assets. Socially responsible investment assets increased 258 percent from 1995 through 2005 from an initial value of $639 billion to $2.29 trillion.

To invest socially, look for companies with good employee relations, a record of community involvement, and accomplished environmental stewardship. You'll also want to consider company track records in maintaining environmental compliance, utilizing alternative energy sources, and handling labor relations. Companies can be evaluated by using some of the resources in this chapter.

Diversifying is important in any portfolio, and this can still be accomplished when the goal is maintaining environmentally friendly investments. To put together a socially responsible collection of stocks and bonds, check out the information on the Social Investment Forum (*www.socialinvest.org*), the Progressive Investor (*www.sustainablebusiness.com*), and SRI World Group's Social Funds (*www.socialfunds.com*). Rather than evaluating companies alone, you can turn to a financial adviser. There are investment groups that specify socially responsible companies, and there are companies that carry a line of environmental investment opportunities along with other funds. Many financial firms that include socially and environmentally responsible companies in their portfolios, such as Calvert Group Ltd, rely on data from sources like the EPA National Environmental Performance Track to select investment options.

Money or Time

Many nonprofit and charity organizations work hard to improve the lives of people and animals and protect the environment. In a move toward a greener lifestyle, you may decide that this is something you want do, not just as a feel-good measure but to help someone or support a cause. A first step is to decide what kind of charity you would like to support. Are you more interested in helping protect land and ecology, farm animals, or impoverished people? Or is there another cause that hits home for you?

Making a Donation

Charities can buy the supplies they need with money donated from individuals. Compared to donating items that have to be stored and distributed, donating money allows the charity to spend as it sees fit. Accounting and tax records indicate how much money is spent and on what.

Often, you can designate how you would like your contributed funds to be distributed. As a rule of thumb, monetary contributions should never be made in cash, and you should be sure to keep records and receipts. You can also choose to support a nonprofit in honor of someone else. Instead of giving a gift, you can give the gift of charity.

When you decide to donate, it's best not to react to situations or make emotional choices. It can be hard when there is a disaster and organizations make pleas for donations. You need to make sure your money will really help those in need and not go to those who are profiting from others' misfortunes. One way to ensure this is to donate to recognized charities with solid reputations.

ALERT!

Charitable organizations are required to be registered in the state in which they operate. You can check on the validity of a charity or organization by contacting your state's Department of State. Many states have an online searchable database. If a charity has asked for contributions but doesn't appear to be registered, you should contact the appropriate department.

Some charities work locally with contributors able to see results first-hand. Is there an animal rescue organization that's in need of supplies, an environmental group trying to purchase a piece of property, or a family hoping for a few presents under the tree?

Beyond the altruistic feeling, an added benefit from donating is writing it off on your taxes. Review your selected charities' financial records to confirm their status as a tax-exempt group under the Internal Revenue Code section 501(c)(3). But just because the charity is tax exempt doesn't mean that contributions will be.

Volunteering

Besides contributing money to charities, you can also volunteer your time. By giving time, you will be able work on projects and meet other people. Projects might include building a house or clearing an area of an invasive species. Volunteering can go beyond task work and include helping run the program, providing some expertise in a specific field, and even being on the board of directors. Many charities do not have staff on their payroll and rely heavily on volunteers to manage the organization. Supporting jobs include filing documents, answering phones, staffing an office, data entry, and other behind-the-scenes tasks.

Time is a valuable commodity that many charities need and appreciate. Giving your time shows that you are concerned and helpful. Some school programs require students to acquire a set number of volunteer hours. This can be used in grading for a class or in determining eligibility for acceptance at certain schools. Volunteer hours in high school are also required for some college or university scholarships. This requirement not only helps the community, it gives students the opportunity to try their hand at volunteering. The lesson might just stick, encouraging students to be lifelong volunteers.

When offering to volunteer for a charity, you will likely be asked what skills you have and when you are available. While volunteering may give you the opportunity to use your skills, it may also give you the chance to learn something new. If you are handy with woodworking or painting, volunteering with Habitat for Humanity could give you the opportunity to learn about wiring and electrical work.

If you decide to donate your time, make sure you show up. If a job is planned, it's hard on those who do show up when others who committed don't come or arrive late, holding up work for others. Treat a volunteer job just as you would any other team activity you're involved with.

Volunteering with some charities may offer the opportunity to travel to other parts of the country or even overseas. There are a variety of organizations available to help you choose a charity or volunteer opportunity if you are looking to expand your boundaries:

- **Action Without Borders** at *www.idealist.org* connects charities with those looking to volunteer all over the world. Volunteers can search the site by location and interest to find an opportunity that meets their goals.
- **SERVEnet** at *www.servenet.org* is a program of Youth Service America (YSA), which provides volunteer opportunities for young people from five to twenty-five years old to help foster citizenship. Opportunities

range from providing office support to local charities to building structures.

- **VolunteerMatch** at *www.volunteermatch.org* allows volunteers to find opportunities nationally, locally, and even virtually. Opportunities can include taking in animals as a foster parent, being a museum docent, and even helping on a fossil dig.
- **Wilderness Volunteers** at *www.wildernessvolunteers.org* brings together hardworking people who love the outdoors with opportunities in forests and parks all over the United States. Each trip lasts one week, and tools and supervision are provided. Downtime is available on most trips for volunteers to enjoy leisure activities like hiking, kayaking, and skiing.

Group volunteering is a great opportunity for organizations such as fraternities and sororities, church groups, school organizations, and businesses to get members working together on something outside their usual routine. It also provides the opportunity for families to work together for a single cause.

Checking on Charities

Whether donating time or money, you will want to make sure you're supporting a worthy charity and one that meets your standards. So before giving to any charity, do your homework. Phone calls may sound convincing, but be careful about giving out any personal information over the phone, especially credit card or social security numbers. There are unscrupulous people who will collect money in the name of charity only to use it for themselves. Unfortunately, these people can give all charities a bad name. There is information available that can be used to determine how forthright a charity is, helping to make sure that your money is going to help legitimate causes.

You can do a background check to see how much of the money collected actually goes to charitable deeds, not to administrative support or fundraising work. Some fundraising companies are for profit and keep a large portion of what they collect for themselves.

ALERT!

Beware of copycat charities. Some charities will intentionally give themselves names similar to other more popular and reputable organizations in the hope that people will be confused. If the name doesn't match exactly, it's not the same charity.

There are a number of organizations that provide valuable information on charities, making donating a safer and more rewarding experience. Here is a list of some of those organizations:

- **Charity Navigator** at *www.charitynavigator.com* rates charities on a scale of one to four stars. Through analysis of federal financial statements, organizations are rated on characteristics such as expenses, earnings, and efficiency. You can search by cause and compare different organizations with each other. The site provides contact information for each organization and offers a portal for donations.

- **BBB Wise Giving Alliance** at *www.give.org* performs analyses of national charities to provide donors with information so they can make informed decisions. Charities that meet standards receive the Alliance's National Charity Seal.

- **GuideStar** at *www.guidestar.org* brings together donors and foundations with businesses and government agencies. The organization maintains a database of information including IRS forms, employee information, and grant activity on charities that is searchable by donors at different membership levels.

- **JustGive** at *www.justgive.org* allows donors to find charities that are important to them. You can give money on the Web site and set up accounts for others to donate to the same charity. JustGive administers wish lists for donors to use, requesting friends and family to give to certain charities.

- The **I Do Foundation** at *www.idofoundation.org* allows happy couples to set up charitable wedding registries. Wedding guests can contribute to charity in lieu of giving a wedding gift. The site also allows the bride and groom to donate in a guest's name instead of giving out wedding favors. The site includes helpful ideas for charitable weddings, including donating wedding dresses, flowers, and leftover food.

Sites like these give credibility to those charities that deserve and improve the altruistic community as a whole. Knowing which organizations will use contributed money most wisely helps donors feel even better about giving.

Chapter 19

Political, Consumer, and Religious Causes

As people work to help the environment and lead greener lives, they can also become involved with others on the same path. Whether for political, consumer, or religious reasons, everyone can be a part of the solution working toward a common goal. This chapter looks at different things you can do to make a difference and maybe even meet some like-minded people along the way.

People Make a Difference

Sometimes in groups, sometimes as individuals, people have worked to promote change. They have bucked the status quo in an effort to make things better either for themselves or for others. The list of people who have made a difference is lengthy, but one individual is worth highlighting. John Muir, considered the original preservationist and father of the national park system, spread the conviction that people need natural space to thrive. Muir helped found the Sierra Club and lobbied politicians against the destruction of resources in the Pacific Northwest. His legacy lives on in numerous schools and protected wilderness areas that bear his name.

If you are looking for inspiration, pick up a biography. Reading how someone else overcame obstacles and followed his or her passion can give you just the boost you need to make some changes in your life. More than likely, you'll see that people who changed the world didn't really set out to do so, but change came one step at a time.

The list of people who have inspired change continues to grow, and one interesting point about nearly all of them is that they weren't born into activism. Something happened in their lives that drove them to work for change. People can be at the forefront of a movement or they can be in the ranks providing support; either way, individuals and groups can make a difference and redirect the course of history. Dr. Rosalie Bertel is a good example. As a mathematician and nun in the order of the Grey Nuns of the Sacred Heart, Dr. Bertel was spurred to action in the mid-1980s after the nuclear reactor meltdown in Chernobyl and the Union Carbide explosion in Bhopal, India. She has become a respected scholar and author and now works on behalf of Native Americans and Gulf War veterans on the effects of depleted uranium and low-level radiation.

Contacting Lawmakers and Regulators

One of the most important political moves you can make is to vote. Politicians are elected as representatives and generally work to promote the beliefs of their constituents—the people they represent and the people who elected them. Before going to the polling precinct, make sure you have done your homework. To get the most from your vote, know the issues and where the candidates stand.

If you want to bring attention to a local issue or if you need a question answered, you can contact your local political leaders and regulators. Contact information should be in the phone book or available on the municipality's or agency's Web site.

Lawmakers

At times, a particular issue is decided by individual states, not by the federal government. In that case, state lawmakers have more influence. If you aren't sure who your representatives or senators are, look up your state government's Web site. It will have information regarding your representatives and how to contact them. The senators and representatives are elected by district. They may have a local office in their district or an office in the state's capital. Depending on the schedule and availability of the legislature, you may receive a call back from an aide rather than the lawmaker you originally contacted.

The Web site *www.speakout.com* has a wealth of information on all aspects of the legislative process and the best ways to communicate with legislators. The site also contains additional information on political activism.

If the issue is on a federal level, you can contact your U. S. senator or representative. Each state has two senators and is divided by population into districts; each district has one representative. Rather than dealing directly with your senator or representative, you will most likely be in contact with one of their assistants. Build a rapport with this person because he or she will likely have a good understanding of the issues and will probably have more time to look into an issue.

Any communication with local, state, or federal politicians should be professional and respectful. Before contacting them, make sure you thoroughly understand the issue. Rumors and misinformation spread quickly. If you are interested in pending legislation, try to contact your legislator before the session begins and the bill is taken to committee.

It's good to remember that written or e-mailed communication is likely to be considered public record, and this includes e-mail addresses. If you contact your congressional leaders, you should consider any potential audience that may read your correspondence—which could include friends, family, and even employers. Regardless of the potential public audience, you'll get further with legislators when you treat them with respect.

Here is a list of tips for contacting a member of the legislature:

- Check your spelling, grammar, and punctuation when writing an e-mail or a letter. It seems obvious, but misspelling your senator or representative's name is a quick way to lose an audience. Poor grammar and punctuation will decrease your credibility.
- Limit your written correspondence to one page and address only one topic; keep your ideas and information concise.
- Back up any claims or assertions with facts. If necessary, attach references.
- If you would like to visit your legislator, make an appointment first. Again, offer a single-page fact sheet on the issue and stick to the topic.

Rather than acting on behalf of a legislative issue that is already being processed, you can also request a public hearing on a local issue. For example, you might request a hearing to inform the public of the potential impacts a new development could have on nearby wetlands. Your letter would include a summary of the project and details about how it will impact the area. In this example, you would describe the development project and specifically how it would impact the wetlands (i.e., increased runoff from paved areas that could cause erosion and reduce the quality of water entering the wetlands). Through the Freedom of Information Act, you can obtain specific information on the project from the regulatory agency responsible for its permitting.

While most agencies will provide documentation to review and copy, some documents may be classified as sensitive material. In the event that documents are not readily available, you will need to submit a formal request to either the agency head or the Freedom of Information Act (FOIA) officer.

In the wetlands example, the letter would also provide a description of the wetlands, including the size and species present, and how it contributes to the community. Applicable laws and regulations should be cited that might include environmental permitting and public notification and involvement.

If you are requesting a public hearing, you should be prepared to make a presentation. Your facts should be in order and organized. Practice your presentation well ahead of time; it may just be the beginning of a political career.

Regulators

Letters can also be written to regulators that are responsible for permitting and monitoring activities. This could range from a letter to the FDA regarding animal testing or to the EPA regarding a nearby superfund site. As with other letters, the tone should be respectful, and while the issue may be emotional, try to present facts. For example, if you are writing a letter to the FDA, you could request that animal testing no longer be used to determine cosmetic ingredient safety and that other means be used. While the plight of animals used in laboratory testing can be emotional, be sure to emphasize the accuracy and availability of alternative measures. You should also include any applicable laws and regulations pertaining to the issue. In this example, you could indicate that while the law may require proof of product safety, it does not specifically require that data be provided through animal testing. You could request regulators to accept the use of alternate tests or data. Even though many of the issues concerning the environment are emotional, it's important to understand the laws and regulations.

Communicating with the Media

If there's an issue that needs to be covered, contact local media outlets. Media coverage is a good way to reach a wider audience, but the media can't cover an event or an issue unless they're kept informed. Many newspapers, radio stations, and television stations list their directory online, making it easier to find contact information. If you get in touch with a specific reporter, determine if the person is aware of the issue and if he or she needs any additional information. If you don't believe the paper has covered a story fairly, contact the editor or a manager. Be sure to list the specific items you took issue with and provide correct facts. Remember that an ongoing relationship with the paper is desirable and that bullying them won't help that relationship. It might even be a good idea to offer to work with them on covering the subject or providing additional information that might be needed.

FACT

Newspapers are widely used in schools as tools in teaching current events and as part of reading, writing, and even math assignments. The Newspaper Association of America (NAA) states that students involved with newspapers in school are more likely to read newspapers as adults. The NAA Foundation administers the News in Education (NIE) program, which helps schools obtain the resources to purchase newspapers for their classrooms.

If you want to see your name in print, write a letter to the editor of the newspaper. Make sure to follow the format required by the newspaper, especially with respect to length and personal information. The letter should be timely and concise, and even though it will go through an editor, make sure to proof it for spelling and grammar. If the letter covers a heated issue, consider how you will feel when it's published in the paper with your name attached. The newspaper may not publish the first letter it gets, but if a topic appears again and again—especially if it's a concern voiced by several writers—it's likely to be recognized.

If you have more to say than can be communicated in a 200-word letter, you can compose a longer piece. Op-ed articles are longer than standard letters to the editor. If it's a topic that's not strictly local, it can be sent to newspapers with wider subscriptions. Larger papers such as the *New York Times* or the *Washington Post* don't routinely accept op-ed articles that have been printed elsewhere; it could be more advantageous to have a letter printed in multiple smaller newspapers than in just one large paper. State the controversial point clearly and present any arguments by sticking to the facts. Keep the audience in mind when you offer solutions. If your intent is to persuade the average person on the street of a stance, don't use complicated facts and figures. Write your letter to the readers. It may be to your advantage to give the piece a catchy title. If not, the newspaper will give it a title that may not accurately reflect your intended position.

Communicating with Companies

Letters to companies could range from encouraging them to take a specific action to requesting that they stop a certain practice. There are generally two approaches to letting a company know you are concerned with its activities and would like to see some changes. You can write a letter as an individual or you can send a letter from a collaborative group, addressed directly to board members. The letter should describe the specific issues of concern and request certain actions as a result. Also, request that the company respond to the letter and explain its stance on the issue. Send the letter so you receive a receipt that it was delivered, preferably knowing who signed for it. If the first letter doesn't get a response, consider writing again.

One way to get involved is with the Adopt-a-Supermarket campaign organized through Co-op America and their Fair Trade Program. This movement gives consumers the tools and suggestions to encourage grocery stores to purchase inventory from companies that practice fair trade. Instead of going it alone, church groups, schools, or community organizations can adopt a store together.

Another method of communicating with companies is through their shareholders. Shareholders own part of the company and have certain rights and privileges. They can request a meeting with the board of directors or attend a shareholders' meeting. They vote on company issues and have the right to vote either in person or through a mailed ballot.

Combining the efforts of other shareholders can also prove effective in changing corporate policies and actions. If a public pension fund invests in a company you take issue with, work with the pension fund and its members to sway company policies. Another alternative is to determine if a university has a vested interest in a company and persuade those in charge to reconsider their investments. The larger the stockholder, the louder the message.

If you own shares in a company through a mutual fund, however, you do not have the same rights as an individual shareholder. In this case, any correspondence to the company should come through your fund provider. The issue can still be tackled, but it has to be handled differently.

Join a Movement

If you want to protect the environment with others, you can join a cause, an organization, a church, or even a political party. It may be that there is already a group working on behalf of a cause that interests you. This could be either a local group dealing with a very specific issue or an international group that takes on many issues at a time.

Activist Groups

There may be a local group that gets together to work on local issues such as land development or animal protection to a very specific area. The group may be working toward building an environmental center or creating educational courses for the community. By joining, you will not only meet other like-minded people, but you will learn a great deal about the politics and activities in the town. It offers the chance to network and may even lead to other activities and endeavors.

Be careful to understand the group's goals and ambitions before join-ing. A small number of activist groups use illegal tactics in promoting their agendas. It's better to find this out before you end up making a phone call from a holding cell downtown.

Joining a larger organization may allow you to be involved in higher profile causes. You might learn about more complex political issues and the key players, such as political and corporate leaders. Many larger organi-zations have local groups that get together and work on more local issues and also join in national and international conventions and gatherings. This would give you the opportunity not only to offer your time and services but to learn a great deal as well.

Churches

Many churches and religious organizations are now looking toward environmental activism as one of their key roles in the community and on the planet. When looking for a congregation to join, you can ask what the church's stance on the environment is and what tasks they have taken to encourage environmental awareness within and outside the church.

Political Parties

Protecting the environment can be a very political issue. The foundation of the Green Party of the United States is based primarily on environmental-ism and social justice. Similarly, the Greens/Green Party USA also promotes sustainability and a balance between people and nature. While these two parties focus primarily on the environment and other social issues, these issues are increasingly becoming a part of the platform of more mainstream political parties. You can consider joining a political organization in your area or volunteering for a candidate who makes the environment an impor-tant aspect of his or her campaign.

Throw a House Party

Many political and activist organizations allow members or those think-ing of joining to go online and link up with others in the area just by plugging in a zip code. If you want to host a party, invitations can be sent to others in the area. House parties are usually scheduled for common times all over the state or country to coincide with the airing of a television show or an announcement. Moveon.org is probably best known for the house parties they have helped organize. The organization relied heavily on house parties to bring political groups together during the 2004 and 2006 elections.

Spearhead a Cause

If you have looked around and there just isn't an organization that seems to fit with your beliefs, or if a specific issue has come up that hasn't been addressed publicly before, you can consider spearheading a cause of your own. You can use some of the tactics mentioned in this chapter, such as writing letters to companies or encouraging politicians to become involved. There are other steps that can be taken to increase awareness and get others involved.

The Michigan Land Use Institute offers activists a tool kit for getting peo-ple involved. The group offers a variety of sample documents, including a sample Freedom of Information Act letter, a sample news release, and sam-ples of testimony letters on their Web site at *www.mlui.org*.

Get Online

Web sites are a great way to disseminate information to the masses. It's a way to link up with other organizations. Creating a Web site is not something everyone feels comfortable with, so it might be worthwhile to search out other group members willing to do it for free. Some Web site designers work regularly with nonprofits, usually charging lower rates than those working with for-profit companies. Web sites should provide up-to-date information on the organization and contact information.

The Internet is also a way to set up regular communications with mem-bers through e-mail lists, bulletin boards, and blogs. Online petitions can be developed that tally responses and send them on to recipients, such as politicians and corporate leaders. A Web site can be used not just to advertise an organization, but also to allow back-and-forth communication between members and others looking for information.

NetAction assists activists with communicating via the Internet. Its Web site (*www.netaction.org*) includes tips on making good use of the Internet and using e-mail as a primary method of communication.

FACT

Affordable Internet Services, Inc. (AISO) is a green energy hosting company that runs its data center and offices on solar power. A green roof is being constructed for the data center that includes three to four inches of dirt topped with drought-resistant plants. The new roof is expected to reduce energy use by 50 percent.

It's important to designate a point person within your group to respond to e-mails and to agree on a response time. Unanswered or late communications are liable to make an organization look disorganized and slapdash. A member should also be responsible for maintaining an updated e-mail list of members and those on the mailing list. This list can be used to send out newsletters and announcements and keep everyone up-to-date.

Demonstrate

Well-run demonstrations can be vital tools in getting the word out to people, sending a message to politicians and community leaders, and giving credibility to a cause. Poorly organized and unattended demonstrations may make the cause appear disorganized and unimportant. Here are some tips for getting the most out of a demonstration:

- Contact the local media well in advance of the demonstration and then follow up with reminder e-mails or phone calls.
- Post flyers strategically in areas where they will be well received.
- Consider contacting another organization to attend, bringing in warm bodies. Be prepared to reciprocate when the request is made.

- Prepare signs that convey the message. Make sure there are enough for people who will spontaneously join in.
- Have a catchy chant ready to call attention to the demonstration. There's always the fall back on the "Hey, hey, ho, ho, so and so has got to go."
- Be prepared to speak. Leaders should make an announcement at the gathering, and if possible, try to schedule community leaders or other activists to speak as well. An unexpected benefit of the karaoke craze is the availability of easily portable microphones and speakers.
- If the demonstration involves a march or a walk, clear it through the proper channels. The finish line should be festive and, if possible, should have booths from other organizations that can offer support and show solidarity. This might be a great opportunity to bring together religious, activist, and public organizations.
- Invite vendors to sell T-shirts and bumper stickers. They should pay an entry fee and/or a percentage of their sales.

Demonstrations can be a fun and motivating experience for those involved as well as for those on the sidelines.

Get on Television

Many cable networks provide local access channels at no cost. You will need to contact the cable provider to find out what is available and what the requirements are for getting on the air. Air time can be used to show a video made by a larger organization or produced by the local organization. If you plan on producing the video, the station will likely have requirements for content and format. The network will most likely provide minimal advertising for the program, so publicize the show much as you would a demonstration. Other ways of getting the word out include newspaper advertisements or even announcements in special-interest newsletters.

Watch Television

Bring together others to watch a special video or movie either at someone's house or in a larger facility. Professionally produced movies could be used to spearhead a more local issue. By watching the movie together, members can discuss the relevant issues, how they apply locally, and the actions to be taken. Having a theme and asking attendees to bring along a potluck dish to share can add a little creativity.

Organize a Lecture or Workshop

One way to promote a cause and give an organization standing is to bring in a well-known expert. Schedule a lecture or workshop featuring a notable speaker or educator, preferably in a low-cost or no-cost location such as a school auditorium, a church fellowship hall, or a lodge. For best attendance, be sure to publicize the event.

Chapter 20

In the End

More and more people are choosing environmental burials for themselves and their family members. New approaches to green burial practices are expanding, and the rise is expected to continue as more people learn their options and make plans for the inevitable. This chapter takes a look at the environmental aspects of dying and offers information and options to consider for green and more Earth-friendly funerals.

Make a Plan

As a general rule, making funeral arrangements isn't easy. But by providing a plan, your final wishes can be carried out more easily, and you'll also alleviate some of the stress involved for your loved ones. Think through the process and make decisions, talk them over with family and friends, and write them down. Make sure your loved ones know how you feel about end-of-life issues such as organ and tissue donation and funeral arrangements.

If a funeral or ceremony is going to be different from the norm, it's best to settle on plans well in advance. There may be issues with state laws, and understanding them ahead of time can save survivors from having to figure it out later. When making arrangements for a green funeral, be sure to consider laws governing embalming or transportation that may become an issue. Community clergy and other religious figures should be familiar with the practices and rites allowed. Funeral directors usually offer guidance and direction through the process, but they may not be aware of all of the alternatives. That's why it's even more important to have a plan.

Organ, Tissue, and Whole-Body Donation

Donating organs so that others live is the ultimate in recycling and reuse. Donate Life America estimates that eighteen people die every day while waiting for a transplant. Organs that can be transplanted include kidneys, lungs, liver, heart, pancreas, and intestines. Skin and bone can also be donated, as can corneas. The United Network for Organ Sharing (UNOS) is a nonprofit company that works under contract with the Department of Health and maintains the database for those needing organs.

FACT

Some organs can be donated without anyone dying. Living donors provide thousands of whole organs such as kidneys or pieces of organs like livers every year. Donors are usually closely related family members. But donations to extended family and friends are not uncommon. Anonymous donations are also possible.

Not just anyone can receive an organ. Patients must have a doctor and transplant team evaluate their condition and attitude and recommend their inclusion in the database. People who are unwilling to give up detrimental habits like smoking and excessive drinking may not be eligible to receive a transplant. In addition, a donor's family must allow the organs to be removed for transplant. In the United States and many other countries, it is illegal to buy and sell organs.

Whole-body donation is another alternative. You may choose to donate your entire body for medical research or education. Whole-body donations are usually run by state governments and universities. You can find a database of whole-body donation programs online at *www.med.ufl.edu/anatbd/usprograms.html*. Generally, health issues don't impact whether a person can donate his or her body. Organs that cannot be used for transplant may still be suitable for research.

Common Funeral Practices

There are standard practices when it comes to handling bodies and preparing them for burial. Following is a description of some of the more common methods that may be recommended at most funeral homes.

Embalming

Laws on embalming vary, but it is not absolutely required in any state. In most states, it is not required unless circumstances such as transporting the body, viewing, or aboveground burial make it necessary. Embalming preserves the body and eliminates some of the postmortem changes the body goes through. It also serves to disinfect the body, destroying bacteria and pathogens. Studies have shown that after a person dies the population of bacteria and pathogens increases greatly. If precautionary measures are not taken, the act of embalming can expose morticians to disease, and embalming fluid decreases the overall chance of transmitting infection from the body to the mortician. Besides potentially protecting funeral and mortician workers, the main purpose of embalming a body is to preserve it long enough for survivors to mourn and pay respects. The practice started during the Civil War when soldiers were embalmed for their journey home. In the event someone dies away from home, embalming allows time for the body to be returned.

ALERT!

Formaldehyde is the main ingredient in embalming fluid and kills most types of bacteria. It is a known carcinogen, and workers inhaling it over a long period have been diagnosed with throat and nose cancer. The Green Burial Council, a nonprofit organization that promotes ethical and sustainable end-of-life measures, considers the practice of embalming and the use of formaldehyde a traditional relic.

Embalming fluid is comprised of a variety of chemicals. Because solutions are patented, specific ingredients are confidential. Generally they include antibacterial compounds, preservatives, fragrances, dyes, solvents, and surfactants. Some in the industry advocate the use of alternative embalming fluids that are capable of disinfecting and preserving bodies while reducing the environmental impact and health concerns for workers. The University of Toledo in Ohio performed limited studies in the vicinity of a number of cemeteries to determine if embalming fluids impacted soil and groundwater. Results indicated that contaminant levels were detected but at minor concentrations.

The process of preserving includes pumping embalming fluid into an incision at the carotid artery and then allowing it to drain from an incision at the jugular vein. Blood and other fluids are then removed from the body cavity. Embalming fluid with a higher concentration of formaldehyde is then pumped into the organs to preserve them. Per the EPA, the fluid-blood mixture requires proper disposal as an industrial wastewater. It must either be flushed down the drain or containerized and taken to a permitted wastewater treatment facility. Funeral homes may also apply for an underground injection control permit that would allow them to discharge to their own septic system.

Refrigeration serves as an alternative to embalming for preserving a body. Cold storage can be provided by the hospital or funeral home. Depending on whether a viewing is to take place or when the funeral is scheduled, embalming may be required.

Coffins or Caskets

There are a variety of coffins available that differ in construction materials as well as cost. A majority of caskets are made out of cardboard, wood, steel, copper, and bronze and range in cost from $200 to over $10,000. Vaults encase caskets and are supposed to keep water and air out, providing additional protection for the body. They are usually made of a concrete shell and lined with asphalt, plastic, stainless steel, bronze, or copper. Vaults are meant to offer protection to the soil and groundwater and the casket; however, it's not always required. If you or a loved one choose not to be buried using a vault, make sure the cemetery chosen doesn't require one.

The environmental impacts of being buried in a coffin include the potential for metals, varnishes, sealers, and preservatives used on wood caskets to be released into the environment. Limited studies showed that arsenic was present in soil but not groundwater and was more than likely caused by older preservation methods or by wood preservatives that contained arsenic. Embalming fluid and wood preservatives no longer contain arsenic, but these changes are relatively new. Many arsenic-treated coffins holding arsenic-embalmed bodies have already been buried. Unlike arsenic, formaldehyde used for embalming today breaks down rather quickly. Arsenic, however, collects in the soil, slowly leaching into groundwater over time.

The materials used to build coffins are frequently harvested from sources that don't comply with sustainable practices. Mary Woodsen with the Pre-Posthumous Society of Ithaca estimated that 30 million board feet of hardwood are buried as caskets every year in the United States. It's difficult to determine if the wood selected for a coffin comes from a reputable source. The easiest way to avoid nonsustainable wood is to avoid exotics such as teak, sandalwood, and ebony and to steer clear of any wood that's harvested from rain forests.

Natural Preparation

Rather than go the standard route, there is a "do it yourself" funeral movement in which survivors take care of their loved ones and bury them on private land. Some find that handling their loved ones after death allows the process to remain personal and loving. Bodies are washed and dressed by close friends and family. Caskets, sometimes homemade, are decorated in favorite colors. Friends and family gather at the house, communing and sharing stories.

If you want to learn more about natural preparation and home burial, check out *Caring for the Dead* by Lisa Carlson. The book starts with stories of regular men and women who choose personal burials for the people they loved. The author then walks readers through the ins and outs of the funeral industry, alternatives, and laws for different states.

While home preparation and burial may seem natural, families must make sure it's handled correctly. By law, the body does belong to the family; however, there are state statutes that must be followed. This means anyone caring for a body is considered the funeral director and must meet all the regulatory requirements a funeral director has to meet. The death certificate has to be completed, embalming or other forms of preservation such as dry ice or refrigeration have to be addressed, a burial permit must be obtained if required by the state, and permits may need to be obtained to move the body.

There are a number of organizations that can provide assistance to anyone planning a funeral to help make sure all the applicable laws are considered. The Funeral Consumers Alliance (*www.funerals.org*) provides information not just on less costly burial alternatives but also on the rights and responsibilities of loved ones. The group can also suggest an advocate to help the survivors if there is confusion or misinformation regarding legalities.

Cremation

Cremation is becoming more popular in the United States, with ashes either being buried or scattered in the sea or the mountains. The decision whether to be cremated may be personal, religious, or societal. A benefit of using cremation prior to a service is that the body need not be preserved and the service can be scheduled at a later time.

Because of the destructive nature of cremation, a death certificate signed by a medical examiner is required before it can take place. Some states require a time limit between death and cremation. If the body is not refrigerated prior to cremation, it must be embalmed. This can be handled directly with a crematorium or through a funeral home.

During cremation, a completely combustible coffin and the body are burned at a very high temperature. Unless otherwise requested by the family, only one body is allowed to be cremated at a time. The cremation of an average size adult results in approximately four to six pounds of ashes. Because bone fragments may be not be completely burned, ashes are processed after cremation and then returned to the family in an urn. The whole process takes several hours to complete. If the funeral ceremony is performed before the body is cremated, funeral homes will likely rent a formal casket for the ceremony.

FACT

More and more people are turning to cremation as a way to handle their pets' remains. Animals can be cremated together or separately, but only the ashes of those cremated alone can be returned to the owner. There are a variety of memorial urns available; some can be customized to look like the deceased.

There are concerns with the air pollution released during cremation. The primary concern with crematorium emissions is mercury released from dental fillings. Crematoriums are required to use what is referred to as the best available technology (BAT) to treat emissions, which includes directing releases through an air scrubber prior to release from a chimney. There are not, however, set air standards for crematoriums to meet.

Green Caskets and Other Alternatives

The casket is one of the more expensive burial components. On the simple end, caskets of cardboard or untreated wood provide the basics without the added expense of chemicals or materials of more opulent coffins. There are many designs available that take the environment into account.

Most of the environmentally friendly caskets available today are manufactured in Europe; however, as green burials gain in popularity, there will likely be more designs available in the United States. Some cemeteries allow the burial of limited types of caskets, so consult your cemetery before you decide on a coffin that may be less mainstream.

Recycled-paper or cardboard caskets are one of the greener burial options. These are generally used for cremation, but they can also be used for burial. Most come in plain brown, but others are more artistic. Ecopods (*www.ecopod.co.uk*), made in the United Kingdom, are 100 percent recycled paper. They have sleek artistic designs and come in a variety of colors. The Cocoon manufactured by the German company Uono (*www.uono.com*) is made of biodegradable jute and is painted with a high-gloss, water-based varnish. It is lightweight and has a contemporary, smooth, almost egg-like, design. These coffins can be purchased and shipped from Europe to the United States.

To get the most out of your wood coffin, you can use it while you're still alive. Coffins can be used as tables, bookshelves, even sofas. Casket furniture is available on ✐*www.casketfurniture.com*, but if it's treated and painted, it may not necessarily be Earth friendly. The site also offers plans for simple pine boxes and casket shelf units, so you can make them yourself using green materials.

There is always the standard pine box that's been used for hundreds of years. They can be purchased through a funeral home or from manufacturers. In fact, there's a company called the Old Pine Box (*www.theoldpinebox .com*) that offers pine coffins and coffins made from other sustainable trees. Some coffins come with metal components, but they can be ordered with rope handles and nontoxic glue. There's also the option of a homemade casket. Casket plans or complete kits can be purchased from companies like the MHP Network (*www.mhp-casketkits.com*). Carpenters or artisans can also be contracted to build a custom casket.

Shrouds are sheets used to wrap a body prior to burial. They are available in a variety of biodegradable fabrics such as silk, cotton, linen, and wool. Biodegradable straps come with purchased shrouds and are used to wrap and lower the body. Shrouds can be purchased but can also come from the family. An heirloom quilt, passed down through generations, may be fitting as a shroud. Remember, though, that some cemeteries are very particular regarding burial practices. If you want to use a shroud or other casket alternative, make sure to confer with the cemetery first.

The Final Resting Place

Even if a loved one is cremated, you'll need to decide what to do with the remains. For decades, burial in a standard cemetery has been the norm, but more and more people are choosing other options. Alternative resting places have actually become businesses in themselves. For those who are cremated, ashes can be spread almost anywhere—sprinkled at sea, scattered in the woods, incorporated into an art piece, even shot into space (although the latter option is not particularly environmentally friendly).

Before spreading ashes, consider whether you'll want to visit the gravesite and what might become of the property where the ashes were placed. Will loved ones feel upset if the open field where the ashes were spread later becomes a discount store?

In the Woods

Preservations are still in their infancy but are growing as alternatives to run-of-the mill manicured and landscaped cemeteries. Considered green cemeteries, preserves let nature take over, leaving many trees in place and planting others as memorials. Birds roost and squirrels skitter about, so these preserved areas are teeming with life not death. As conservation areas, most preserves allow hiking and bird watching, giving the public the opportunity to appreciate a sacred area.

Nature preserves require that the deceased not be embalmed and that only environmentally friendly caskets or shrouds be used. Caretakers can usually help interested parties find acceptable products and materials. Although embalmed bodies are generally not accepted for burial, exceptions may be made if the deceased was embalmed against their wishes. Graves are marked with simple stones or native plants and can be documented with a global positioning system. Pets can also be buried on the property, so owners and their dogs, cats, or other pets can spend eternity side by side. Trails and boardwalks offer pathways for visitors who are coming to see a grave, taking a relaxing walk, or enjoying a bird-watching expedition.

Green cemeteries are unregulated, so take care in choosing one. The Green Burial Council (*www.greenburialcouncil.org*) is working to begin certifying conservation burial grounds and natural burial grounds. A conservation burial ground offers a natural setting, provides for future conservation measures, and is located near parks, wildlife corridors, or permanently protected areas. A portion of the proceeds is set aside for perpetual care, and the grounds are protected by a conservation easement, which means that legally the land cannot be developed. Natural burial grounds are similar, but they only provide protection of the burial ground, not the surrounding areas.

The Glendale Nature Preserve (*www.glendalenaturepreserve.org*) in Florida owns more than 350 acres of countryside, allowing burials to be more natural and peaceful. The preserve includes an open-air chapel, boardwalks, and bamboo groves. Tractor-drawn hay-wagon tours are available to explore the property. The preserve also has a sawmill on the property that is used to make caskets. Burial shrouds can also be purchased through the preserve.

Other green burial locations, state laws, and more information can be found at *www.forestofmemories.org*.

Under the Sea

It is possible to be buried at sea without being cremated. As part of the Clean Water Act, the EPA requires that burials at sea take place at least three miles offshore and where water is at least 600 feet deep. Remains must be in a container that will not float. If remains are cremated, they must still be taken three miles offshore, but there is no minimum water depth.

Burial at sea has become its own industry, offering reef memorials and boating services. Eternal Reefs (*www.eternalreefs.com*) offers a concrete casting in which the remains are mixed with the concrete. Once the mixture is cast, family and friends can place their handprints or write messages on the outside of the form that will eventually rest on the ocean floor. The concrete forms can form an artificial reef and marine habitat.

Professional services can be contracted with to assist in the burial, but it is also perfectly acceptable to arrange the service personally. Loved ones' remains can be scattered from a private boat in a personal ceremony that exemplifies a tribute to their life.

What's Left Behind

Many people believe that funeral services should emulate the deceased's life, and their legacy should as well. If you are able to plan your own memorial, you can be sure that a favorite poem is read or memorable music is played.

QUESTION?

How can I make my memorial more memorable?
One way to let your legacy live on is to give your friends and other family members a piece of memorabilia. If you have a collection of things like snow globes or sunbursts, have loved ones come by the house and pick one out. More than just giving them a piece of art or a knickknack, you are giving them a piece of yourself.

There are a variety of alternatives to receiving flowers at the memorial service. Friends can be asked to donate native plants to a church, school, park, or center. Books that illustrate the deceased's environmental beliefs can be purchased for the local library. Money can be donated to an environmental charity in the name of the deceased. A scholarship can be set up for environmental studies to benefit a deserving student.

Appendix A

Green Resources

If you are interested in learning more about a particular topic, this appendix has lists of resources to check out. There are detailed books and magazines that present a variety of information on various topics. You may be surprised at how many experts are trying to protect the environment with efforts that range from extreme to pragmatic. Some authors have written numerous books on environmental topics, so be sure to check out other titles. Web sites provide the latest information and are a good source for local causes and events.

Books

Anderson, Ray. *Mid-Course Correction: Toward a Sustainable Enterprise: The Interface Model*. Penguin Press, April 2006.

Carlson, Lisa. *Caring for the Dead: Your Final Act of Love*. Upper Access, March 1997.

Carson, Rachel. *Silent Spring*. 40th anniversary ed. Mariner Books, October 2002.

Cherry, Lynne. *The Great Kapok Tree: A Tale of the Amazon Rain Forest*. Reprint ed. Voyager Books, March 2000.

Colborn, Theo, Dianne Dumanoski, and John Peterson Myers. *Our Stolen Future: Are We Threatening Our Fertility, Intelligence and Survival? A Scientific Detective Story*. Reprint ed. Plume, March 1997.

Flannery, Tim. *The Weather Makers: How Man Is Changing the Climate and What It Means for Life on Earth*. Atlantic Monthly Press, February 2006.

Glickman, Marshall. *The Mindful Money Guide: Creating Harmony Between Your Values and Your Finances*. Wellspring/Ballantine, May 1999.

Goodell, Jeff. *Big Coal: The Dirty Secret Behind America's Energy Future*. Houghton Mifflin, June 2006.

Gore, Al. *An Inconvenient Truth*. Viking Juvenile, February 2007.

Harr, Jonathon. *A Civil Action*. First Vintage Books Edition, August 1996.

Hawken, Paul. *The Ecology of Commerce.* Reprint ed. HarperCollins, August 1994.

Hollender, Jeffrey, and Stephen Fenichell. *What Matters Most: How a Small Group of Pioneers Is Teaching Social Responsibility to Big Business, and Why Big Business Is Listening.* New Ed ed. Basic Books, January 2006.

Kolbert, Elizabeth. *Field Notes from a Catastrophe.* Bloomsbury USA, March 2006.

Louv, Richard. *Last Child in the Woods: Saving Our Children from Nature-Deficit Disorder.* Algonquin Books, April 2005.

Miller, Benjamin. *Fat of the Land: The Garbage of New York—The Last Two Hundred Years.* Four Wall Eight Windows, October 2000.

Paine, Lynn Sharp. *Value Shift: Why Companies Must Merge Social and Financial Imperatives to Achieve Superior Performance.* 1st ed. McGraw-Hill, September 2003.

Pearce, Fred. *When the Rivers Run Dry: Water—The Defining Crisis of the Twenty-First Century.* Beacon Press, March 2006.

Pollan, Michael. *Omnivore's Dilemma.* Penguin Press, April 2006.

Rathje, William, and Cullen Murphy. *Rubbish!* University of Arizona Press, March 2001.

Rivoli, Pietra. *The Travels of a T-Shirt in the Global Economy: An Economist Examines the Markets, Power, and Politics of World Trade.* New ed. Wiley, June 2006.

Royte, Elizabeth. *Garbage Land: On the Secrete Trail of Trash.* Little, Brown and Company, July 2005.

Scheckel, Paul. *The Home Energy Diet: How to Save Money by Making Your House Energy Smart.* New Society Publishers, May 2005.

Schlosser, Eric. *Fast Food Nation.* Harper Perennial, July 2005.

Singer, Peter, and Jim Mason. *The Way We Eat: Why Our Food Choices Matter.* Rodale Books, May 2006.

Zoellner, Tom. *The Heartless Stone: A Journey Through the World of Diamonds, Deceit and Desire.* St. Martin's Press, May 2006.

Magazines and Associated Web Sites

Audubon. National Audubon Society, Inc. ✐*www.audubonmagazine.com*

E/The Environmental Magazine. Earth Action Network, Inc. ✐*www.emagazine.com*

Earth Island Journal. Earth Island Institute. ✐*www.earthisland.org*

Ecological Home Ideas. Invisible Ink Publishing. ✐*www.ecologicalhomeideas.com*

Grist (online only). ✍*www.grist.org*

Mother Earth News. Ogden Publications, Inc. ✍*www.motherearthnews.com*

Mother Jones. The Foundation for National Progress. ✍*www.motherjones.com*

National Geographic. National Geographic Society. ✍*www.nationalgeographic.com*

National Geographic Kids. National Geographic Society. ✍*www.nationalgeographic.com/kids*

National Wildlife. National Wildlife Federation. ✍*www.nwf.org/nationalwildlife*

Natural Home. Ogden Publications, Inc. ✍*www.naturalhomeandgarden.com*

OnEarth. Natural Resources Defense Council. ✍*www.nrdc.org/onearth*

Sierra. Sierra Club. ✍*www.sierraclub.org*

Treehugger (online only). ✍*www.treehugger.com*

Utne Reader. Ogden Publications, Inc. ✍*www.utne.com*

Wildlife Conservation. Wildlife Conservation Society. ✍*www.wildlifeconservation.org*

Environmentally Conscious Businesses and Other Helpful Sites

When striving to lead a greener lifestyle, you'll want to patronize companies that operate with the environment in mind. Here's a list of companies that do just that. Some of the companies are listed under one category, but carry a variety of items. Be sure to check out their whole site. Also included are sites that provide information to help you choose environmental products or that have additional information.

Art

Aaron Foster Designs
✍*www.aaronfoster.com*

Bill Clark, Robotman Futuristic Sculptures
✍*www.robotman.0me.com*

Cracked Pots
✍*www.crackedpots.org*

Eco-artware.com
✍*www.eco-artware.com*

Bedding

Earthsake
✍*www.earthsake.com*

Gaiam
✐*www.gaiam.com*

Hollander EcoBedroom
✐*www.bedroom.com*

Natural Home Design Center
✐*www.naturalhomeproducts.com*

White Lotus Home
✐*www.whitelotus.net*

Building and Construction Materials

AFM Naturals
✐*www.afmsafecoat.com*

American Clay
✐*www.americanclay.com*

Collins Companies
✐*www.collinswood.com*

Hayward Lumber
✐*www.haywardlumber.com*

Ice Stone
✐*www.icestone.biz*

Burials and Caskets

Casket Furniture
✐*www.casketfurniture.com*

Eco Casket
✐*www.environmentalcaskets.com*

Forest of Memories
✐*www.forestofmemories.org*

Glendale Memorial Nature Preserve
✐*www.glendalenaturepreserve.org*

Memorial Ecosystems, Inc.
✐*www.memorialecosystems.com*

MHP-Casket Kits
✐*www.mhp-casketkits.com*

Woodland Caskets in the USA
✐*www.kentcasket.com*

Business Equipment

RyzexGroup
✐*www.ryzex.com*

Careers and Education

Action Without Borders, The Career Center
✐*www.idealist.org*

The Environmental Education Directory
✐*www.enviroeducation.com*

Gradschools.com
✐*www.gradschools.com*

SustainableBusiness.com
✐*www.sustainablebusiness.com*

Carpooling and Ride-Sharing

Carpoolconnect.com
www.carpoolconnect.com

City Car Share
www.citycarshare.org

eRideShare.com
www.erideshare.com

Flexcar
www.flexcar.com

iCarPool.com
www.icarpool.com

Zipcar
www.zipcar.com

Charity Information

BBB Wise Giving Alliance
www.give.org

Charity Navigator
www.charitynavigator.org

GuideStar
www.guidestar.org

JustGive
www.justgive.org

Children and Family

Childsake
www.childsake.com

ClothDiaper.com
www.clothdiaper.com

Cotton Babies
www.cottonbabies.com

Eco-dipes
www.ecodipes.com

ERGO Baby
www.ergobaby.com

KidBean.com
www.kidbean.com

Laptop Lunches by Obentec
www.laptoplunches.com

Mother-Ease
www.mother-ease.com

One Hot Mama
www.onehotmama.com

Peppermint
www.peppermint.com

The Sling Station
www.theslingstation.com

Soft Cloth Bunz
www.softclothbunz.com

Wholesome Baby Food
www.wholesomebabyfood.com

Yosemite National Institutes
www.yni.org

Cleaning Products

Eco-Source
www.eco-source.com

Household Products Database
www.householdproducts.nlm.nih.gov

Natural Choices, Home Safe Products, LLC
www.oxyboost.com

Seventh Generation
www.seventhgen.com

Sun and Earth, Inc.
www.sunandearth.com

Clothing

American Apparel
www.americanapparel.net

downBound.com
www.downbound.com

Patagonia
www.patagonia.com

Round Belly Clothing
www.roundbelly.com

Teko Socks
www.tekosocks.com

Zoots (dry cleaner, carpet cleaning)
www.zoots.com

Consultants and Designers

EnerTech Environmental
www.enertech.com

GreenOrder
www.greenorder.com

Healthy Home Center
www.healthyhome.com

IBC Engineering Services
www.ibcengineering.com

Michelle Kaufman Designs
www.mkd-arc.com

Electronics

ReCellular
www.recellular.net

Voltaic Systems
www.voltaicsystems.com

Energy

Affordable Solar Group
www.affordable-solar.com

The Alternative Energy Story
www.altenergy.com

BlackLight Power, Inc.
www.blacklightpower.com

Cilion
www.cilion.com

CoalTek
www.coaltek.com

Database of State Incentives for Renewables & Efficiency
www.dsireusa.org

Energy Innovations
www.energyinnovations.com

Energy Star
www.energystar.gov

Find Solar
www.findsolar.com

GreatPoint Energy
www.greatpointenergy.com

GreenFuel Technologies Corp.
www.greenfuelonline.com

Gridpoint, Inc.
www.gridpoint.com

Nanosolar
www.nanosolar.com

Prometheus Energy
www.prometheus-energy.com

Solar Direct
www.solardirect.com

Southwest Windpower
www.windenergy.com

SPG Solar
www.sunpowergeo.com

Verdant Power
www.verdantpower.com

Environmental Information

AIRNow
www.airnow.gov

California Urban Water Conservation Council
www.cuwcc.org

The Conservation Fund
www.conservationfund.org

Co-op America
www.coopamerica.org

Earth 911
www.earth911.org

Environmental Working Group
www.ewg.org

Green Festival
www.greenfestivals.org

Green Options
www.greenoptions.com

IdealsWork, Inc.
www.idealswork.com

Living Green Expo
www.livinggreen.org

Office of the Federal Environmental Executive
www.ofee.gov

Flooring

Hendricksen Natürlich Flooring
www.naturalfloors.net

Interface, Inc.
www.interfaceinc.com

Natural Home Design Center
www.naturalhomeproducts.com

Teragren
www.teragren.com

Food and Drink

Blue Sky Beverage Company
www.drinkbluesky.com

Brewers Association
www.beertown.org

Burgerville
www.burgerville.com

Choice Organic Teas
www.choiceorganicteas.com

CLIF BAR
www.clifbar.com

EatWild
www.eatwild.com

Eden Foods
www.edenfoods.com

Environmental Protection Agency Fish Advice
www.epa.gov/waterscience/fishadvice

Fantastic World Foods
www.fantasticfoods.com

Fiddler's Green Farm
www.fiddlersgreenfarm.com

Fresh Farm Market
www.freshfarmmarket.com

Frey Vineyards
www.freywine.com

Frog's Leap Winery
www.frogsleap.com

Dr. Temple Grandin
www.grandin.com

Green Restaurant Association
www.dinegreen.com

Grounds for Change
www.groundsforchange.com

Healthy Beverage Company
www.steaz.com

Horizon Organic
www.horizonorganic.com

R.W. Knudsen
www.knudsenjuices.com

Local Harvest
www.localharvest.org

Monterey Bay Aquarium
www.mbayaq.org

New Belgium Brewing Company
www.newbelgium.com

Otter Creek Brewing
www.wolavers.com

Santa Cruz Organic
www.scojuice.com

Seven Bridges Cooperative
www.breworganic.com

Stonyfield Farm
www.stonyfield.com

TransFair
www.transfairusa.org

Gifts

Global Exchange Fair Trade Online Store
http://store.gxonlinestore.org

Global Gifts
www.globalgifts.org

Peaceful Valley
www.peacefulvalleygreetings.com

Ten Thousand Villages
www.tenthousandvillages.com

Home Furnishings and Appliances

Cabin Furniture and Décor
www.1cabinfurniture.com

Ecowork
www.ecowork.com

el Environmental Language
www.el-furniture.com

GREENCulture
www.eco-furniture.com

Herman Miller, Inc.
www.hermanmiller.com

Vivavi, Inc.
www.vivavi.com

Investing

The Progressive Investor
www.sustainablebusiness.com

Social Funds
www.socialfunds.com

The Social Investment Forum
www.socialinvest.org

Sustainable Business Institute
www.sustainablebusiness.org

Jewelry

greenKarat
www.greenkarat.com

Moonrise Jewelry
www.moonrisejewelry.com

Lawn and Garden

Composters.com
www.composters.com

Hobbs & Hopkins Ltd
www.protimelawnseed.com

NaturaLawn of America
www.nl-amer.com

No Mow Grass
www.nomowgrass.com

Prairie Nursery
www.prairienursery.com

Stepables
www.stepables.com

TerraCycle
www.terracycle.net

Wildflower Farm
www.wildflowerfarm.com

Paper, Printing, and Office Supplies

Ecoprint
www.ecoprint.com

Excellent Packaging & Supply
www.excellentpackaging.com

New Leaf Paper
www.newleafpaper.com

Printedgreen
www.printedgreen.com

Personal Care

The Alchemist's Apprentice
www.alchemistsapprentice.com

Aubrey Organics
www.aubrey-organics.com

The Body Shop
www.thebodyshop.com

Burt's Bees
www.burtsbees.com

California Baby
www.californiababy.com

CanaryCosmetics.com
www.canarycosmetics.com

The Coalition for Consumer Information on Cosmetics
www.leapingbunny.org

J. P. Durga
www.jpdurga.com

EcoColors
www.ecocolors.net

Environmental Working Group Skin Deep Report
www.ewg.org/reports/skindeep2

Feminine Options
www.feminineoptions.com

Greenfeet
www.greenfeet.com

Dr. Hauschka Skin Care
www.drhauschka.com

Kiss My Face
www.kissmyface.com

Natural Woman
www.natural-woman.com

Nature's Gate
www.natures-gate.com

Noah's Naturals
www.noahsnaturals.com

ONEwithEarth Organics
www.onewithearth.com

The Organic Make-up Company
www.organicmakeup.com

Pandora Pads
www.pandorapads.com

PeaceKeeper
www.iamapeacekeeper.com

Preserve
www.recycline.com

Terressentials
www.terressentials.com

Tom's of Maine
www.tomsofmaine.com

A Wild Soap Bar
www.awildsoapbar.com

Pet Products

GreenPets.com
www.greenpets.com

Holistic Pet Food
www.holisticfood4pets.biz

Only Natural Pet Store
www.onlynaturalpet.com

PetDIETS.com
www.petdiets.com

Purrfectplay
www.purrfectplay.com

Politics

Michigan Land Use Institute

✎*www.mlui.org*

NetAction

✎*www.netaction.org*

SpeakOut.com

✎*www.speakout.com*

Recycling

The Freecycle Network

✎*www.freecycle.org*

Shopping Bags

Eco Bags Products, Inc.

✎*www.ecobags.com*

Enviro-Tote

✎*www.enviro-tote.com*

ReusableBags.com

✎*www.reusablebags.com*

Toys and Sports

Comet Skateboards

✎*www.cometskateboards.com*

Vehicles and Driving

Extengine Transport Systems

✎*www.extengine.com*

fueleconomy.gov

✎*www.fueleconomy.gov*

IdleAire

✎*www.idleaire.com*

Tesla Motors

✎*www.teslamotors.com*

Volunteer Opportunities

Action Without Borders

✎*www.idealist.org*

HumaneTeen

✎*www.humaneteen.org*

SERVEnet

✎*www.servenet.org*

VolunteerMatch

✎*www.volunteermatch.org*

Wilderness Volunteers

✎*www.wildernessvolunteers.org*

Waste Handling

Seahorse Power Company

✎*www.seahorsepower.com*

Webhosting

Affordable Internet Services Online, Inc.

✎*www.aiso.net*

Appendix B

Glossary

acid rain
Nitric and sulfuric acid in precipitation; combustion of fossil fuels contributes to the problem

alternative fuels
Power for vehicles that does not rely on fossil fuels (e.g., ethanol and biodiesel)

biodegradable
Organic material that is able to be broken down by living things

biodiversity
The variety of living organisms found in a particular area or ecosystem

biomass
The production of energy from plant or animal materials; an alternative fuel source

borax
An alkali that can be used as a cleaning agent

carbon monoxide
Deadly, odorless gas produced during the incomplete combustion of carbon

carbon trading
Related to offsetting carbon emissions; companies that emit more greenhouse gases than they are allowed can buy credits from companies that produce less

carcinogen
Cancer-causing agent

chlorofluorocarbons (CFCs)
Ozone-depleting, heat-trapping chemicals once prevalent in aerosols and cleaning solvents

coal gasification
A method of using coal for energy that produces fewer emissions than traditional burning, in which coal is subjected to high temperatures, intense pressure, and a controlled flow of oxygen to break down the carbon and produce energy

combustion
The process of burning fuels to produce energy

cooperative
Also called a co-op; a group that works together for the members' economic, social, and cultural benefit

dioxin
A toxic chemical by-product of some industrial operations

ecosystem
A chain of life in a given area; a balance between living organisms

ecotourism
Travel that includes environmental considerations, respecting the environment and local cultures

effluent
Wastewater from human lives; usually refers to treated sewage

emission
Release of gases into the atmosphere

endocrine disruptor
Chemicals that block or mimic hormones when absorbed by the body

erosion
Wearing away of Earth's surface

exotics
Non-native species

fair trade
A partnership that supports better trading conditions particularly for under-represented workers

fescue grass
Transitional grass that can survive in both warm and cool climates

fluorinated gases
Global-warming gases produced from various industrial processes

fossil fuels
Non-renewable energy sources such as coal and petroleum that are derived from fossilized plants and animals and that emit greenhouse gases when burned

geothermal
Natural source of power obtained from Earth's heat, which is derived from rock and liquid in Earth's crust

geotourism
A form of travel that encourages visitors to appreciate the natural features and cultures of destinations

global warming
Gradual increases in the planet's air and water temperatures resulting in changes to the climate

green living
The act of being environmentally responsible; making decisions to benefit the environment or curtailing harmful practices

greenhouse gases
Agents of global warming that trap heat within the atmosphere instead of allowing it to escape into outer space; include carbon dioxide, methane, nitrous oxide, and fluorinated gases

growth hormone
Supplements fed to livestock to help them grow larger and more quickly

humus
Composted waste

kinetic energy
Power derived from movement; windmills use this type of energy

Kyoto Protocol
An international pact that aims to reduce greenhouse gas emissions by capping emissions rates

low-emissivity
A type of coating applied to windows to regulate the amount of heat the windows allow into rooms

methane
The simplest form of hydrocarbon; a greenhouse gas formed by both natural and human activities; highly combustible; can be used to generate electricity

natural food
Edible products grown without help from synthetic hormones or additives

natural resources
Land, forests, mineral deposits, and other raw materials supplied by nature

nitrous oxides
Reactive gases formed during the combustion of fuel; can form ground-level ozone and acid rain

offgas
The vaporizing or evaporating chemicals from treated surfaces

offset
The process of negating harmful environmental practices by engaging in beneficial practices, such as offsetting greenhouse gas emissions by planting trees

organic
Growing, raising, or processing of food without drugs, synthetic chemicals, or hormones by using methods that conserve natural resources and limit effects on the environment

ozone
A gas made up of three atoms of oxygen found in the atmosphere; in its naturally occurring state, it protects Earth from the sun's harmful UV rays. Ground-level ozone is a pollutant that contributes to urban smog and causes respiratory problems.

parabens
Chemicals used as preservatives in cosmetic products; linked to rare allergies; hotly debated studies reported traces of parabens in breast cancer tumors

particulate matter
Pollutants present in the air in the form of small particles and liquid droplets

pesticide
Chemicals used to control pests (e.g., spraying DDT to kill insect populations)

phthalate
Chemicals added to plastics to increase flexibility; controversial studies linked them to decreased sperm counts in men and other reproductive problems

pollution
Contamination of air, water, or soil by harmful agents

radon
A naturally occurring cancer-causing gas that's emitted from the soil and can collect in structures

renewable energy
Power derived from sources whose supplies are not limited (e.g., wind or solar energy)

smog
Ground-level air pollution associated with respiratory problems and hazy skies

sulfites
Preservatives in wine and some food products; linked to relatively rare allergies

sulfur dioxide
A pollutant produced during combustion of fossil fuels like coal and oil; prevalent in acid rain

surfactant
Organic molecules that get in between grime and fabric, separating the two; a major component of detergents and soaps

sustainability
The balance between continuing a way of life or standard of living while protecting the environment and its resources

sustainable energy
Power sources that cannot be easily depleted (e.g., wind or solar energy)

synthetic
Any artificially made material

transpiration
The process of plants releasing water into the atmosphere

vegan
A lifestyle that rejects the use of any products or foods made from animals

vegetarian
A lifestyle that relies on nonanimal products for food

volatile organic compounds (VOCs)
Chemical compounds that easily vaporize into the atmosphere or are absorbed into the soil or water; include harmful pollutants and greenhouse gases like methane

whole foods
Foods that undergo as little processing as possible

Appendix C

A Quiz: How Big Is Your Eco-Footprint?

So, just how "green" are you? Most people want to tread lightly on the planet, but they really aren't sure how big an impact they are making. If you are curious to see if you are a help or hindrance to the planet, take this quiz and find out. Just pick the answer that best suits your lifestyle.

The Questions

1. How often do you recycle?

a. I am a recycling nut. I recycle everything I can: paper, aluminum, printer cartridges, you name it.

b. I recycle when it's convenient as long as it doesn't require any excessive thought or effort on my part.

c. I don't have the time or the patience to recycle. I'm a very busy person.

2. Do you use recycled products?

a. I try to reduce what I need, but when I do have to make purchases, I opt for recycled products whenever possible.

b. If I remember to look for the recycle triangle logo, I will usually buy that product.

c. So that's what they're doing with all the stuff other people recycle?

3. How many of your appliances have the Energy Star label?

a. Every single one of them that's available with the Energy Star label. I only buy products that are energy-efficient.

b. When I'm out shopping, I look for the Energy Star label. I try to purchase efficient appliances, but I won't sacrifice what I ultimately want.

c. I buy the appliances I want and need regardless of whether they're efficient. If there's an Energy Star label on one of my appliances, it's pure coincidence.

4. How much of your house is made from sustainable materials?

a. My entire house is made of recycled or sustainable materials. In fact, it is LEED certified.

b. My house wasn't built using sustainable materials, but every time I renovate, I use sustainable and recycled materials.

c. I leave all the purchasing decisions to the builders. If they want to use sustainable or recycled materials, they can. It doesn't matter to me.

5. Do you use any form of renewable energy in your home?

a. I purchase renewable energy from the local utility that's generated from landfill gas. Otherwise, I'd have a windmill or solar cells.

b. I'm evaluating different options. My local utility just started a renewable energy option. It costs a little more, but it's worth it. I'm also looking at adding solar cells to the house.

c. I think I heard something about the local utility using renewable energy, but I think it costs more, so I don't think I'll sign up for it.

6. What kind of gas mileage does your car get?

a. I don't own a car.

b. Fifty miles to the gallon, baby!

c. I'm not really sure, but I'm guessing about fifteen.

7. How often to do you eliminate car trips?

a. I don't own a car. My primary means of transportation are my feet, my bike, and mass transit.

b. I try to eliminate at least one car trip a day by riding my bike or walking. I also try to carpool when car trips are really necessary.

c. My car is an extension of me. I wouldn't think of using any other kind of transportation.

8. How often do you eat meat?

a. I really don't eat meat. Sometimes on rare occasions, I'll have a taste.

b. I do eat it regularly, but I try to buy local meat that's raised organically.

c. I eat meat like Cookie Monster eats cookies.

9. What kind of seafood do you eat?

a. I rarely eat meat, seafood included, but when I do eat seafood, it's usually clams or mussels.

b. I eat seafood every couple of weeks, and it's usually shrimp that's been caught in the wild or farmed in the United States.

c. I love Atlantic halibut and flounder and eat it every chance I get.

10. What kind of pet do you have?

a. I got my two dogs from the local animal shelter. I got my cat from a purebred rescue group.

b. My dog came from the animal shelter, but I really wanted a purebred cat with papers, so I bought it from a breeder.

c. I checked, but my local animal shelter didn't have any Amazon parrots, so I bought some online. I had a boa constrictor, but it got too big so I let it go.

Scoring:

For every *a* answer, give yourself 2 points.
For every *b* answer, give yourself 1 point.
For every *c* answer, give yourself 0 points.

How Big Is Your Footprint?

If you scored:

20 to 15 points: You have a petite and delicate footprint. Earth needs more inhabitants like you!

14 to 9 points: Your footprint shows potential. Just a few more eco-friendly acts and you'll be reducing your shoe size.

8 to 0 points: Your footprint rivals that of Sasquatch. You are hereby challenged to stop stomping around on the planet.

Index

THE EVERYTHING SERIES!

BUSINESS & PERSONAL FINANCE

Everything® Accounting Book
Everything® Budgeting Book, 2nd Ed.
Everything® Business Planning Book
Everything® Coaching and Mentoring Book, 2nd Ed.
Everything® Fundraising Book
Everything® Get Out of Debt Book
Everything® Grant Writing Book, 2nd Ed.
Everything® Guide to Buying Foreclosures
Everything® Guide to Mortgages
Everything® Guide to Personal Finance for Single Mothers
Everything® Home-Based Business Book, 2nd Ed.
Everything® Homebuying Book, 2nd Ed.
Everything® Homeselling Book, 2nd Ed.
Everything® Human Resource Management Book
Everything® Improve Your Credit Book
Everything® Investing Book, 2nd Ed.
Everything® Landlording Book
Everything® Leadership Book, 2nd Ed.
Everything® Managing People Book, 2nd Ed.
Everything® Negotiating Book
Everything® Online Auctions Book
Everything® Online Business Book
Everything® Personal Finance Book
Everything® Personal Finance in Your 20s & 30s Book, 2nd Ed.
Everything® Project Management Book, 2nd Ed.
Everything® Real Estate Investing Book
Everything® Retirement Planning Book
Everything® Robert's Rules Book, $7.95
Everything® Selling Book
Everything® Start Your Own Business Book, 2nd Ed.
Everything® Wills & Estate Planning Book

COOKING

Everything® Barbecue Cookbook
Everything® Bartender's Book, 2nd Ed., $9.95
Everything® Calorie Counting Cookbook
Everything® Cheese Book
Everything® Chinese Cookbook
Everything® Classic Recipes Book
Everything® Cocktail Parties & Drinks Book
Everything® College Cookbook
Everything® Cooking for Baby and Toddler Book
Everything® Cooking for Two Cookbook
Everything® Diabetes Cookbook
Everything® Easy Gourmet Cookbook
Everything® Fondue Cookbook
Everything® Fondue Party Book
Everything® Gluten-Free Cookbook
Everything® Glycemic Index Cookbook
Everything® Grilling Cookbook
Everything® Healthy Meals in Minutes Cookbook
Everything® Holiday Cookbook
Everything® Indian Cookbook
Everything® Italian Cookbook

Everything® Lactose-Free Cookbook
Everything® Low-Carb Cookbook
Everything® Low-Cholesterol Cookbook
Everything® Low-Fat High-Flavor Cookbook
Everything® Low-Salt Cookbook
Everything® Meals for a Month Cookbook
Everything® Meals on a Budget Cookbook
Everything® Mediterranean Cookbook
Everything® Mexican Cookbook
Everything® No Trans Fat Cookbook
Everything® One-Pot Cookbook
Everything® Pizza Cookbook
Everything® Quick and Easy 30-Minute, 5-Ingredient Cookbook
Everything® Quick Meals Cookbook
Everything® Slow Cooker Cookbook
Everything® Slow Cooking for a Crowd Cookbook
Everything® Soup Cookbook
Everything® Stir-Fry Cookbook
Everything® Sugar-Free Cookbook
Everything® Tapas and Small Plates Cookbook
Everything® Tex-Mex Cookbook
Everything® Thai Cookbook
Everything® Vegetarian Cookbook
Everything® Whole-Grain, High-Fiber Cookbook
Everything® Wild Game Cookbook
Everything® Wine Book, 2nd Ed.

GAMES

Everything® 15-Minute Sudoku Book, $9.95
Everything® 30-Minute Sudoku Book, $9.95
Everything® Bible Crosswords Book, $9.95
Everything® Blackjack Strategy Book
Everything® Brain Strain Book, $9.95
Everything® Bridge Book
Everything® Card Games Book
Everything® Card Tricks Book, $9.95
Everything® Casino Gambling Book, 2nd Ed.
Everything® Chess Basics Book
Everything® Craps Strategy Book
Everything® Crossword and Puzzle Book
Everything® Crossword Challenge Book
Everything® Crosswords for the Beach Book, $9.95
Everything® Cryptic Crosswords Book, $9.95
Everything® Cryptograms Book, $9.95
Everything® Easy Crosswords Book
Everything® Easy Kakuro Book, $9.95
Everything® Easy Large-Print Crosswords Book
Everything® Games Book, 2nd Ed.
Everything® Giant Sudoku Book, $9.95
Everything® Giant Word Search Book
Everything® Kakuro Challenge Book, $9.95
Everything® Large-Print Crossword Challenge Book
Everything® Large-Print Crosswords Book
Everything® Lateral Thinking Puzzles Book, $9.95
Everything® Literary Crosswords Book, $9.95
Everything® Mazes Book
Everything® Memory Booster Puzzles Book, $9.95
Everything® Movie Crosswords Book, $9.95

Everything® Music Crosswords Book, $9.95
Everything® Online Poker Book
Everything® Pencil Puzzles Book, $9.95
Everything® Poker Strategy Book
Everything® Pool & Billiards Book
Everything® Puzzles for Commuters Book, $9.95
Everything® Puzzles for Dog Lovers Book, $9.95
Everything® Sports Crosswords Book, $9.95
Everything® Test Your IQ Book, $9.95
Everything® Texas Hold 'Em Book, $9.95
Everything® Travel Crosswords Book, $9.95
Everything® TV Crosswords Book, $9.95
Everything® Word Games Challenge Book
Everything® Word Scramble Book
Everything® Word Search Book

HEALTH

Everything® Alzheimer's Book
Everything® Diabetes Book
Everything® First Aid Book, $9.95
Everything® Health Guide to Adult Bipolar Disorder
Everything® Health Guide to Arthritis
Everything® Health Guide to Controlling Anxiety
Everything® Health Guide to Depression
Everything® Health Guide to Fibromyalgia
Everything® Health Guide to Menopause, 2nd Ed.
Everything® Health Guide to Migraines
Everything® Health Guide to OCD
Everything® Health Guide to PMS
Everything® Health Guide to Postpartum Care
Everything® Health Guide to Thyroid Disease
Everything® Hypnosis Book
Everything® Low Cholesterol Book
Everything® Menopause Book
Everything® Nutrition Book
Everything® Reflexology Book
Everything® Stress Management Book

HISTORY

Everything® American Government Book
Everything® American History Book, 2nd Ed.
Everything® Civil War Book
Everything® Freemasons Book
Everything® Irish History & Heritage Book
Everything® Middle East Book
Everything® World War II Book, 2nd Ed.

HOBBIES

Everything® Candlemaking Book
Everything® Cartooning Book
Everything® Coin Collecting Book
Everything® Digital Photography Book, 2nd Ed.
Everything® Drawing Book
Everything® Family Tree Book, 2nd Ed.
Everything® Knitting Book
Everything® Knots Book
Everything® Photography Book
Everything® Quilting Book

Everything® Sewing Book
Everything® Soapmaking Book, 2nd Ed.
Everything® Woodworking Book

HOME IMPROVEMENT

Everything® Feng Shui Book
Everything® Feng Shui Decluttering Book, $9.95
Everything® Fix-It Book
Everything® Green Living Book
Everything® Home Decorating Book
Everything® Home Storage Solutions Book
Everything® Homebuilding Book
Everything® Organize Your Home Book, 2nd Ed.

KIDS' BOOKS

All titles are $7.95

Everything® Fairy Tales Book, $14.95
Everything® Kids' Animal Puzzle & Activity Book
Everything® Kids' Astronomy Book
Everything® Kids' Baseball Book, 5th Ed.
Everything® Kids' Bible Trivia Book
Everything® Kids' Bugs Book
Everything® Kids' Cars and Trucks Puzzle and Activity Book
Everything® Kids' Christmas Puzzle & Activity Book
Everything® Kids' Connect the Dots
         Puzzle and Activity Book
Everything® Kids' Cookbook
Everything® Kids' Crazy Puzzles Book
Everything® Kids' Dinosaurs Book
Everything® Kids' Environment Book
Everything® Kids' Fairies Puzzle and Activity Book
Everything® Kids' First Spanish Puzzle and Activity Book
Everything® Kids' Football Book
Everything® Kids' Gross Cookbook
Everything® Kids' Gross Hidden Pictures Book
Everything® Kids' Gross Jokes Book
Everything® Kids' Gross Mazes Book
Everything® Kids' Gross Puzzle & Activity Book
Everything® Kids' Halloween Puzzle & Activity Book
Everything® Kids' Hidden Pictures Book
Everything® Kids' Horses Book
Everything® Kids' Joke Book
Everything® Kids' Knock Knock Book
Everything® Kids' Learning French Book
Everything® Kids' Learning Spanish Book
Everything® Kids' Magical Science Experiments Book
Everything® Kids' Math Puzzles Book
Everything® Kids' Mazes Book
Everything® Kids' Money Book
Everything® Kids' Nature Book
Everything® Kids' Pirates Puzzle and Activity Book
Everything® Kids' Presidents Book
Everything® Kids' Princess Puzzle and Activity Book
Everything® Kids' Puzzle Book
Everything® Kids' Racecars Puzzle and Activity Book
Everything® Kids' Riddles & Brain Teasers Book
Everything® Kids' Science Experiments Book
Everything® Kids' Sharks Book
Everything® Kids' Soccer Book
Everything® Kids' Spies Puzzle and Activity Book
Everything® Kids' States Book
Everything® Kids' Travel Activity Book
Everything® Kids' Word Search Puzzle and Activity Book

LANGUAGE

Everything® Conversational Japanese Book with CD, $19.95
Everything® French Grammar Book
Everything® French Phrase Book, $9.95
Everything® French Verb Book, $9.95
Everything® German Practice Book with CD, $19.95
Everything® Inglés Book
Everything® Intermediate Spanish Book with CD, $19.95
Everything® Italian Practice Book with CD, $19.95
Everything® Learning Brazilian Portuguese Book with CD, $19.95
Everything® Learning French Book with CD, 2nd Ed., $19.95
Everything® Learning German Book
Everything® Learning Italian Book
Everything® Learning Latin Book
Everything® Learning Russian Book with CD, $19.95
Everything® Learning Spanish Book
Everything® Learning Spanish Book with CD, 2nd Ed., $19.95
Everything® Russian Practice Book with CD, $19.95
Everything® Sign Language Book
Everything® Spanish Grammar Book
Everything® Spanish Phrase Book, $9.95
Everything® Spanish Practice Book with CD, $19.95
Everything® Spanish Verb Book, $9.95
Everything® Speaking Mandarin Chinese Book with CD, $19.95

MUSIC

Everything® Bass Guitar Book with CD, $19.95
Everything® Drums Book with CD, $19.95
Everything® Guitar Book with CD, 2nd Ed., $19.95
Everything® Guitar Chords Book with CD, $19.95
Everything® Harmonica Book with CD, $15.95
Everything® Home Recording Book
Everything® Music Theory Book with CD, $19.95
Everything® Reading Music Book with CD, $19.95
Everything® Rock & Blues Guitar Book with CD, $19.95
Everything® Rock & Blues Piano Book with CD, $19.95
Everything® Songwriting Book

NEW AGE

Everything® Astrology Book, 2nd Ed.
Everything® Birthday Personology Book
Everything® Dreams Book, 2nd Ed.
Everything® Love Signs Book, $9.95
Everything® Love Spells Book, $9.95
Everything® Paganism Book
Everything® Palmistry Book
Everything® Psychic Book
Everything® Reiki Book
Everything® Sex Signs Book, $9.95
Everything® Spells & Charms Book, 2nd Ed.
Everything® Tarot Book, 2nd Ed.
Everything® Toltec Wisdom Book
Everything® Wicca & Witchcraft Book, 2nd Ed.

PARENTING

Everything® Baby Names Book, 2nd Ed.
Everything® Baby Shower Book, 2nd Ed.
Everything® Baby Sign Language Book with DVD
Everything® Baby's First Year Book
Everything® Birthing Book

Everything® Breastfeeding Book
Everything® Father-to-Be Book
Everything® Father's First Year Book
Everything® Get Ready for Baby Book, 2nd Ed.
Everything® Get Your Baby to Sleep Book, $9.95
Everything® Getting Pregnant Book
Everything® Guide to Pregnancy Over 35
Everything® Guide to Raising a One-Year-Old
Everything® Guide to Raising a Two-Year-Old
Everything® Guide to Raising Adolescent Boys
Everything® Guide to Raising Adolescent Girls
Everything® Mother's First Year Book
Everything® Parent's Guide to Childhood Illnesses
Everything® Parent's Guide to Children and Divorce
Everything® Parent's Guide to Children with ADD/ADHD
Everything® Parent's Guide to Children with Asperger's Syndrome
Everything® Parent's Guide to Children with Asthma
Everything® Parent's Guide to Children with Autism
Everything® Parent's Guide to Children with Bipolar Disorder
Everything® Parent's Guide to Children with Depression
Everything® Parent's Guide to Children with Dyslexia
Everything® Parent's Guide to Children with Juvenile Diabetes
Everything® Parent's Guide to Positive Discipline
Everything® Parent's Guide to Raising a Successful Child
Everything® Parent's Guide to Raising Boys
Everything® Parent's Guide to Raising Girls
Everything® Parent's Guide to Raising Siblings
Everything® Parent's Guide to Sensory Integration Disorder
Everything® Parent's Guide to Tantrums
Everything® Parent's Guide to the Strong-Willed Child
Everything® Parenting a Teenager Book
Everything® Potty Training Book, $9.95
Everything® Pregnancy Book, 3rd Ed.
Everything® Pregnancy Fitness Book
Everything® Pregnancy Nutrition Book
Everything® Pregnancy Organizer, 2nd Ed., $16.95
Everything® Toddler Activities Book
Everything® Toddler Book
Everything® Tween Book
Everything® Twins, Triplets, and More Book

PETS

Everything® Aquarium Book
Everything® Boxer Book
Everything® Cat Book, 2nd Ed.
Everything® Chihuahua Book
Everything® Cooking for Dogs Book
Everything® Dachshund Book
Everything® Dog Book, 2nd Ed.
Everything® Dog Grooming Book
Everything® Dog Health Book
Everything® Dog Obedience Book
Everything® Dog Owner's Organizer, $16.95
Everything® Dog Training and Tricks Book
Everything® German Shepherd Book
Everything® Golden Retriever Book
Everything® Horse Book
Everything® Horse Care Book
Everything® Horseback Riding Book
Everything® Labrador Retriever Book
Everything® Poodle Book
Everything® Pug Book

Everything® Puppy Book
Everything® Rottweiler Book
Everything® Small Dogs Book
Everything® Tropical Fish Book
Everything® Yorkshire Terrier Book

REFERENCE

Everything® American Presidents Book
Everything® Blogging Book
Everything® Build Your Vocabulary Book, $9.95
Everything® Car Care Book
Everything® Classical Mythology Book
Everything® Da Vinci Book
Everything® Divorce Book
Everything® Einstein Book
Everything® Enneagram Book
Everything® Etiquette Book, 2nd Ed.
Everything® Guide to C. S. Lewis & Narnia
Everything® Guide to Edgar Allan Poe
Everything® Guide to Understanding Philosophy
Everything® Inventions and Patents Book
Everything® Jacqueline Kennedy Onassis Book
Everything® John F. Kennedy Book
Everything® Mafia Book
Everything® Martin Luther King Jr. Book
Everything® Philosophy Book
Everything® Pirates Book
Everything® Private Investigation Book
Everything® Psychology Book
Everything® Public Speaking Book, $9.95
Everything® Shakespeare Book, 2nd Ed.

RELIGION

Everything® Angels Book
Everything® Bible Book
Everything® Bible Study Book with CD, $19.95
Everything® Buddhism Book
Everything® Catholicism Book
Everything® Christianity Book
Everything® Gnostic Gospels Book
Everything® History of the Bible Book
Everything® Jesus Book
Everything® Jewish History & Heritage Book
Everything® Judaism Book
Everything® Kabbalah Book
Everything® Koran Book
Everything® Mary Book
Everything® Mary Magdalene Book
Everything® Prayer Book
Everything® Saints Book, 2nd Ed.
Everything® Torah Book
Everything® Understanding Islam Book
Everything® Women of the Bible Book
Everything® World's Religions Book

SCHOOL & CAREERS

Everything® Career Tests Book
Everything® College Major Test Book
Everything® College Survival Book, 2nd Ed.
Everything® Cover Letter Book, 2nd Ed.
Everything® Filmmaking Book
Everything® Get-a-Job Book, 2nd Ed.
Everything® Guide to Being a Paralegal
Everything® Guide to Being a Personal Trainer
Everything® Guide to Being a Real Estate Agent
Everything® Guide to Being a Sales Rep
Everything® Guide to Being an Event Planner
Everything® Guide to Careers in Health Care
Everything® Guide to Careers in Law Enforcement
Everything® Guide to Government Jobs
Everything® Guide to Starting and Running a Catering Business
Everything® Guide to Starting and Running a Restaurant
Everything® Job Interview Book, 2nd Ed.
Everything® New Nurse Book
Everything® New Teacher Book
Everything® Paying for College Book
Everything® Practice Interview Book
Everything® Resume Book, 3rd Ed.
Everything® Study Book

SELF-HELP

Everything® Body Language Book
Everything® Dating Book, 2nd Ed.
Everything® Great Sex Book
Everything® Self-Esteem Book
Everything® Tantric Sex Book

SPORTS & FITNESS

Everything® Easy Fitness Book
Everything® Fishing Book
Everything® Krav Maga for Fitness Book
Everything® Running Book, 2nd Ed.

TRAVEL

Everything® Family Guide to Coastal Florida
Everything® Family Guide to Cruise Vacations
Everything® Family Guide to Hawaii
Everything® Family Guide to Las Vegas, 2nd Ed.
Everything® Family Guide to Mexico
Everything® Family Guide to New England, 2nd Ed.
Everything® Family Guide to New York City, 3rd Ed.
Everything® Family Guide to RV Travel & Campgrounds
Everything® Family Guide to the Caribbean
Everything® Family Guide to the Disneyland® Resort, California Adventure®, Universal Studios®, and the Anaheim Area, 2nd Ed.
Everything® Family Guide to the Walt Disney World Resort®, Universal Studios®, and Greater Orlando, 5th Ed.
Everything® Family Guide to Timeshares
Everything® Family Guide to Washington D.C., 2nd Ed.

WEDDINGS

Everything® Bachelorette Party Book, $9.95
Everything® Bridesmaid Book, $9.95
Everything® Destination Wedding Book
Everything® Father of the Bride Book, $9.95
Everything® Groom Book, $9.95
Everything® Mother of the Bride Book, $9.95
Everything® Outdoor Wedding Book
Everything® Wedding Book, 3rd Ed.
Everything® Wedding Checklist, $9.95
Everything® Wedding Etiquette Book, $9.95
Everything® Wedding Organizer, 2nd Ed., $16.95
Everything® Wedding Shower Book, $9.95
Everything® Wedding Vows Book, $9.95
Everything® Wedding Workout Book
Everything® Weddings on a Budget Book, 2nd Ed., $9.95

WRITING

Everything® Creative Writing Book
Everything® Get Published Book, 2nd Ed.
Everything® Grammar and Style Book, 2nd Ed.
Everything® Guide to Magazine Writing
Everything® Guide to Writing a Book Proposal
Everything® Guide to Writing a Novel
Everything® Guide to Writing Children's Books
Everything® Guide to Writing Copy
Everything® Guide to Writing Graphic Novels
Everything® Guide to Writing Research Papers
Everything® Improve Your Writing Book, 2nd Ed.
Everything® Writing Poetry Book